I have made for you a song,

And it may be right or wrong,

But only you can tell me if it's true

I have tried for to explain

Both your pleasure and your pain,

And, Thomas, here's my best respects to you!

r.k.

EX LIBRIS   D. R. THOMAS

ON FAME'S ETERNAL
CAMPING GROUND

On Fame's Eternal Camping Ground

*A study of First World War epitaphs
in the British cemeteries of the Western Front*

Trefor Jones

Published by T.G.Jones, 9 Moss Close, Pinner, Middlesex, HA5 3AY

ISBN 978 0 9527458 2 2

Designed and typeset by the author

Printed and bound by
Cromwell Press Ltd, Trowbridge, Wiltshire

On Fame's eternal camping ground
Their silent tents are spread,
And Glory guards, with solemn round,
The bivouac of the dead.

Theodore O'Hara (1820-1867)
'The Bivouac of the Dead'

Introduction

THE TITLE OF THIS BOOK IS THE EPITAPH OF CAPTAIN C.S. JEFFRIES, VC, a young Australian infantry officer whose parents chose it as the personal inscription for his military headstone in Tyne Cot Cemetery, Belgium. The words are from *The Bivouac of the Dead*, a poem written by the American soldier-poet Theodore O'Hara to commemorate his fellow-Kentuckians who died at the Battle of Buena Vista in February 1847.

Clarence Jeffries, 22 years old when he was killed in the action for which he was posthumously awarded the Victoria Cross, is not alone in Tyne Cot: the remains of 11,952 other First World War soldiers of the United Kingdom and its Empire lie in what is the largest British war cemetery in the world. The bodies of almost exactly 70 per cent of those men were found but could not be identified – grisly testimony to the unimaginable horror of the battles in which they fought and the conditions in which they fell.

The conflict of 1914-1918 is the monstrous backdrop to this book, which however is not *'about'* the war. It offers no analysis of political decision-making or military tactics, no description of life in the trenches, no catalogue of weaponry or equipment. Its sole purpose is to examine, and marvel at, the response of bereaved families when given the opportunity to choose an epitaph for a young son/husband/brother, to be inscribed on a headstone on foreign soil which in most cases they would never see.

Altogether, the theatre of war familiarly known as the Western Front claimed the lives of nearly three-quarters of a million men of the British Empire. A total of approximately 411,600 of that astronomical number of casualties have named graves in France and Belgium; about 158,700 other graves contain remains which were not identified; and the names of about 313,700 men are listed on Memorials to the Missing. The arithmetic here indicates that something like 155,000 bodies were either blown to smithereens or still lie undiscovered.

The overwhelming majority of these victims of war were either in the flower of young manhood or, in many cases, hadn't even reached it. A strict official policy of 'no repatriation' of the dead, regardless of rank or family wealth and influence, means that their graves are in western Belgium and northern France.

Bodies which were recovered from the battlefields, and those of men who died behind the front lines from wounds or other causes, lie in immaculately maintained graves marked by headstones which are identical in shape and size. A similar uniformity applies to the factual information inscribed on them, consisting at most of name, rank, number, decorations, regiment or corps, date of death, and age. On each headstone is also engraved the appropriate regimental or corps badge and an emblem of religious faith – always a Christian cross unless the next-of-kin expressed a wish to have this excluded or, in the case of a Jew, replaced with the Star of David. Otherwise, the sole concession to individuality is a 'personal inscription' chosen by the next-of-kin. A representative selection of these family tributes, encompassing an astonishing variety of profoundly moving responses from the bereaved, are presented in the pages which follow.

The Commonwealth War Graves Commission

The organization now known as the Commonwealth War Graves Commission is responsible for the graves of all members of the armed forces of the British Empire and Commonwealth who died on active service in the two World Wars, and for the commemorative monuments on which are engraved the names of those whose bodies were never identified or never even found. The Commission grew out of what began in the very early days of the First World War as a Red Cross unit. It soon came under army control as the Graves Registration Commission, which in turn led, in May 1917, to the incorporation under Royal Charter of the Imperial War Graves Commission. ('Imperial' became 'Commonwealth' in 1950.)

The inspiration and driving force behind the whole concept was Fabian Ware, a distinguished and influential man who was too old for army service. He led the original Red Cross unit in 1914 and went on to serve the Commission as its vice-chairman from the date of its foundation until his retirement in 1948. It was Ware who had first recognized and urged upon others the importance of marking and recording the graves of men killed and buried on the battlefields. No mere figurehead, he presided over the Commission's affairs with a visionary sense of purpose and an energetic attention to detail.

The Graves and Their Headstones

Until the work of erecting headstones got under way, each grave was marked with a simple wooden cross, but within a year or two of the end of the war the Commission began the task of contacting next-of-kin via regimental record offices. A circular letter set out the policy which had been decided with regard to the headstones and what was to be engraved on them – *ie* the basic information outlined above. Next-of-kin were also asked to confirm or correct the Commission's particulars of the deceased's name, initials, decorations, *etc*, and to notify his age if it was desired that this should be added. *(Therefore an incorrect age on a headstone – and there are such instances – can in most cases be assumed to have come from this source.)*

The letter contained one further item, and it was one that caused a good deal of resentment. It read as follows (words in bold type in the letter are printed here in the same form):

*The Commission draw your attention to the fact that three lines have been reserved at the foot of the headstone for a **personal inscription**.*

Should you wish to take advantage of this privilege, would you please write the desired inscription in the space (b) provided opposite, following these instructions:-

Inscriptions requiring the use of special alphabets such as Greek, etc., cannot be accepted.

The length of the inscription is limited by the space on the stone.

It cannot therefore exceed a certain number of letters.

The number of letters is 66, less the number of spaces between the words of the inscription.

For instance, if you choose an inscription of twelve words, the total number of letters permissible is 66, less 11, or 55 letters.

*The inscribing of this inscription will be at **your** expense.*

At the current rates the cost per letter will be 3½d, and is subject to future fluctuations of cost.

An adjusted claim for the amount due to the Imperial War Graves Commission for the inscription will be sent to you when the construction of the cemetery in question is taken in hand.

*Unless you **state otherwise** in the space (c) opposite, a cross will be engraved in the centre of the stone.*

What caused the kerfuffle, of course, was the charge for the 'optional extra', which was inconsistent with the sensitivity that otherwise characterized the Commission's approach to its task, and the use of bold type to emphasize 'at **your** expense' seems particularly unnecessary. To a great many people at the time the sums involved were not the trifling amounts they seem now, and a harrowing illustration of this is provided by a form returned to the War Graves Commission by the mother of a soldier of the King's Own Yorkshire Light Infantry who had been killed on the first day of the Battle of the Somme. This lady, living in Brisbane, Australia, wrote her chosen epitaph on the form ('IN LOVING MEMORY OF MY BOY'), but then crossed it through and added: *"I am more than sorry I cannot afford a stone on my boy's grave. I am absolutely without means just now. I'm sorry I made this mistake."* She then signed the form under words: *"A soldier's daughter who is proud of her soldier son who died for his country."*

The Canadian authorities decided at the outset not to impose any charge on their families, the cost of whose personal epitaphs was met by the Canadian Government. The British went ahead as planned, but subsequently decided that the charge should after all be voluntary, although the controversy rumbled on, and an indication of the confused state of affairs is that as late as 1927 the father of the war-poet Isaac Rosenberg was told that it would cost him 3d per character (not 3½d) to have a chosen inscription ('ARTIST & POET') added to his son's headstone - and there was no mention of the 'voluntary' nature of the charge, either. Another 1927 letter asked a next-of-kin for 3½d per character but imposed a charge of 6/5d for 22 characters – *ie* nothing for the spaces. More inconsistency, therefore - and again there's no mention of 'voluntary'.

And there was inconsistency in respect of other factors, too – notably the stipulated maximum length of the epitaph – 66 characters, less the number of spaces between words. A spectacular anomaly is that concerning Private Edward Rust, whose headstone in Hazebrouck Communal Cemetery in France is filled with an account of his activities in action in the final days of his life which, remarkably and unaccountably, runs to no fewer than exactly 400 characters and spaces.

It was intended that the opportunity for a personal inscription should be offered to the families of all those who died while serving with the British armed forces and those of the Dominions (plus Newfoundland, which although now a province of Canada, was then a separate colony). The New Zealand authorities, however, stood out against the decision on the grounds that, it being inevitable that not all families could or would request an epitaph, *none* should be allowed to do so. *(Inexplicably, though, one New Zealand grave actually __does__ have a personal inscription.)* Therefore it is the dead of only the British, Australian, Canadian, Newfoundland and South African forces whose graves bear family tributes.

The Cemeteries

The British cemeteries on the Western Front all occupy land which, in both Belgium and France, has been freely granted in perpetuity as a resting-place for those who are buried there. They vary in size from the largest, Tyne Cot, on the site of the Battle of Passchendaele, to tiny enclosures with just a few dozen graves. In design and construction they all have a great deal in common, but at the same time each and every cemetery retains an individual serenity and solemn beauty which can hardly fail to move any visitor. The supremely apt sobriquet 'Silent Cities' was applied to them by Rudyard Kipling, who served on the War Graves Commission and whose own son was killed at Loos in 1915. That distinguished literary figure was also responsible for the words which adorn the headstones of all 'Unknown' burials *(see under* 'Epitaphs', *below)* and for choosing from *Ecclesiasticus* (a book of *Apocrypha*) the phrase 'THEIR NAME LIVETH FOR EVERMORE' to be inscribed on the altar-like Stone of Remembrance which, together with a Cross of Sacrifice, is a feature of all but the smallest cemeteries.

A considerable number of cemeteries are purpose-built extensions of Belgian and French churchyards and burial grounds. (In many of the latter can also be found British graves among those of local citizens, rather than in separate sections, but with headstones in the unique War Graves Commission style. And incidentally, the designation *'communal* cemetery' in France derives from the noun *'commune'*, which is an administrative unit equating to the British parish.) The British sections of some French cemeteries are very large indeed, examples being those of Bailleul and Rouen (St Sever), which are the resting-place of several thousand soldiers of the British and Empire armies. The total number of burial grounds in Belgium and France which contain Commonwealth War Graves Commission graves of the Great War is about 2,200.

Unless forewarned, anyone to whom Belgian Flanders is not familiar territory is likely to be confused by the Flemish names of many towns and villages which are now used instead of the former French ones. Some of the changes are fairly obvious – Passchendaele is now Passendale, and Dickebusch is Dikkebus – but others less so, *eg* Furnes/Veurne, Warneton/Waasten and Roulers/Roeselare. The old versions are perpetuated in the names of some British war cemeteries, which has created anomalies such as, for instance, Ypres Reservoir Cemetery, which is in the town now called Ieper, and La Clytte Military Cemetery in the village now known as De Klijte. Equally confusing, or potentially so – don't expect to find anywhere called Bandaghem, Dozinghem or Mendinghem. These authentic-looking but totally bogus 'Flemish' linguistic constructions survive in the names of British war cemeteries as examples of the humour of the troops, who originally applied them in jest (bandage 'em, dosing 'em, mending 'em) to three casualty clearing stations in the area north-west of Poperinge where these three cemeteries are situated.

In respect of the British presence in Belgium from 1914 to 1918, it is a bizarre fact that the theatre of war which is always popularly referred to as the Western Front was only ever officially designated 'France and Flanders'. The absence therein of any specific mention of Belgium is heavy with irony, the precise reason for Britain's entry into the war having been none other than to honour a commitment to protecting Belgian neutrality when Germany invaded in 1914. It is, in any case, simply daft to talk of France *and* Flanders as though they were different territories, since a substantial part of Flanders is actually *in* France. This geographical confusion, to the detriment of 'poor little Belgium', is also apparent in a number of epitaphs containing reference to burials in France which are actually in Belgium. (And by the same token, in view of their sacrifices and contribution to the war effort, the Irish, Scots and Welsh have every reason to resent the inappropriate references to 'England' in many epitaphs.)

The Epitaphs

On the headstone of every grave containing an unidentified body is inscribed 'A SOLDIER OF THE GREAT WAR' (or a variation in accordance with any known detail such as rank, regiment or nationality) and 'KNOWN UNTO GOD'. The phrases were chosen by Kipling.

In respect of the 'named' graves, about 45% have an epitaph chosen by the families, and the percentage is considerably higher for officers (whose families by and large were more likely to be traceable, and better able to afford the cost) than for other ranks. Australians have the highest overall rate (about 55%), and it comes as no surprise that some of their epitaphs are particularly rich in direct, down-to-earth sentiments and tributes, while time and again there are robust proclamations of loyalty to the mother-country. Those close ties, in fact, applied equally throughout the Empire, where so many of those who fought were first-generation immigrants who had been born in the British Isles.

The absence of a personal inscription can be attributed in many cases to a failure to trace the next-of-kin. Others who *were* traced and did reply to the Commission's circular, for financial or whatever other reason did not request a personal inscription.

The themes of most of the epitaphs can be broadly categorized as grief, Christian faith, pride, patriotism, duty, sacrifice and heroism. Sometimes anger, too. Often two of these categories were combined. Infinitely varied forms of expression were used, from the elegant and lyrical, with biblical and poetic texts particularly prominent, to simple statements of fact ('LATE BUTCHER OF HORSFORTH, NR. LEEDS'). Many of the latter were probably an acknowledgement by the bereaved of the inadequacy of words to convey the depth of their feelings. The verse offerings range from well-known lines by great writers to simple rhyming couplets which would never win poetry prizes but lack for nothing in sincerity and emotion. *(Throughout the book the author has attributed some of the quotes to the works from which they were taken. Doubtless, readers will recognize other sources.)*

Anyone chancing upon a Western Front war cemetery knowing nothing of the events of 1914-1918, and wishing to know why all these men gave their lives, would be little the wiser after wandering among the headstones. Consider the following, just a small sample of the reasons attributed to a willingness to fight and to die: *for England's honour, for democracy, for France and liberty, for one and all, for me, for the Empire, for King and Constitution, for the honour of Bristol, for the freedom of small nations, for his wife and little son, for his friends, for you and me, for simple love of home, for the world, for Ulster, for Church and King, for home and duty, for our tomorrows, for righteousness, for love, to help the maple leaf to live, for posterity, for Australia, in defence of hearth and home, for humanity's sake, for love of kindred, for justice and right, for mother's honour, for Scotland, for lasting peace.* Any attempt to rationalize this bewildering miscellany would be inappropriate, except simply to acknowledge them to be all equally valid as heartfelt sentiments borne of tragedy and grief, in the context of attitudes which make that era, not yet entirely gone from living memory, seem impossibly remote.

The words are sometimes addressed directly to the deceased ('SLEEP LAD, SLEEP, THY WORK IS WELL DONE'), while others are in a form as if spoken *by* the deceased ('TELL ENGLAND THAT WE WHO DIED SERVING HER REST HERE CONTENT'). There are also entreaties to the passer-by ('TREAD GENTLY O'ER MY SON'S GRAVE, FOR A MOTHER'S LOVE LIES SLEEPING HERE'). The distances of the graves from the men's homelands was the theme chosen by many families – not least, of course, those in the far-flung Dominions ('THE MIDNIGHT STARS ARE GLEAMING OVER THE GRAVE WE MAY NEVER SEE').

Burial grounds everywhere have an atmosphere of dignified and solemn beauty, and headstones can always be interesting, but those under examination here are significantly different from those in a local churchyard or cemetery back home. It is essential, for instance, to bear in mind that the epitaphs were chosen several years after the death – not, as is usually the case, in its immediate aftermath ('SEVEN YEARS HAVE PASSED, OUR HEARTS STILL SORE, AS TIME ROLLS ON WE MISS HIM MORE'). Moreover, the inspiration for these expressions of mourning is not the normal one of the sad but inevitable loss of an elderly relation. Life offers no worse fate, it's often said, than to be predeceased by a son or daughter – a particularly potent observation in the context of war victims, almost exclusively sons, husbands and brothers cut down in, or even before, the prime of life, and buried far from home in graves which thousands and thousands of families knew they would never be able to visit. These factors are prominent themes on Western Front headstones, the grieving mother being a constantly recurring and especially powerful image ('THE ONLY SON OF HIS MOTHER, AND SHE A WIDOW').

Pride is expressed sometimes by reference to the fact that a soldier had *volunteered* for military service. The form of such words is usually simple and factual, and nobody would have deliberately set out to cause distress or offence, but the parents who chose to proclaim emphatically of a fallen son: 'NO CONSCRIPT', were insensitive to the feelings of families visiting the graves of many dead conscripts who lie around him in the same cemetery. The stridency of that phrase sits uneasily with the Commission's guiding principle of 'equality in death', irrespective of rank, race or creed – and certainly also irrespective of volunteer or conscript. There are echoes here of the pre-conscription days, when abuse and white feathers were thrust on young men on the streets of Britain who were not wearing military uniform. Compare that epitaph with the understated tribute in Vlamertinghe Military Cemetery to a corporal who became one of a quarter of a million British soldiers who perished in the Ypres Salient. 'JUST A VOLUNTEER' was the simple, dignified choice of words of the parents of this holder of the Military Medal.

Attributing responsibility for wholesale slaughter on the Western Front to the Almighty would not suit Christian theologians, who argue that the evils of the world arise from mankind's misuse of its God-given free will, but grieving families will simply have drawn strength from their Christian faith without concerning themselves with finer points of religious doctrine. Thus appeared great numbers of epitaphs on the lines of 'THY WILL, O LORD, NOT MINE' and 'GOD MOVES IN A MYSTERIOUS WAY'.

The military metaphor abounds in Christian literature, of course, and countless families who were sustained in their loss by religious faith used it as a singularly appropriate medium for their tributes. Lines from familiar hymns and biblical references to battles, warfare, Christian soldiers, the armour of God, *etc, etc*, appear time and time again. One biblical text in particular, although not 'military' in context, occurs more frequently throughout the Western Front cemeteries than any other personal inscription: the words of Jesus in *The Gospel According to St John*, Chapter 15, Verse 13. So apt is 'GREATER LOVE HATH NO MAN THAN THIS, THAT HE LAY DOWN HIS LIFE FOR HIS FRIENDS' that it might almost have been written expressly for this purpose, and it appears constantly, either complete or in abbreviated or amended form.

Having considered how epitaphs can reasonably be pigeonholed in various specific categories, it remains to be said that there is occasionally one which defies any attempt at interpretation altogether. What are we to make of, for instance, 'YES, DAD'? Clearly the families not only understood what they were saying, but knew that the deceased would have understood as well. And when all's said and done, nothing else matters.

Attempts at interpretation can also be hindered by the style in which the inscriptions were cut. All lettering on the headstones is in capitals, for example, and punctuation is spasmodic. Although a question might be obvious despite the absence of a question mark (a common occurrence), and the omission of an apostrophe need be nothing more than an irritation, the absence of a comma or two here and there can lead to doubt or confusion. In this connection it should be noted that the epitaphs included in the book are reproduced with line-breaks inserted where they occur on the headstones, and with only the most indisputable errors corrected.

The pages which follow present more than 1,500 epitaphs selected from cemeteries throughout the Western Front. No attempt has been made to arrange them by 'category', since page after page of tributes focusing on, say, patriotism, and another section with an exclusively religious theme, would eventually pall. They are instead listed under their respective cemeteries and thus offered to the reader as an unsorted miscellany, which in that regard replicates the experience of anyone visiting the cemeteries in person.

Let the epitaphs now speak for themselves. Inspired by human tragedy on a grotesquely vast scale, these brief private tributes combine to provide in their many forms a sublime demonstration of the beauty and power of language.

Abeele Aerodrome Military Cemetery

237516 Gunner
James Henry ELLENS
Royal Field Artillery
Died 26 July 1918, aged 24

IN LOVING MEMORY
OF MY DEAR DADDY
WHO GAVE HIS LIFE
FOR THE GREAT CAUSE

60692 Private
James Congreve FERN
1st Battalion, West Yorkshire Regiment
(Prince of Wales's Own)
Died 31 July 1918, aged 19

OLD PAL
WHY DON'T YOU ANSWER ME

(A plea from Private Fern's father in Halifax,
Yorkshire.)

Acheux British Cemetery

70471 Private
William Richard HOOPER
17th Battalion, Royal Welsh Fusiliers
Died 29 June 1918, aged 19

STRONG AS A ROCK
THROUGH STRIFE AND FEAR
HE SERVED HIS LORD
TILL DEATH

24359 Private
Arthur Albert HUNT
6th Battalion, Dorsetshire Regiment
Died 15 June 1918, aged 20

HIS WAR IS O'ER
HIS SUN IS SET
BUT ONES WHO LOVED HIM
CANNOT FORGET

THEIR NAME LIVETH
FOR EVERMORE

107847 Gunner
Fred RAWNSLEY
231st Siege Battery, Royal Garrison Artillery
Died 30 April 1918, aged 33

LIVED FOR HOME.
DIED FOR HOME.
GONE HOME.
FROM HIS LOVING WIFE ANNIE

75524 Gunner
Walter Ralph SEYMOUR
88th Battery, Royal Field Artillery
Died 17 July 1916, aged 23

MY ONLY BELOVED CHILD
YOU HAVE DONE YOUR DUTY.
I AM WAITING TO MEET YOU.
MOTHER

44819 Private
William Joseph SHOULER
1st Garrison Battalion, Hampshire Regiment
Died 22 April 1918, aged 22

SNAPPED LIKE A FLOWER
IN EARLY BLOOM
FROM HIS SORROWING
FATHER AND MOTHER

Adanac Military Cemetery

703922 Corporal
Thomas Bourchier CAVE
102nd Battalion, Canadian Infantry
(Central Ontario Regiment)
Died 11 November 1916, aged 27

THE BETTER DAYS
OF LIFE WERE OURS
THE WORST CAN BUT BE MINE

(Each year on Armistice Day the widowed Mrs
Cave would have been only too well aware that it
was also the anniversary of her husband's death.)

65433 Private
James HAYES
24th Battalion, Canadian Infantry
(Quebec Regiment)
Died 17 September 1916, aged 18

BELOVED SON
PROUD CANADIAN
R.I.P.

(This young soldier and his elder brother, Francis
Joseph Hayes, enlisted together and served in the
same battalion. Private F.J.Hayes also died in
service, five months earlier.)

S/11523 Private
Thomas Alexander JACKSON
11th Battalion, Argyll & Sutherland Highlanders
Died 9 October 1916, aged 39

ONLY SON
OF MRS. ALEXR. JACKSON
THORNLIE BANK

(Playing as an amateur in professional football,
Private Jackson had reached the highest levels of the
game, representing St Mirren and Middlesbrough,
and winning six Scotland caps.)

132163 Private
William Patrick RYAN
13th Battalion, Canadian Infantry
(Quebec Regiment)
Died 8 October 1916, aged 31

THOSE WHO LIVED
AND THOSE WHO DIED
THEY WERE ONE
IN NOBLE PRIDE

180344 Private
William SIME
28th Battalion, Canadian Infantry
(Saskatchewan Regiment)
Died 29 September 1916, aged 35

HE DIED
SO THAT LIFE MIGHT BE
A SWEETER THING TO ALL
HE LIVETH

178197 Private
Adon SMITH
87th Battalion, Canadian Infantry
(Quebec Regiment)
Died 21-22 October 1916, aged 26

HE GAVE HIS ALL FOR FREEDOM
THE WHOLE WIDE WORLD TO SAVE

Adelaide Cemetery

491 Private
Charles Frederick BARNARD
18th Battalion, Australian Infantry
Died 1 August 1918, aged 20

FATHER AND BROTHERS
ARE PROUD OF YOU DEAR CHARLIE
DOING YOUR DUTY

7050 Private
William Charles DURRANT
25th Battalion, Australian Infantry
Died 17 July 1918, aged 40

HE HEARD THE DISTANT "COOEE"
OF HIS MATES ACROSS THE SEA

3160 Private
Percy James GORE
50th Battalion, Australian Infantry
Died 25 April 1918, aged 24

HIS BRAVE YOUNG LIFE HE GAVE
THAT BRITONS STILL MIGHT LIVE

3326 Private
Hugh Grahame HENDERSON
35th Battalion, Australian Infantry
Died 4 April 1918, aged 18

HUGH BORN 23/4/99
NOBLE & LOVING
MAY GOD BE THY PORTION
BELOVED

(Hugh Henderson died five days before his brother
Ronald [see below] and they lie in adjacent graves.)

Lieutenant
Ronald Grahame HENDERSON, *MC*
18th Battalion, Australian Infantry
Died 9 April 1918, aged 25

RONALD BORN 5/7/92
PURE & BEAUTIFUL
GOD BE THY PORTION, BELOVED

(See Private H.G. Henderson, above.)

741397 Gunner
Joseph SNOWDEN
'D' Battery, 290th Brigade, Royal Field Artillery
Died 24 April 1918, aged 36

NOT FAULTLESS
BUT MANY VIRTUES
ONE OF THE BEST
FROM HIS WIFE & CHILD

19562 Sapper
John Arthur STIRLING
7th Field Company, Australian Engineers
Died 17 July 1918, aged 18

HE WAS THE LOVED OF ALL
YET NONE
O'ER HIS LOW BED MAY WEEP

(For Sapper Stirling's parents in Sydney, a visit to
their young son's grave half a world away was out of
the question.)

Adinkerke Military Cemetery

701528 Gunner
Joseph Albert ELLIOTT
'B' Battery, 330th Brigade, Royal Field Artillery
Died 7 August 1917, aged 26

GRIEVE NOT DEAR PARENTS
BUT BE CONTENT
FOR TO YOU I WAS BUT LENT

250951 Private
Peter HOGG
5th/6th Battalion, Royal Scots
Died 28 August 1917, aged 29

HE GIED HIS A'

37227 Private
Frank ROBERTS
'C' Company, 2nd/8th Battalion,
Lancashire Fusiliers
Died 5 September 1917, aged 24

HIS DUTY DONE, THE ORDEAL O'ER
HE HAS MARCHED
THROUGH HEAVEN'S GATE

Aeroplane Cemetery

43351 Corporal
John DAVIDSON
5th Battalion, Cameron Highlanders
Died 28 September 1918, aged 19

CONCEALED
IN THE CLIFT OF THE ROCK

3246 Private
William Roy DOUGHAN
55th Battalion, Australian Infantry
Died 26 September 1917, aged 23

A MOTHER'S PART
IS A BROKEN HEART
AND BURDEN OF LONELY YEARS

26576 Private
Luke Clegg LEADBEATER
1st/5th Battalion,
Duke of Wellington's (West Riding Regiment)
Died 22 November 1917, aged 19

UNTIL THE DAY BREAKS

(For Private Leadbeater's fiancée Jessy, the day
broke 84 years later. She died in July 2001, aged
100. Her ashes were scattered on his grave, on
which was placed the photograph of her which he
had been carrying when he was killed.)

4500 Private
John Ernest ORR
28th Battalion, Australian Infantry
Died 1 November 1917, aged 35

A PRAISE FOR THOSE
WHO FOUGHT AND FELL
TO SAVE THE EMPIRE'S NAME

6581 Private
Walter John SAYERS
7th Battalion, Australian Infantry
Died 4 October 1917, aged 34

WHEN ALIVE THEY WOULD NOT
TAKE YOUR PLACE
THEY CANNOT HAVE IT NOW
MY SON

5424 Lance Corporal
James Henry SMITH
24th Battalion, Australian Infantry
Died 4 October 1917, aged 41

WITH EVERY VICTORY WON
HE HAS RECEIVED
THE GLAD "WELL DONE"

Lieutenant
Richard WALMESLEY
3rd Battalion, attached 2nd Battalion,
Yorkshire Regiment
Died 21 October 1914, aged 23

AND THE ARMIES
WHICH ARE IN HEAVEN
FOLLOWED HIM
UPON WHITE HORSES

(Adapted from Revelation, *Chapter 15, Verse*
14.)

Agny Military Cemetery

Second Lieutenant
Harold Torrance BURGESS
3rd Battalion, London Regiment (Royal Fusiliers)
Died 2 April 1917, aged 23

HE SLEEPS THE SLEEP OF THOSE
WHO BRAVELY DIED

Second Lieutenant
Richard GREENLAND
9th Battalion, Durham Light Infantry
Died 13 April 1917, aged 25

HE TROD THE PATH OF DUTY
A VOLUNTEER OF AUGUST 1914

R/21078 Rifleman
George James JIGGINS
9th Battalion, King's Royal Rifle Corps
Died 29 January 1917, aged 34

YES, IT IS OURS!
THE FIELD IS WON
LIFT FROM THE GROUND
MY NOBLE SON

Second Lieutenant
Philip Edward THOMAS
244th Siege Battery, Royal Garrison Artillery
Died 9 April 1917, aged 39

POET

*(Edward Thomas established his literary reputation
before the war, but only in 1914, aged 36, began to
write poetry. Although acknowledged as one of the
'war poets', he actually wrote little war poetry.)*

AIF Burial Ground

3951 Private
James DAWSON
49th Battalion, Australian Infantry
Died 5 September 1916, aged 23

HAPPY SON, THY BARK IS PAST
BEYOND ROUGH FOAM

19957 Private
Charles John ELLIS
'D' Company, 26th Battalion, Royal Fusiliers
Died 18 September 1916, aged 20

SOLDIER LAY THY WEAPON DOWN
QUIT THE SWORD FOR THE CROWN

Lieutenant Colonel
The Right Honourable
Charles William Reginald Duncombe,
Earl of FEVERSHAM
Yorkshire Hussars,
commanding 21st Battalion,
King's Royal Rifle Corps
Died 15 September 1916, aged 37

IN LIFE LOYAL
IN DEATH FEARLESS
IN FAITH CERTAIN
IN HOPE SECURE

(Lord Feversham fell in action. A future Prime Minister, Anthony Eden, of the same battalion, supervised the search for his commanding officer's body, which was missing on the battlefield. It was found nearly a month later.)

36624 Sergeant
William John GRAHAM
'D' Battery, 183rd Brigade, Royal Field Artillery
Died 14 October 1916, aged 28

IT IS SOWN IN DISHONOUR
IT IS RAISED IN GLORY
IT IS SOWN IN WEAKNESS
IT IS RAISED IN POWER

(From I Corinthians, Chapter 15, Verse 43.)

Second Lieutenant
Gerald William HIRST
3rd Battalion, The King's (Liverpool Regiment)
Died 26 February 1917, aged 19

FOR THE SAFETY, HONOUR
AND WELFARE OF OUR SOVEREIGN
AND HIS DOMINIONS

767107 Private
William Lawrence HUTCHINSON
28th Battalion, London Regiment (Artists' Rifles)
Died 27 August 1918, aged 19

OUR DEAR SON
OF ST JOSEPH'S RECTORY
BARBADOS B.W.I.
FELL NEAR BAPAUME
LOVE NEVER FAILETH

2479 Private
Australian Peter JENSEN
31st Battalion, Australian Infantry
Died 27 October 1916, aged 36

YOU DIED FOR US
SHALL WE NOT LIVE FOR YOU?

(The family's strong sense of patriotism, evident in Private Jensen's name, is reflected also in the name of the house in Five Dock, New South Wales, in which his widow continued to live: 'Austral'.)

4748 Private
Harry Lemin Hepburn PAGE
12th Battalion, Australian Infantry
Died 9 December 1916, aged 19

AN AUSTRALIAN'S GIFT
TO FRANCE
LET NO FOEMAN
DESECRATE ITS SOIL

Aix-Noulette Communal Cemetery Extension

657661 Private
Joseph Edgar HORNIBROOK
2nd Battalion, Canadian Pioneers
Died 13 August 1917, aged 27

HE IS NOT DEAD
HE ONLY SLEEPETH
RESTING FROM THE BATTLE MOIL

678619 Private
William Edward LLOYD
116th Battalion, Canadian Infantry
(Central Ontario Regiment)
Died 28 August 1917, aged 33

THIS BE THY RECORD
WHEREIN PEACE THOU LIEST

210613 Private
Harry MUNRO
58th Battalion, Canadian Infantry
(Central Ontario Regiment)
Died 26 August 1917, aged 20

AND WITH A CHEERY SMILE
AND WAVE OF THE HAND
HE HAS WANDERED
INTO AN UNKNOWN LAND

490291 Pioneer
Albert NORMINGTON
2nd Battalion, Canadian Pioneers
Died 15 August 1917, aged 33

A MAN IN A WORLD OF MEN
LOVED BY ALL

Albert Communal Cemetery Extension

22/1744 Private
David BEST
22nd (Tyneside Scottish) Battalion,
Northumberland Fusiliers
Died 3 July 1916, aged 17

IT IS A FAR, FAR BETTER THING
THAT I DO
THAN I HAVE EVER DONE

(It might be expected that this quote from Dickens's
A Tale of Two Cities would also be found
elsewhere in the Western Front cemeteries, but no
other example was discovered in the course of
research for this book.)

Second Lieutenant
Richard William Byrd LEVETT
1st Battalion, King's Royal Rifle Corps
Died 10 March 1917, aged 19

SO PASSED A BRAVE SOLDIER
A GALLANT GENTLEMAN
AND A RADIANT SOUL

Alençon (St Leonard) Cemetery

2203395 Private
Noel SEYMOUR
42nd Company, Canadian Forestry Corps
Died 10 June 1918, aged 33

BRITISH COLUMBIA INDIAN
DIED FOR KING AND COUNTRY

(Private Seymour was born and lived in Indian
reservations in Canada.)

Ancre British Cemetery

CZ/536 Able Seaman
John Carruthers FARQUHARSON
Royal Naval Volunteer Reserve,
Nelson Battalion, Royal Naval Division
Died 13 November 1916, aged 19

WE'LL MEET AGAIN
WHEN THE BARRAGE LIFTS

TZ/3290 Able Seaman
Cecil Rhodes HUNTLEY
Royal Naval Volunteer Reserve,
Nelson Battalion, Royal Naval Division
Died 13 November 1916, aged 19

LEAD KINDLY LIGHT
FOR I AM FAR FROM HOME
LEAD THOU ME ON

(From The Pillar of Cloud: Lead Kindly
Light, *by Cardinal John Henry Newman.)*

Arras Road Cemetery

3210 Private
Benjamin Thomas HATTON
1st/5th Battalion, Leicestershire Regiment
Died 13 October 1915, aged 21

I WAS BRITISH

Artillery Wood Cemetery

30739 Private
Charles Sydney JENKINS
16th Battalion, Lancashire Fusiliers
Died 24 March 1918, aged 31

THO' THE WARRIORS' SUN HAS SET
ITS LIGHT SHALL LINGER
ROUND US YET

Lieutenant
Harold George JOHNSON
1st Battalion, Grenadier Guards
Died 7 August 1917, aged 20

"I HAVE FOUGHT A GOOD FIGHT
I HAVE FINISHED MY COURSE
I HAVE KEPT THE FAITH"
2 TIM. IV.7.

Second Lieutenant
Herbert Berwick TAYLOR
4th Battalion, London Regiment (Royal Fusiliers)
Died 31 July 1917, aged 22

WAR HAS NOT MARRED THEM
NOR DEATH
DESTROYED THEIR BEAUTY

18663 Guardsman
Walter TURNER
2nd Battalion, Coldstream Guards
Died 31 July 1917, aged 29

HE LOVED
HE SERVED

7748 Guardsman
Richard WALSH
2nd Battalion, Irish Guards
Died 9 October 1917, aged 27

MOTHER'S LOVE

(An only son. In November 2002 an ornate silver-coloured pillbox containing two locks of brown hair was found on this grave, having worked its way to the surface. It was reburied by the Commonwealth War Graves Commission.)

15953 Guardsman
Herbert Clarence WRIGHT
'G' Company, 2nd Battalion, Scots Guards
Died 14 September 1917, aged 20

A SACRIFICE TO RIGHT
AGAINST MIGHT
OUR BERT

Aubers Ridge British Cemetery

723478 Private
Lawrance Herbert HEBDITCH
24th Battalion, London Regiment
Died 14 October 1918, aged 21

WHAT CRUEL FOLLY IS WAR.
IT ROBS US OF OUR DEAREST

34485 Private
Arthur Robert MUSK
15th (Suffolk Yeomanry) Battalion,
Suffolk Regiment
Died 15 October 1918, aged 31

HE HAS JOINED
THE INVISIBLE ARMY
WHERE KHAKI GIVES PLACE
TO PURE WHITE

Aubigny British Cemetery

3755 Private
David Edward ARNOLD
55th Battalion, Australian Infantry
Died 16 April 1918, aged 20

THE SHIPS CAME BACK
WITH HONOURED BRAVE
BUT NONE CAME BACK
WITH OUR DAVE

3040 Private
John Albert EMMETT
33rd Battalion, Australian Infantry
Died 17 June 1918, aged 46

FATE LIES HID
BUT NOT THE DEEDS
THAT TRUE MEN DARED AND DID

2707 Private
Arthur Jefferson LANE
60th Battalion, Australian Infantry
Died 25 April 1918, aged 21

BOYS, YE FOUGHT
AS HEROES FIGHT
AND DIED AS MEN

(Private Lane had been decorated by France with the Croix de Guerre.)

Auchonvillers Military Cemetery

9349 Corporal
John George DUNLEA
'C' Company, 2nd Battalion,
Royal Dublin Fusiliers
Died 31 October 1915, aged 34

"AN IRISH VOLUNTEER"
HE DIED FOR THE FREEDOM
OF SMALL NATIONS

4221 Private
Henry HAWORTH
2nd Battalion, Hampshire Regiment
Died 17 July 1916, aged 20

OF SUCH WAS ENGLAND
AND OF SUCH IS
THE KINGDOM OF HEAVEN

4267 Private
Christopher MABER
'Z' Company, 2nd Battalion, Hampshire Regiment
Died 17 July 1916, aged 18

FOR ENGLAND'S SAKE
LOST ALL
BUT ENGLAND'S PRAISE
R.I.P.

Authuile Military Cemetery

Captain
Herbert Graham BARBER, *MC*
4th Battalion, York & Lancaster Regiment
Died 7 July 1916, aged 31

DEATH IS ONLY
AN INCIDENT IN LIFE

Lieutenant
Frank Robson BEST
4th Battalion, Loyal North Lancashire Regiment
Died 2 January 1916, aged 21

DEEDS NOT WORDS

Awoingt British Cemetery

203422 Private
Frederick BURDEN
5th (Reserve) Battalion, Lancashire Fusiliers
Died 23 October 1918, aged 32

THE MIDNIGHT STARS
ARE GLEAMING
OVER THE GRAVE
WE MAY NEVER SEE

28561 Private
Harry HART
1st Battalion, East Surrey Regiment
Died 29 October 1918, aged 29

THAT HE MAY PLEASE HIM
WHO HATH CHOSEN HIM
TO BE A SOLDIER
2 TIM. 11. 21

41025 Private
Andre Alexandre HILL
'B' Company, 1st/5th Battalion,
Duke of Cornwall's Light Infantry
Died 2 November 1918, aged 19

MODEST PIONEER OF VICTORY
HE DIED LIKE A MAN
DOING A MAN'S WORK

(Private Hill was born in Paris to a French mother
– hence the Christian names.)

9027 Guardsman
Arthur Edward HINTON
1st Battalion, Grenadier Guards
Died 7 November 1918, aged 38

FOR AS MUCH AS YE KNOW
YOUR LIFE WAS NOT SACRIFICED
IN VAIN

56549 Lance Corporal
Robert TAYLOR
1st Battalion, The Cameronians (Scottish Rifles)
Died 24 October 1918, aged 18

DIED SO YOUNG
WITH ALL HIS WEALTH OF YOUTH

Bailleul Communal Cemetery

L/8270 Private
William Benbow HUGHES
1st Battalion, East Surrey Regiment
Died 10 March 1915, aged 29

FOR ALL THY SAINTS
A NOBLE THRONG
WHO FELL BY FIRE AND SWORD

(From C.F.Alexander's hymn For All Thy
Saints, a Noble Throng.*)*

Bailleul Communal Cemetery Extension

14968 Private
William BARNETT
6th Battalion, Royal Scots Fusiliers
Died 12 March 1916, aged 20

HOW THE BROTHER SPIRIT BINDS
ALL WHO WEAR
THE SCOUT LIKE SIGN

---

117 Private
Thomas Andrew Joseph BYRNES
47th Battalion, Australian Infantry
Died 7 July 1917, aged 27

THE WHITEST OF THEM ALL
MY SON

3023 Private
James Thomas Roy EASTON
14th Battalion, Australian Infantry
Died 4 July 1916, aged 25

OUR ROY
APPROVED UNTO GOD
A WORKMAN THAT NEEDED NOT
TO BE ASHAMED

---

550 Sergeant
Thomas Lumley FRANKISH
5th Battalion, Yorkshire Regiment
Died 24 June 1915, aged 22

THIS SOLDIER FOUGHT
FOR THE LAW OF HIS GOD
EVEN UNTO DEATH

Second Lieutenant
John Everatt GOODMAN
53rd Squadron, Royal Flying Corps
Died 14 August 1917, aged 19

OUR NOBLE SON
IT IS WELL WITH YOU
AMONG THE VERY BRAVE
THE VERY TRUE

1686 Private
James GRICE
1st/4th Battalion, East Yorkshire Regiment
Died 20 June 1916, aged 18

REMEMBRANCE
A FLOWER THAT NEVER FADES
WHEN WATERED
BY A MOTHER'S TEARS

38527 Driver
Robert Stewart *OAKES*
(*served as* HOLMES)
64th Company, Royal Engineers
Died 1 May 1916, aged 19

HE SLEEPS
NOT IN HIS NATIVE LAND
BUT 'NEATH SOME FOREIGN SKIES

3386 Lance Corporal
William Ewart HOPKINSON
9th Battalion, London Regiment
(Queen Victoria's Rifles)
Died 6 June 1915, aged 24

WE REMEMBER
THOUGH THE WORLD FORGET

5031 Private
Ivor Grafton JONES
10th Battalion, Royal Welsh Fusiliers
Died 2 May 1916, aged 22

DEATH TO ME
SHORT WARNING GAVE
THEREFORE BE CAREFUL
HOW YOU LIVE

16684 Private
Harold Ernest KITCHEN
8th Battalion, Lincolnshire Regiment
Died 27 January 1916, aged 20

HE DIED FOR US
IS IT IN VAIN?

1396 Sergeant
Thomas MOTTERSHEAD, *VC, DCM*
20th Squadron, Royal Flying Corps
Died 12 January 1917, aged 24

NOT ONCE OR TWICE
IN OUR ROUGH ISLAND STORY
WAS THE PATH OF DUTY
THE WAY TO GLORY

(The epitaph is based on lines by Tennyson in Ode
on the Death of the Duke of Wellington.
Sergeant Mottershead's age is incorrectly inscribed
on the headstone as 27. The VC was awarded
posthumously. When on a flying patrol he was
attacked at 9,000 feet and his aircraft was set on
fire. He landed it behind Allied lines, but was
trapped in the burning cockpit and died.)

Lieutenant
Geoffrey Cowper Spencer PRATT
14th Anti-Aircraft Section, Royal Horse Artillery
Died 27 November 1915, aged 22

"STRONG AND COURAGEOUS
LOVELY AND PLEASANT
IN HIS LIFE"
II SAMUEL CHAP.1

Second Lieutenant
Archibald David REID
5th Battalion, attached 4th Battalion,
Middlesex Regiment
Died 8 August 1917, aged 24

"I'VE ALWAYS TRIED
AND DONE MY BEST
AT EVERYTHING"
ARCHIE

3/5930 Private
Harry Walter WAITE
'A' Company, 1st Battalion,
Somerset Light Infantry
Died 4 May 1915, aged 23

AT ENGLAND'S CALL
I TOOK MY CHANCE
ONLY TO FALL
ON THE SOIL OF FRANCE

L/10671 Private
Henry WATERS
8th Battalion,
The Queen's Own (Royal West Kent Regiment)
Died 7 May 1916, aged 17

OH MEMORIES
THAT BLESS AND BURN

(This is a line from The Rosary, *a poem by*
Robert Cameron Rogers.)

Bailleulmont Communal Cemetery

10495 Private
Albert INGHAM
18th Battalion, Manchester Regiment
Died 1 December 1916, aged 24

SHOT AT DAWN
ONE OF THE FIRST TO ENLIST
A WORTHY SON
OF HIS FATHER

(Many executed soldiers have epitaphs, but this one
is unique in its reference to the circumstances of
death. Private Ingham's parents were originally told
simply that he had "died of wounds", and only
years later found out the full truth. He was found
guilty of desertion with his friend and former work
colleague, Albert Longshaw, who was also executed
and is buried alongside him.)

Bailleul Road East Cemetery

45773 Private
Herbert Henry GARRATT
25th (Tyneside Irish) Battalion,
Northumberland Fusiliers
Died 21 March 1918, aged 20

IN ME, PEACE
IN THE WORLD, TRIBULATION

Second Lieutenant
Francis Mott LAWLEDGE
Royal Engineers, attached Royal Flying Corps
Died 10 October 1916, aged 38

A SON OF ENGLAND – FROM CANADA
GIVEN TO THE EMPIRE

Bapaume Australian Cemetery

3754 Private
Frank Leslie SEXTON
51st Battalion, Australian Infantry
Died 2 April 1917, aged 23

OH, WHY ARE WE DEAD
WE YOUTH?
ALL YE THAT PASS BY
FORGET NOT

Bapaume Post Military Cemetery

Lieutenant
Bruce Hosmer Acton BURROWS
12th Field Company, Canadian Engineers
Died 25 November 1916, aged 23

HE GAVE HIS MERRY YOUTH AWAY
FOR COUNTRY AND FOR GOD

Second Lieutenant
Charles EDWARDS
6th Battalion, East Yorkshire Regiment
Died 29 January 1917, aged 23

HE RESPONDED TO
LORD KITCHENER'S APPEAL
AUGUST 1914
AND DIED FOR HIS COUNTRY

Major
Cecil WEDGWOOD, *DSO*
8th Battalion, North Staffordshire Regiment
Died 3 July 1916, aged 53

AS THE SHADOW
OF A GREAT ROCK
IN A WEARY LAND

(From Isaiah, *Chapter 32, Verse 2.)*

Barlin Communal Cemetery Extension

Lieutenant
Joseph GRIFFITHS, *MC*
73rd Battalion, Canadian Infantry
Died 2 March 1917, aged 29

THE DEATH HE DIED TO SAVE US
VICTOR IN THAT AWFUL STRIFE

Beacon Cemetery

240883 Sergeant
Lionel Arthur BROADBRIDGE
7th Battalion, The Buffs (East Kent Regiment)
Died 7 August 1918, aged 26

DEAREST BOY
ALL IS OVER AND LONG GONE
BUT LOVE IS NOT OVER
AND WHAT LOVE, O MY SON

87 Private
Arthur Claude GIBBS
34th Battalion, Australian Infantry
Died 18 August 1918, aged 39

THE WHITE GIFT OF HIS LIFE
HE GAVE UNGRUDGINGLY

7090 Sergeant
Edwin Thomas OBERG
17th Battalion, Australian Infantry
Died 14 May 1918, aged 33

"GONE"
WHAT SADNESS IN THAT WORD

1212 Private
Burton Pearson Septimus POWELL
34th Battalion, Australian Infantry
Died 22 August 1918, aged 29

HE DIED
WEARING THE WHITE FLOWER
OF AN HONOURED LIFE

Beaumont Hamel British Cemetery

8449 Sergeant
Norman BLISSETT
'A' Company, 1st Battalion, Hampshire Regiment
Died 1 July 1916, aged 23

YOUTH HAD SCARCELY WRITTEN
HIS NAME ON HER PAGE

Bécourt Military Cemetery

Second Lieutenant
Robert Astley Franklin EMINSON
6th Battalion, King's Royal Rifle Corps,
attached Machine Gun Corps (Infantry)
Died 20 July 1916, aged 24

THE NOBLE ARMY OF MARTYRS
PRAISE THEE

(From The Book of Common Prayer: *Te*
Deum Laudamus.)

27421 Lance Corporal
Arthur FINNEGAN
1st Battalion, Gloucestershire Regiment
Died 28 November 1916, aged 30

STOP TRAVELLER
A HERO LIES HERE

Second Lieutenant
Hugh Reginald FRESTON
3rd Battalion, attached 6th Battalion,
Royal Berkshire Regiment
Died 24 January 1916, aged 25

AUTHOR OF "THE QUEST OF TRUTH"
AND OTHER POEMS

1274 Private
Alexander McISAAC
'B' Company, 1st/8th Battalion,
Argyll & Sutherland Highlanders
Died 31 August 1915, aged 20

HE FOUGHT
FOR THE HONOUR OF BRITAIN
AND DIED
FOR THE GLORY OF FRANCE

4577 Private
Lyell POCOCK
6th Battalion, Australian Infantry
Died 15 August 1916, aged 17

IN DREAMS WE SEE YOU
ON THE BATTLE PLAIN
WOUNDED CALLING IN VAIN

---

154 Private
John PRENTICE
10th Battalion, The Cameronians (Scottish Rifles)
Died 23 August 1916, aged 27

HERE LIES A FATHER'S HOPE
A MOTHER'S PRIDE
AND A WIFE'S DEPENDENCE

A SOLDIER
OF THE GREAT WAR

Bedford House Cemetery

Captain
George Fenwick Hedley CHARLTON
10th Battalion, South Wales Borderers
Died 6 October 1916, aged 24

SLEEP LIGHTLY LAD
THOU ART KING'S GUARD
AT DAYBREAK

(This officer's brother, Lieutenant W.G.Charlton,
is buried in Warlencourt British Cemetery and has
the same epitaph.)

Second Lieutenant
Herbert Edward DUDLEY
6th Battalion, Somerset Light Infantry
Died 23 August 1917, aged 21

O NOT IN VAIN BRAVE SOUL
YE LIVED AND DIED

Second Lieutenant
Bernard Roy EDGAR
23rd Battalion, Machine Gun Corps (Infantry)
Died 31 July 1917, aged 20

HE FREELY GAVE
HIS PURE YOUNG RADIANT LIFE
THAT WE MAY LIVE IN PEACE

2321 Rifleman
Ernest William ELVIN
12th Battalion, London Regiment (The Rangers)
Died 21 April 1915, aged 20

VIVAS TO THE UNKNOWN HEROES
EQUAL TO
THE GREATEST HEROES KNOWN

(The epitaph is a much-condensed version of a stanza from Leaves of Grass *by Walt Whitman.)*

10143 Private
Edwin FITZPATRICK
1st Battalion, Royal Welsh Fusiliers
Died 20 October 1914, aged 31

CAN HONOUR'S VOICE
PROVOKE THE SILENT DUST
OR FLATTERY SOOTHE
THE DULL COLD EAR OF DEATH?

(From Thomas Gray's Elegy *Written in a Country Churchyard.)*

16702 Private
Hamilton GEDDES
'E' Company, 2nd Battalion,
Royal Dublin Fusiliers
Died 12 May 1915, aged 21

HE WENT FROM HIS HOME
IN THE FLOWER OF YOUTH

12885 Private
Thomas Morton HEALEY
9th Battalion,
Duke of Wellington's (West Riding Regiment)
Died 2 March 1916, aged 20

WAR'S CRUEL REAPER GATHERED
OUR TREASURED FLOWER

5857 Private
Archibald IZZATT
'D' Company, 1st Battalion,
The Black Watch (Royal Highlanders)
Died 31 October 1914, aged 38

PEACE HATH HIGHER TESTS
OF MANHOOD
THAN BATTLE EVER KNEW

Captain
Alfred Johnson LEEMING
6th Battalion, Royal Fusiliers
Died 31 July 1917, aged 28

SLEEP IN THY PERFECT PEACE
O SON OF ENGLAND
W.S.L.

652025 Rifleman
Peter Thomas REDMOND
21st Battalion, London Regiment
(1st Surrey Rifles)
Died 3 May 1917, aged 24

THERE'S A COTTAGE HOME
IN ENGLAND
WHERE HIS MOTHER SITS AND
WEEPS

(These words offer a rather different picture from that of a 1915 recruiting poster on which a white-haired lady at a cottage door urges her son to volunteer, proclaiming "It's your duty, lad!")

11058 Private
Walter Charles RUE
1st Battalion, Somerset Light Infantry
Died 30 May 1915, aged 20

BRAVE DEEDS NEVER DIE

4092 Private
Leslie Arthur SIDDINS
4th Battalion, Australian Infantry
Died 9 October 1916, aged 26

OUR BRAVE YOUNG LAD'S LIFE
NOBLY ENDED

Lieutenant
Philip Comfort STARR
154th Field Company, Royal Engineers
Died 20 February 1918, aged 28

ONE OF AMERICAN
HARVARD VANGUARD
ENTERING CANADIAN SERVICE
IN 1916

Belgian Battery Corner Cemetery

8140 Company Sergeant Major
Abraham DRAGE
2nd Battalion, Northamptonshire Regiment
Died 5 July 1917, aged 31

A SOLDIER STILL
BUT JOINED
IN A HIGHER SERVICE
FROM HIS LOVING WIFE KEZY

1979 Driver
John Charles HERITAGE
4th Divisional Ammunition Column,
Australian Field Artillery
Died 22 October 1917, aged 37

FOR GOD AND EMPIRE
BELOVED SON
OF J.C. & M.A. HERITAGE
OF EUSTON

(The Euston in question here is in New South Wales.)

41375 Private
Reginald Alexander TILLCOCK
2nd Battalion, Middlesex Regiment
Died 28 June 1917, aged 24

THE DEAD DO NOT NEED US
BUT FOR EVER AND EVER MORE
WE NEED THEM

Bellicourt British Cemetery

220 Private
John William HAYS
31st Battalion, Australian Infantry
Died 29 September 1918, aged 29

GOD GRANT THAT ERE
HIS SPIRIT FLED
HE SAW
THAT NOT IN VAIN HE BLED

Lieutenant Colonel
Bernard William VANN, *VC, MC & Bar*
8th Battalion, attached 1st/6th Battalion,
Sherwood Foresters
(Nottinghamshire & Derbyshire Regiment)
Died 3 October 1918, aged 31

CROIX DE GUERRE AVEC PALME
"A GREAT PRIEST
WHO IN HIS DAYS
PLEASED GOD"

(This highly accomplished man won a hockey blue
at Cambridge, was ordained as a priest, taught
history at a public school [Wellingborough], played
as an amateur in the Football League and later
turned professional, served as a First World War
army officer, won two MCs and a Croix de Guerre,
and was killed by a sniper three days after the
action for which he was posthumously awarded the
VC. He left a widow, and a baby son he never
saw.)

Berks Cemetery Extension

3091 Private
Arthur BELLGROVE
1st/5th Battalion, Royal Warwickshire Regiment
Died 31 May 1915, aged 39

STILL WAITING

10325 Private
Harold Frederick GIBBONS
11th Battalion,
The Queen's Own (Royal West Kent Regiment)
Died 15 June 1916, aged 23

CALLED HOME
IN THE MORNING OF HIS DAYS
IN GOD'S HANDS NOW HE RESTS

---

858 Gunner
Henry John HUDSON
1st Battery, Australian Siege Artillery
Died 3 February 1918, aged 20

THY WORK IS DONE
THOU'ST LAID
THINE ARMOUR DOWN
FOUGHT THE GOOD FIGHT

18011 Private
Harry HURST
15th Battalion, Hampshire Regiment
Died 4 August 1916, aged 32

A DAY'S MARCH NEARER HOME

435324 Private
James Fingland HYSLOP
10th Battalion, Canadian Infantry
(Alberta Regiment)
Died 18 March 1916, aged 27

HE PREFERRED A NOBLE LIFE
BEFORE A LONG

2244 Lance Corporal
William James MacFARLANE
'B' Company, 2nd Battalion, Seaforth Highlanders
Died 2 April 1915, aged 23

FORGET THEM NOT
O LAND FOR WHICH THEY FELL
MAY IT GO WELL WITH ENGLAND
STILL GO WELL

108402 Private
Cecil MUMFORD
'C' Company, 3rd Canadian Mounted Rifles
Died 1 December 1915, aged 22

THE FIGHT THAT YE
SO WELL BEGUN
IS FINISHED NOW
AND NOBLY WON

2137 Private
Herbert William ROHDE
38th Battalion, Australian Infantry
Died 29 November 1917, aged 32

REST ON IN PEACE
AUSTRALIAN HERO
TILL THE BUGLE SOUNDS AGAIN

6402 Private
Laurence Ralph STONE
28th Battalion, Australian Infantry
Died 30 December 1917, aged 24

HE DIED FOR ITS COLOURS
AND SHED HIS HEART'S BLOOD
FOR THE FLAG

C/12262 Rifleman
Herbert Spencer TRAFFORD
'D' Company, 21st Battalion,
King's Royal Rifle Corps
Died 24 June 1916, aged 19

19 YEARS – SHORT – BUT CROWNED

Bernafay Wood British Cemetery

4102 Private
John ROAMS
30th Battalion, Australian Infantry
Died 2 March 1917, aged 31

OUR HERO GONE WEST

1183 Private
George Silvester SMITH
2nd Battalion, Australian Infantry
Died 25 December 1916, aged 46

TOO FAR AWAY
YOUR GRAVE TO SEE
BUT NOT TOO FAR
FOR MY MEMORY

(Private Smith died of wounds on Christmas Day.)

Bertangles Communal Cemetery

Second Lieutenant
James Arthur MILLER
24th Squadron, Royal Flying Corps
Died 28 March 1918, aged 24

AND BRIGHT
WITH MANY AN ANGEL
AND ALL THE MARTYR THRONG

(The only British war-grave in this cemetery is that
of an American. Second Lieutenant Miller, who
was born in Hawaii, was killed when his SE5A
crashed. His epitaph is from the hymn Jerusalem
the Golden, *a translation by John M.Neale from*
the medieval Latin of Bernard of Morlais.)

Bertrancourt Military Cemetery

18/343 Private
Frank PLOWS
18th Battalion, Durham Light Infantry
Died 25 June 1916, aged 18

TRUMPETER
WHAT ARE YOU SOUNDING NOW

Bethleem Farm East Cemetery

2581 Private
Fred HAMPTON
43rd Battalion, Australian Infantry
Died 3 July 1917, aged 32

THE HOURS I'VE SPENT
WITH THEE DEAR HEART
ARE AS A STRING OF PEARLS
TO ME

Bethleem Farm West Cemetery

6068 Private
Arthur William RENNIE
37th Battalion, Australian Infantry
Died 8 June 1917, aged 20

TRUE AND LOYAL TO EMPIRE
AND GOOD PRINCIPLE

251 Private
Sidney Calton WARD
42nd Battalion, Australian Infantry
Died 10 June 1917, aged 21

INSCRIBE HIS NAME
ON THE SCROLL OF FAME
IN LETTERS OF PUREST GOLD

Béthune Town Cemetery

11056 Private
Edward Thomas BROWNE
9th Battalion, Essex Regiment
Died 14 March 1916, aged 17

REST OUR BRAVE BOY
UNTIL THE DAY BREAK
AND WARS CEASE

Lieutenant
Frank Alexander DE PASS, *VC*
34th (Prince Albert Victor's Own) Poona Horse
Died 25 November 1914, aged 27

SON OF ELIOT
AND BEATRICE DE PASS
BORN 26TH APRIL 1887
LOVED
GONE PROUDLY FRIENDED

(This lieutenant's posthumous VC was awarded for his attack on an enemy trench when under heavy fire, and his rescue of a wounded sepoy from the battlefield later the same day. He survived these actions, but was shot dead by a sniper the following day. The final words of the epitaph are from The Dead, *a poem by fellow-Rugbeian Rupert Brooke.)*

26541 Corporal
Archibald DEVLIN
14th Battalion, Canadian Infantry
(Quebec Regiment)
Died 22 May 1915, aged 32

LYING TONIGHT
BESIDE THE BRAVE
SLEEPS MY BROTHER
IN A SOLDIER'S GRAVE

Lieutenant
Bruce Francis Sholto DOUGLAS
2nd Battalion, South Staffordshire Regiment
Died 14 April 1915, aged 18

HAVING GIVEN ALL CHEERFULLY
HE ENTERS NEW LIFE
WELL EQUIPT

14383 Private
Albert Edward FREER
2nd Battalion, Worcestershire Regiment
Died 19 March 1915, aged 17

THE CLARION CALLED
HE OBEYED

Second Lieutenant
Cecil Boyce GRUNDY
1st Battalion, Middlesex Regiment
Died 16 November 1915, aged 21

AGE 21
AND FOR SUCH SONS AS THESE
BE PRAISE TO GOD

Lieutenant
Duncan Stuart Ross MACPHERSON
7th Gurkha Rifles
Died 23 November 1914, aged 25

AGED 25
ONLY CHILD OF MAJOR GENERAL
SIR W.G. MACPHERSON
AND ELIZABETH ANNE
MACPHERSON

(This is one of three adjacent graves of sons of high-ranking officers.)

S/8720 Private
John REID
2nd Battalion, Gordon Highlanders
Died 17 May 1915, aged 16

OUR ONLY REGRET
"TOO YOUNG"

2235 Private
William Rendle SMITH
1st/24th Battalion, London Regiment
Died 5 May 1915, aged 21

HE DIED FOR A HIGH IDEAL
THEREIN LIES
THE ONE CONSOLATION

Beuvry Communal Cemetery

Lieutenant
Charles Loaring CLARK
3rd Battalion, Canadian Infantry
(Central Ontario Regiment)
Died 17 June 1915, aged 21

AND THEY RISE TO THEIR FEET
AS HE PASSES BY
GENTLEMEN UNAFRAID

(From a Rudyard Kipling poem, To Wolcott Balestier.)

Captain
George John Lorne SMITH
1st Battalion, Canadian Infantry
(Western Ontario Regiment)
Died 15 June 1915, aged 32

I COUNT MY LIFE WELL LOST
TO SERVE MY COUNTRY BEST

Beuvry Communal Cemetery Extension

10067 Lance Corporal
Albert Henry GARDNER
1st Battalion, Gloucestershire Regiment
Died 17 April 1918, aged 22

WE MARCH TO THE BATTLE FIELD
THE FOE IS NOW BEFORE US

743 Lance Corporal
Douglas GORDON
'C' Company, 17th Battalion, Royal Fusiliers
Died 14 August 1917, aged 25

"HE LIVED & DIED
A GALLANT GENTLEMAN SOLDIER"
A COMRADE'S TRIBUTE

Birr Cross Roads Cemetery

1945 Private
William Gilbert GRACE
7th Battalion, Australian Infantry
Died 20 September 1917, aged 38

THE ILLS OF LIFE
HE PATIENTLY BORE
WILL NEVER DISTRESS HIM AGAIN

Second Lieutenant
Raymond LODGE
2nd Battalion, attached 3rd Battalion,
South Lancashire Regiment
Died 14 September 1915, aged 26

RAYMOND WHO HAS HELPED
MANY TO KNOW
THAT DEATH IS NOT THE END

5494 Gunner
John Clegg TAYLOR
1st Brigade, Australian Field Artillery
Died 3 November 1917, aged 23

STRONG IN ARMS
FAITHFUL IN PEACE
HIS MOTHER

Bleuet Farm Cemetery

113893 Gunner
Ernest CALLAGHAN
145th Siege Battery, Royal Garrison Artillery
Died 4 September 1917, aged 20

VICTORIOUS TOO SHALL RISE
THEY WHO HAVE DRUNK
THE CUP OF SACRIFICE

127865 Gunner
John George PEARSON
232nd Siege Battery, Royal Garrison Artillery
Died 19 September 1917, aged 32

ONLY SON
INTO THINE HANDS O GOD
INTO THINE HANDS

Bois-Grenier Communal Cemetery

1908 Private
Ernest JOHNSON
1st/4th Battalion,
King's Own Yorkshire Light Infantry
Died 18 May 1915, aged 20

FOREVER HERE
MY REST SHALL BE
CLOSE TO THY BLEEDING SIDE

Captain
Thomas TODRICK
8th Battalion, Royal Scots
Died 14 December 1914, aged 34

PSALM 144

('Blessed be the Lord my strength, which teacheth
my hands to war, and my fingers to fight … ')

Bonnay Communal Cemetery Extension

Captain
Jack DE MEZA, *MC*
19th (County of London) Battalion,
London Regiment
Died 23 March 1918, aged 27

BELOVED HUSBAND OF
DAISY DE MEZA
YOU HAD THE DEATH YOU WISHED

Bootham Cemetery

553138 Rifleman
Arthur Horace NEWMAN
16th Battalion, London Regiment
(Queen's Westminster Rifles)
Died 14 April 1917, aged 19

A NOBLE BOY
A GALLANT GENTLEMAN
LOVED AND ADMIRED BY ALL

Borre British Cemetery

Second Lieutenant
Henry James FORBES
'C' Company, 3rd Battalion,
attached 1st Battalion,
King's Own Scottish Borderers
Died 18 August 1918, aged 22

A GREAT COMPANION
A GALLANT SOLDIER
AND GENTLEMAN
COL. BEATY-POWNALL

(Lieutenant Colonel G.E.Beaty-Pownall,
commanding officer of Second Lieutenant Forbes's
battalion, was to become the last British officer to be
killed in the Ypres Salient when he met his own
death less than two months later.)

Lieutenant
Muirton Warrand FORBES
2nd Battalion, Australian Infantry
Died 24 May 1918, aged 19

THE EARTH HOLDS
NO BRAVER GENTLEMAN

(This officer's older brother, Lieutenant
J.W.Forbes, who died eight months earlier and is
buried in Perth Cemetery [China Wall], has the
same epitaph.)

Captain
Lindon Howard Russell HIGINBOTHAM
3rd Battalion, Australian Infantry
Died 21 June 1918, aged 28

OUR TURN HERE IS FINISHED
LAST WORDS IN HIS DIARY
18/6/18

Lieutenant
Elmer Winfred Drake LAING, *MC*
12th Battalion, Australian Infantry
Died 8 May 1918, aged 25

FOR HIS ENGLISH AND FRENCH
BROTHERS AND SISTERS

440 Private
Albert Victor LARSEN
12th Battalion, Australian Infantry
Died 28 May 1918, aged 21

BEING UNABLE TO VIEW
THIS PLAIN
BUT BY THE GRACE OF GOD
WE'LL MEET AGAIN

3898 Private
Aeneas MURRAY
11th Battalion, Australian Infantry
Died 31 July 1918, aged 33

ONE WHO HAS HELPED
TO WRITE AUSTRALIA'S HISTORY
IN BLOOD

(A tribute which reflects as strongly as any the
significance to Australia's young nationhood of the
contribution and sacrifice of her servicemen in the
Great War.)

1634 Corporal
William Horace Floyd ROBERTS
9th Battalion, Australian Infantry
Died 19 July 1918, aged 33

NOT DEAD, PROMOTED
MERELY CHANGED HIS REGIMENT
HIS DUTY NOBLY DONE

---

487 Second Corporal
William Albert SNELL, *MM*
3rd Field Company, Australian Engineers
Died 31 May 1918, aged 37

WEEP NOT MOTHER DEAR
NOT DEAD BUT SLEEPETH HERE

Boulogne Eastern Cemetery

6356 Private
Thomas Percival BLAKEMAN
'D' Company, 2nd Battalion,
South Staffordshire Regiment
Died 24 February 1915, aged 28

AGE 28
HE HUMBLED HIMSELF
BECOMING OBEDIENT UNTO
DEATH

(From Philippians, *Chapter 2, Verse 8.)*

9962 Private
William DOUGLAS
1st Battalion, Cheshire Regiment
Died 16 February 1915, aged 17

HERO OF OURS
BY NOBLE PURPOSE LED
REST THOU IN PEACE
ONE OF THE HONOURED DEAD

11712 Private
Douglas FLEMING
1st Battalion, The King's (Liverpool Regiment)
Died 16 January 1915, aged 19

MAN'S INHUMANITY TO MAN
MAKES
COUNTLESS THOUSANDS MOURN
BURNS

(From Robert Burns's poem Man Was Made To
Mourn.*)*

1370 Sergeant
William FLEMING
1st Battalion, Irish Guards
Died 4 November 1914, aged 27

BY HONOUR BOUND
FOR WEAL OR WOE
WHAIT'ER SHE BID
HE DARED TO DO

Captain
Reginald Harry Myburgh HANDS
South African Heavy Artillery
attached Royal Garrison Artillery
Died 20 April 1918, aged 29

BELOVED ELDEST SON OF
SIR HARRY & LADY HANDS
CLAREMONT, CAPE TOWN

(One of a trinity of talented sporting brothers,
Captain Hands was a double-international, having
represented England at rugby union and South
Africa as a Test cricketer.)

38

10242 Private
Robert John HOOPER
2nd Battalion, Wiltshire Regiment
Died 6 April 1915, aged 17

HIS LIFE
WAS FREELY GIVEN
DEFENDING BRAVELY, HONOUR
TRUTH AND RIGHT

Second Lieutenant
Alfred John HUNT
30th Battery, Royal Field Artillery
Died 28 November 1914, aged 23

EVERYWHERE
WHERE DUTY AND GLORY LEAD

Captain
Theodore Stewart LUKIS
13th (Kensington) Battalion, London Regiment
Died 15 March 1915, aged 29

WE GRUDGE NOT OUR LIFE
IF IT GIVES LARGER LIFE
TO THEM THAT DO LIVE

9840 Private
James Crawford Eaglesome MacKINNON
1st Battalion, Leicestershire Regiment
Died 31 October 1914, aged 23

STRANGERS, TREAD LIGHTLY
OVER JAMIE'S GRAVE
HERE LIES
ONE OF THE GLORIOUS BRAVE

1348 Corporal
Kenneth Charles Ernest MacRAE
1st/14th Battalion, London Regiment
(London Scottish)
Died 26 November 1914, aged 21

HE GAVE WITHOUT STINT
HE FOUGHT WITHOUT MALICE
HE DIED WITHOUT FEAR

Bouzincourt Communal Cemetery Extension

Lieutenant
William Setten GOFF, *MC*
7th Battalion, Royal Welsh Fusiliers
Died 22 April 1918, aged 36

DEAR OLD BILL, GOD BLESS YOU

(It was Lieutenant Goff's brother who offered this
fond and simple greeting.)

593370 Rifleman
William Walter HEWETT
'C' Company, 1st/18th Battalion,
London Regiment
(London Irish Rifles)
Died 5 April 1918, aged 26

THERE SHALL BE NO FORSAKING
OF THOSE WHO NOBLY FOUGHT
AND FIGHTING DIED

Second Lieutenant
Hubert Franklin MADDERS
168th Brigade, Royal Field Artillery
Died 1 July 1916, aged 35

WHOSO TAKES THE WORLD'S LIFE
ON HIM
AND HIS OWN LAYS DOWN
… LIVES

(From A.C.Swinburne's poem Super Flamina
Babylonis.*)*

20441 Sergeant
Stanley Trevelyan REES
10th Battalion, South Wales Borderers
Died 27 April 1918, aged 21

A BRITON AYE, A HERO TOO
HIS MOTTO "BE PREPARED"
KEPT TRUE

56129 Private
Albert SHINTON
17th Battalion, Royal Welsh Fusiliers
Died 13 August 1918, aged 23

HE SLEEPS
'MID THE POPPIES IN FLANDERS
HIS BED A SOLDIER'S GRAVE

Bouzincourt Ridge Cemetery

46990 Private
William Wilson SIMPSON
6th Battalion, Northamptonshire Regiment
Died 18 August 1918, aged 24

SOME DAY
GOD'S VOICE WILL SPEAK
AND TELL US WHY

Brandhoek Military Cemetery

21772 Private
Hugh CAMERON
7th Battalion, Cameron Highlanders
Died 8 July 1917, aged 20

LIVE ON BRAVE LAD
THE LORD OF LIFE ALONE
KNOWS TO WHAT GOAL OF GOOD

202296 Private
George DOW
4th/5th Battalion,
The Black Watch (Royal Highlanders)
Died 9 July 1917, aged 24

ONE OF
THE UNRETURNING HEROES;
ONE OF
GOD'S HONOURED DEAD

12424 Guardsman
George William EDWARDS
3rd Company, 4th Battalion, Coldstream Guards
Died 15 April 1916, aged 21

AGED 21
THIS BE THY RECORD
HE GAVE HIS LIFE THAT
ENGLAND'S SOUL MIGHT LIVE

16220 Private
Thomas ELWELL
7th Battalion, Yorkshire Regiment
Died 6 November 1915, aged 31

O GOD GIVE ME
THE HERO'S MOTHER
STRENGTH TO SAY
THY WILL BE DONE

745 Guardsman
Harry HEATH
4th Company, 1st Battalion, Welsh Guards
Died 2 July 1916, aged 23

OH MAY IT DRY
HIS MOTHER'S TEARS
TO SEE HIM HONOURED
THUS FOR YEARS.

28473 Private
Robert Naylor McNEILLY
10th Battalion, The Cameronians (Scottish Rifles)
Died 22 July 1917, aged 19

HE PLAYED THE MAN

2306 Private
George Augustus MASCORD
Honourable Artillery Company
Died 20 September 1915, aged 26

PRO PATRIA MORI (HOOGE)
AN ONLY SON
MELBOURNE, AUSTRALIE
BARNES, LONDRES

(An epitaph which encompasses three languages –
Latin [pro patria mori = died for his country],
English – and French rather than Flemish,
although Private Mascord died and is buried in
Flemish-speaking Flanders.)

Captain
Henry Evelyn Arthur PLATT
2nd Company, 1st Battalion, Coldstream Guards
Died 15 May 1916, aged 32

… FRIEND, JUST SAY
"HE TRIED"

1800 Guardsman
William Owen PRITCHARD
1st Battalion, Welsh Guards
Died 18 July 1916, aged 27

GOD WATCHETH OVER
EACH LOVED SOLDIER'S GRAVE
BENEATH A FOREIGN SUN

1154 Guardsman
Reginald SMITH
1st Battalion, Welsh Guards
Died 22 June 1916, aged 21

A GRAVE IN FRANCE
WHERE A BRAVE HERO SLEEPS
A HOME IN ENGLAND
WHERE LOVED ONES WEEP

(Wales, France and England all feature on the
headstone, but not Belgium, which is where the
soldier is buried. Why this error – and there are
several other similar ones – was not picked up and
corrected somewhere along the way is a mystery.)

R/32841 Rifleman
Percy William WARDEN
17th Battalion, King's Royal Rifle Corps
Died 28 June 1917, aged 30

NOT LEFT TO LIE
LIKE FALLEN TREE,
NOT DEAD

Captain
Edward Arthur WICKSON
51st Battalion, Canadian Infantry,
attached Royal Flying Corps
Died 16 June 1917, aged 33

HE WHO DIES FOR OTHERS
DIES A PERFECT MAN

Brandhoek New Military Cemetery

240207 Private
Francis Emile BISSAT
1st/5th Battalion,
Duke of Cornwall's Light Infantry
Died 19 August 1917, aged 21

MY KING, MY COUNTRY
'TIS FOR THEE

96136 Driver
Bert BROWN
8th Divisional Ammunition Company,
Royal Field Artillery
Died 3 August 1917, aged 20

REST WELL BRAVE HEART
BY STREAM AND HILL
WHERE MANY A HERO'S GRAVE
GROWS GREEN

Captain
Noel Godfrey CHAVASSE, *VC & Bar, MC*
Royal Army Medical Corps,
attached 1st/10th Battalion,
The King's (Liverpool Regiment)
Died 4 August 1917, aged 32

"GREATER LOVE
HATH NO MAN THAN THIS
THAT A MAN LAY DOWN
HIS LIFE FOR HIS FRIENDS"

(While the epitaph itself is the most common of all
on British war-graves, this headstone is unique in
displaying two Victoria Crosses. Only three men
have won the decoration twice, and the other two
survived their respective wars. Captain Chavasse, a
son of the Bishop of Liverpool, repeatedly treated
wounded men on the battlefield while under heavy
fire. He died exactly a month after his brother
Aidan, who is commemorated on the Menin Gate
Memorial to the Missing.)

41378 Private
James Aulinne GRAY
108th Field Ambulance,
Royal Army Medical Corps
Died 9 August 1917, aged 17

HEAVEN IS FULL OF
GAY AND CARELESS FACES
NEW-WAKED FROM
DREAMS OF DREADFUL THINGS

(Despite his extreme youth, Private Gray was not a
newcomer to the ranks. He joined up when he was
14, which would have meant lying about his age, as
so many boys did when the minimum age for
enlistment was 18.)

97507 Bombardier
Charles HADFIELD
202nd Siege Battery, Royal Garrison Artillery
Died 6 August 1917, aged 21

MAY ANGELS GUARD
THAT LONELY PLACE
WHERE MY DEAR SON SLUMBERS

35529 Private
Charlie William JAMES
10th Battalion, Essex Regiment
Died 13 August 1917, aged 37

HE WAS GOOD TO HIS MOTHER

20853 Private
Ivor Idris LEWIS
15th Battalion, Welsh Regiment
Died 1 August 1917, aged 23

BRIEF, BRAVE AND GLORIOUS
WAS HIS YOUNG CAREER

785792 Acting Bombardier
Thomas MOUNTFORD
'C' Battery, 232nd Army Brigade,
Royal Field Artillery
Died 31 July 1917, aged 23

EVERY NOBLE LIFE
LEAVES ITS FIBRE INTERWOVEN
IN THE WORK OF THE WORLD

49590 Gunner
Horatio Nelson ORMEROD
30th Siege Battery, Royal Garrison Artillery
Died 28 July 1917, aged 29

WHAT A NOBLE DEATH
FIGHTING FOR GOD
RIGHT AND LIBERTY

5457 Lance Corporal
Lewis Milford SCAWEN
7th Battalion, Leinster Regiment
Died 5 August 1917, aged 39

HIS KING AND COUNTRY
CALLED HIM
HIS ANSWER WAS "I'LL GO"
HE DIED THAT WE MIGHT LIVE

Brandhoek New Military Cemetery No 3

41951 Private
William BRADBURY
8th Battalion, Royal Inniskilling Fusiliers
Died 17 August 1917, aged 19

SLAIN BY THE HAND
OF A RUTHLESS FOE
OUR BOY IS AT REST
WITH GOD WE KNOW

75069 Private
Frederick BUNKHALL
126th Company, Labour Corps
Died 20 August 1917, aged 44

HE DIED FIGHTING
TO KILL THE WRONG
AND THRONE THE RIGHT

534173 Private
John Gilbert GILL
4th (London) Field Ambulance,
Royal Army Medical Corps
Died 18 August 1917, aged 21

I HAVE ONLY DONE MY DUTY
AS A MAN IS BOUND TO DO
"GIBBIE"

340164 Gunner
Maitland Harold GORING
4th Divisional Ammunition Column,
Canadian Field Artillery
Died 19 October 1917, aged 17

AGE 17 YRS.
1 MON. 10 DYS.
IN THY KEEPING
OUR FATHER

KNOWN UNTO GOD

118642 Gunner
William Henry HOLLIDAY
'B' Battery, 173rd Brigade, Royal Field Artillery
Died 18 August 1917, aged 28

WATCHMAKER
WIGAN, LANCASHIRE

Second Lieutenant
Arthur Leslie Gwynne JONES
252nd Siege Battery, Royal Garrison Artillery
Died 4 May 1918, aged 20

AGE 20 OF LLANDAFF
FAITHFUL UNTO DEATH
IN THE SERVICE OF THE GUNS

Second Lieutenant
Richard Douglas MILES, *MC*
9th Battalion, Royal Irish Fusiliers
Died 17 August 1917, aged 27

THANK GOD: WE KNOW
THAT HE BATTLED WELL
IN THE LAST
GREAT GAME OF ALL

(Before obtaining a commission in the Royal Irish
Fusiliers, Second Lieutenant Miles had attained the
rank of sergeant major while serving with the 31st
Battalion, Canadian Infantry [Alberta Regiment.])

211770 Gunner
Walter William WARREN
'B' Battery, 245th Brigade, Royal Field Artillery
Died 25 April 1918, aged 20

DIED WITH THE BRAVE
BURIED WITH THE HEROES

Bray Military Cemetery

3509A Private
John Francis Cecil GALLAGHER
35th Battalion, Australian Infantry
Died 23 August 1918, aged 23

HIS LIFE
ON THE BATTLEFIELD SPENT
AUSTRALIA RAISES
THIS MONUMENT

47281 Driver
Fred SEDGWICK
'B' Battery, 181st Brigade, Royal Field Artillery
Died 28 February 1917, aged 29

WE LITTLE KNEW
AS WE SAID GOOD-BYE
WE WERE PARTED FOR EVER
AND YOU WERE GOING TO DIE

Bronfay Farm Military Cemetery

92915 Private
Frederick Robert AGATES
2nd/2nd Battalion, London Regiment
(Royal Fusiliers)
Died 26 August 1918, aged 18

STILL ON GUARD
WITH JESUS MY CAPTAIN

Lieutenant Colonel
Hubert Pulteney DALZELL-WALTON
8th Battalion, Royal Inniskilling Fusiliers
Died 9 September 1916, aged 50

HIS WARFARE IS ACCOMPLISHED
HIS REST SHALL BE GLORIOUS

(The first line of the epitaph is adapted from
Isaiah, Chapter 40, Verse 2. This veteran officer
had served in the Bechuanaland Expedition of
1884-85, the Burma War of 1886-89, in which
he was twice wounded, and the Boer War.)

Brown's Road Military Cemetery

2658 Battery Sergeant Major
John Marks GILBERT
114th Heavy Battery, Royal Garrison Artillery
Died 2 November 1914, aged 42

PRAY FOR THE SOUL OF HIM
WHO DIED FOR CHURCH AND
KING
R.I.P.

(A veteran of 21 years' service, Battery Sergeant
Major Gilbert had been Mentioned in Despatches
during the Boer War. He was also Assistant
Organizing Secretary to Lord Roberts in the
National Service League.)

Second Lieutenant
Bertram Gilbert HILL
3rd Battalion, attached 2nd Battalion,
Royal Warwickshire Regiment
Died 25 September 1915, aged 18

HE IS THE SILENCE FOLLOWING
GREAT WORDS OF PEACE

Major
Reginald Trevor ROPER
1st Battalion, Dorsetshire Regiment
Died 12 October 1914, aged 42

QUIT YOU LIKE MEN
BE STRONG
1 COR. 16. 13

Lieutenant
Arthur Nugent WEBSTER
203rd Squadron, Royal Air Force
Died 5 June 1918, aged 19

FELL IN AERIAL BATTLE
"THEY SHALL MOUNT UP
WITH WINGS AS EAGLES"

(The source of the quotation is Isaiah, *Chapter 40,*
Verse 31.)

Buffs Road Cemetery

Second Lieutenant
Arnold William RASH
5th Battalion, Suffolk Regiment
Died 31 July 1917, aged 25

HE GAVE UP ALL
EVEN LIFE ITSELF
FOR THE IDEALS
OF TRUTH & JUSTICE

Bulls Road Cemetery

5655 Private
Stanley Franklyn BROADBENT
3rd Battalion, Australian Infantry
Died 5 November 1916, aged 18

HE WAS PREPARED
FOR HIS NOBLE DEATH
AMONGST MEN

C/7572 Rifleman
Thomas Ernest WALTON
18th Battalion, King's Royal Rifle Corps
Died 15 September 1916, aged 42

JESUS, MY REST
AMID EARTH'S BATTLEFIELDS

Bully-Grenay Communal Cemetery British Extension

267056 Private
Reginald George ALDRIDGE
5th Battalion, Canadian Infantry
(Saskatchewan Regiment)
Died 16 March 1918, aged 25

SCATTER THOU THE PEOPLE
THAT DELIGHT IN WAR

(Psalms, Chapter 68, Verse 30.)

27415 Sergeant
Charles COX
113th Battery, Royal Field Artillery
Died 31 May 1916, aged 39

WHAT GREATER SACRIFICE
THAN HIS OWN LIFE
TO SAVE A HORSE

(A massive number of horses were lost in the Great
War. Estimates vary widely – some well into six
figures and others in millions. Most died from
exposure, disease and starvation, but a great many
also were 'killed in action', which presumably was
the fate said here to have been averted by Sergeant
Cox at the cost of his own life.)

718608 Lance Corporal
Frederick Charles DAVIES
107th Battalion, Canadian Pioneers
Died 4 March 1918, aged 19

GVANDVIEN, MAN.
BRAVE BUGLER BOY

(The erroneously-inscribed first line of the epitaph
should be a reference to the soldier's home town -
Grand View, Manitoba.)

104960 Private
Richard Russell REEVE
16th Battalion, Canadian Infantry
(Manitoba Regiment)
Died 4 March 1918, aged 23

HE DIED TO HELP
THE MAPLE LEAF TO LIVE

Bus House Cemetery

Lieutenant
Eric Douglas DOYLE, *MC*
190th Brigade, Royal Field Artillery
Died 29 July 1917, aged 23

HIS RADIANT SPIRIT
SERVES WITH THE BATTALIONS
OF THE SUPREME RULER

67022 Private
Fred LAYLAND
96th Field Ambulance,
Royal Army Medical Corps
Died 21 September 1917, aged 23

SUCH GRAVES AS HIS
ARE PILGRIM-SHRINES

Buttes New British Cemetery

49297 Private
William GRANT
20th Battalion, Manchester Regiment
Died 8 October 1917, aged 19

SACRED SPOT
TREAD GENTLY
A MOTHER'S LOVE LIES HERE

Lieutenant
Harold Rowland HILL
25th Battalion, Australian Infantry
Died 4 October 1917, aged 22

"I'M ALL RIGHT MOTHER
CHEERIO"

40272 Private
Alfred John PATCHETT
7th Battalion, Leicestershire Regiment
Died 5 October 1917, aged 19

THE DAYS OF HIS YOUTH
HAST THOU SHORTENED

(From Psalms, Chapter 89, Verse 45.)

---

928 Private
William TOWNSEND
22nd Battalion, Australian Infantry
Died 4 October 1917, aged 42

JUST AS I AM
WITHOUT ONE PLEA
BUT THAT THY BLOOD
WAS SHED FOR ME

(The opening lines of Charlotte Elliott's hymn Just
As I Am, Without One Plea.*)*

Cabaret Rouge British Cemetery

9074 Corporal
Thomas Healy BATES
1st Battalion, Royal Warwickshire Regiment
Died 31 March 1918, aged 27

THE FIGHT IS O'ER
& VICTORY WON
AND MANY A MOTHER
HAS LOST HER SON

Major
Hugh Reginald BELL
11th Battalion, Tank Corps
Died 3 September 1918, aged 39

CHORISTER
SCHOOLMASTER
SOLDIER

Captain
Braxton BIGELOW
170th Tunnelling Company, Royal Engineers
Died 23 July 1917, aged 30

AN AMERICAN

THEIR NAME LIVETH
FOR EVERMORE

S/40115 Private
Douglas James Henderson BLACK
'C' Company, 7th Battalion, Seaforth Highlanders
Died 9 April 1917, aged 19

WOE TO THE WORLD
SHOULD HE DIE IN VAIN

25822 Private
William BREMNER
2nd Battalion, Highland Light Infantry
Died 28 April 1917, aged 27

LOOK ON US THOU WHO PASS BY
FROM OUR DEAD HANDS
THY FREEDOM CAME

2332 Private
Arthur William CALLANDER
14th Battalion, London Regiment
(London Scottish)
Died 9 May 1915, aged 28

NATURE MIGHT STAND UP
AND SAY TO ALL THE WORLD
THIS WAS A MAN!

(From William Shakespeare's Julius Caesar, Act
5, Scene 5.)

512581 Private
Frank CARBUTT
14th Battalion, London Regiment
(London Scottish)
Died 2 June 1917, aged 20

… AT TWENTY COULD DIE
IN THE OLD AGE
OF A COMPLETE UNSPOTTED LIFE

Captain
Arthur Reginald FRENCH
5th Baron DE FREYNE
3rd Battalion, attached 1st Battalion,
South Wales Borderers
Died 9 May 1915, aged 35

THE PITY OF IT

Second Lieutenant
Samuel Lawrence GLOVER
10th Battalion,
Duke of Wellington's (West Riding Regiment)
Died 12 January 1916, aged 20

I FEAR NO FOE
WITH THEE AT HAND TO BLESS

(From Henry Francis Lyte's hymn Abide With
Me.*)*

Captain
Roy Scott GREIG
14th Battalion, London Regiment
(London Scottish),
attached 6th Battalion, Cameron Highlanders
Died 28 March 1918, aged 24

WOUNDED MESSINES 1914
GOMMECOURT 1916
ARRAS (MORTALLY) 1918

S/9185 Private
Robert GRIERSON
9th Battalion,
The Black Watch (Royal Highlanders)
Died 9 April 1917, aged 20

THE WARRIOR FOR THE TRUE
THE RIGHT
FIGHTS IN LOVE'S NAME

Second Lieutenant
Percy William HUBBARD, *MM*
16th Battalion, Lancashire Fusiliers,
Died 6 June 1918, aged 37

A GREAT HEARTED SPORTSMAN
SUNNY, CHIVALROUS & STRONG
SO BRAVE IN PERIL
CONSTANT IN TRIBULATION
AND IN ALL CHANGES OF
FORTUNE
LOYAL AND LOVING

(This resounding tribute to Second Lieutenant
'Peter' Hubbard, who had twice been severely
wounded, runs well beyond the stipulated maximum
length. He enjoyed success at cricket, rugby and
boxing in both civilian and army life, and before
being commissioned had been promoted to sergeant
at the capture of Ovillers in 1916.)

2399 Lance Corporal
Charles Vernon JASON
57th Battalion, Australian Infantry
Died 13 August 1916, aged 22

ONE OF GOD'S BRAVEST
GONE WEST WITH THE GLORY
OF THE SETTING SUN

58096 Private
David John JONES
6th Battalion, Northamptonshire Regiment
Died 29 September 1918, aged 29

WHO KNOWS AT WHAT GREAT COST
OUR LIBERTY WAS WON?
A MOTHER WHO HAS LOST
HER ONLY SON

(Mrs Jones of Abercynon was also a widow.)

8471 Lance Sergeant
Alfred Edward LENNOX
1st Regiment, South African Infantry
Died 18 October 1916, aged 40

THESE ARE THE SOULS
TO WHOM HIGH VALOUR GAVE
GLORY UNDYING

(Having served with the Cape Mounted Police in
the Boer War and received the Queen's Medal with
Clasp, Lance Sergeant Lennox began the First
World War in the South African Mounted Rifles,
taking part in the campaign in German South-
West Africa.)

---

85 Private
Alexander Vernon MARTIN
5th Field Ambulance,
Australian Army Medical Corps
Died 6 May 1917, aged 27

HE DIED INSTEAD OF ME

6388 Private
Robert MORRISSEY
'F' Company, 2nd Battalion, Royal Irish Regiment
Died between 19 and 21 October 1914, aged 38

HE DIED FOR ENGLAND'S GLORY
AWAY FROM ERIN'S ISLE

(Private Morrissey, whose parents' home was in
County Kilkenny, was a Boer War veteran.)

Buried near this spot
2906 Private
Frederick Willie OPPERMAN
1st/24th Battalion, London Regiment
Died 26 May 1915, aged 31

SO HE IS GONE
HIS SMILE, HIS FUN
WE LOVED HIM
BETTER THAN WE KNEW

4338 Rifleman
Alec Percival PLUMMER
8th Battalion, London Regiment
(Post Office Rifles)
Died 22 March 1916, aged 31

HE SERVED HIS KING
UNTIL
THE KING OF KINGS CALLED HIM

249325 Driver
William Frederick SMITH
'B' Battery, 72nd Brigade , Royal Field Artillery
Died 26 June 1918, aged 21

YOUR DEATH WAS EASY
WHEN THE SUMMONS CAME
AND LIKE A HERO DIED

669581 Pioneer
George Candlish TAYLOR
Canadian Pioneers
Died 30 April 1917, aged 24

ENTERED TO REST
ON HIS 24TH BIRTHDAY
ASLEEP IN JESUS

R/2875 Rifleman
Francis George Swann WALTERS
7th Battalion, King's Royal Rifle Corps
Died 13 March 1916, aged 19

NOTHING BUT WELL AND FAIR
AND WHAT MAY QUIET US
IN A DEATH SO NOBLE

(From John Milton's Samson Agonistes.*)*

Caestre Military Cemetery

23777 Private
Albert AMBLER
5th Battalion, Cameron Highlanders
Died 26 May 1918, aged 24

GONE TO HIS REST
THROUGH THE PATHWAY OF DUTY

19191 Private
Edgar HORNSHAW
11th Battalion, East Yorkshire Regiment
Died 18 May 1918, aged 24

WAR'S BITTER COST
A DEAR ONE LOST

S/25142 Private
Jack Bluett TURNER
7th Battalion, Seaforth Highlanders
Died 20 July 1918, aged 19

DEATH CLAIMED HIM
IN THE PRIDE
OF HIS BOYHOOD DAYS

Calais Southern Cemetery

108378 Acting Bombardier
Thomas Marshall BEADMAN
221st Siege Battery, Royal Garrison Artillery
Died 7 August 1917, aged 35

A BETTER HUSBAND
NEVER LIVED
A KINDER FATHER
NEVER DIED

Second Lieutenant
Robert BLAGDEN
10th Battalion, attached 7th Battalion,
Norfolk Regiment
Died 12 May 1916, aged 36

WHITE ROBES WERE GIVEN
UNTO EVERY ONE OF THEM

(From Revelation, *Chapter 6, Verse 11.)*

592068 Rifleman
Francis DAVIES
1st/18th Battalion, London Regiment
(London Irish Rifles)
Died 10 April 1917, aged 20

SLEEP PEACEFULLY BOY
THY DUTY IS WELL DONE

245204 Sapper
Joseph GREGORY
Railway Operating Department, Royal Engineers
Died 4 September 1917, aged 18

HE HAS FOUGHT
THE GALLANT FIGHT
IN DEATH'S COLD ARMS
HE PERSEVERED. R I P

(Adapted from The Queen of Purgatory, *a*
poem by Father Faber.)

129462 Pioneer
Edward Henry Filmer HANSON
5th Battalion, Special Brigade, Royal Engineers
Died 28 April 1916, aged 17

THOUGH ONLY A BOY
HIS DEATH WAS BRAVE
NOW HE RESTS
IN A SOLDIER'S GRAVE

21807 Private
Edward James McCONNELL
15th Battalion, Royal Welsh Fusiliers
Died 17 June 1916, aged 18

YOU ANSWERED
YOUR COUNTRY'S CALL
I AM PROUD OF
MY SOLDIER BOY. MOTHER

122225 Lance Corporal
Charles Bellenden POWELL
Inland Water Transport, Royal Engineers
Died 24 January 1916, aged 36

IN LOVING MEMORY OF
MY DEAR HUSBAND CHARLIE
DROWNED ON ACTIVE SERVICE

6144 Private
David ROLLE
4th Battalion, British West Indies Regiment
Died 3 August 1917, aged 30

I GAVE MY ONLY SON
THAT ENGLAND MIGHT NOT DIE
R I P

(Private Rolle was from San Salvador in the
Bahamas.)

32429 Private
Ernest Ryder SHARMAN
2nd Battalion, York & Lancaster Regiment
Died 5 July 1917, aged 34

HE LIES WITH MANY
OF ENGLAND'S FLOWERS
YET YOU KNOW
HE WAS JUST OURS

879 Private
Albert SHAW
16th Battalion,
West Yorkshire Regiment (Prince of Wales's Own)
Died 4 September 1916, aged 29

OUR LAD DID HIS DUTY

15803 Private
Harry Alfred TAYLOR
1st Battalion, The Buffs (East Kent Regiment)
Died 7 May 1917, aged 49

FRANCIS GIDEON HIS ONLY SON
K.R.R.C.
KILLED IN ACTION 10.1.15
AGED 18

(The son has no known grave and is commemorated
on the Le Touret Memorial to the Missing.)

648914 Private
William TURNER
52nd Battalion, Canadian Infantry
(Manitoba Regiment)
Died 6 July 1917, aged 35

AN INDIAN
TO HIS COUNTRY'S CALL
DOING HIS DUTY, THAT IS ALL

Cambrin Churchyard Extension

15594 Private
Horace BINDLEY
1st Battalion, Middlesex Regiment
Died 1 September 1915, aged 18

IT WAS FOR YOU

PS/6330 Private
Clifford Percival CALCUTT
No 2 Company, 19th Battalion, Royal Fusiliers
Died 22 January 1916, aged 18

HE LIVED A LOYAL SOLDIER
AND DIED A BRAVE ONE

G/4387 Private
Eugène de la Haye DUPONSEL
2nd Battalion,
The Queen's (Royal West Surrey Regiment)
Died 3 October 1915, aged 26

MORT GLORIEUSEMENT
POUR LA FRANCE
SEIGNEUR AYEZ
PITIE DE LUI

(Born in Mauritius, this soldier had been in Buenos Aires when war broke out, and left for England in order to enlist. His epitaph translates from the French as: 'Died gloriously for France; Lord have pity on him'.)

22/914 Private
Robert LAIDLER
22nd Battalion, Durham Light Infantry
Died 30 July 1916, aged 42

HE DIED
FOR HIS KING AND COUNTRY
AND IS LAID WITHIN
A BRITISH SOLDIER'S GRAVE

21662 Private
Thomas Leslie MARSTON
'C' Company, 11th Battalion,
Leicestershire Regiment
Died 10 December 1916, aged 22

ALAS! THAT YOUTH'S
SWEET-SCENTED MANUSCRIPT
SHOULD CLOSE

(An extract from The Rubaiyyat of Omar Khayyam, *by Edward Fitzgerald.)*

Captain
Arthur Legge SAMSON, *MC*
2nd Battalion, Royal Welsh Fusiliers
Died 25 September 1915, aged 33

OF ALL THY BRAVE ADVENTURES
THIS WAS THE LAST, THE BRAVEST
WAS THE BEST

Cambrin Military Cemetery

Captain
Alan Geoffrey FOX
Royal Engineers, attached Royal Flying Corps
Died 9 May 1915, aged 27

ONE OF
THE PIONEERS OF FLIGHT
HIS LIFE WAS SERVICE
HIS DEATH GLORY

(Captain Fox was one of the first five officers in the army to be taught to fly.)

36704 Sapper
James Joseph LEONARD
157th Field Company, Royal Engineers
Died 12 October 1918, aged 30

NO KING OR SAINT
HAD TOMB SO PROUD
AS HE WHOSE FLAG
BECOMES HIS SHROUD

Canada Farm British Cemetery

Second Lieutenant
Archie Seaward ARMFIELD
2nd Battalion, Irish Guards
Died 31 July 1917, aged 38

BOER WAR
RHODESIA. MAFEKING

37359 Driver
John Lewis DAVIES
20th Divisional Ammunition Column,
Royal Field Artillery
Died 11 September 1917, aged 22

BUT THE VERY HAIRS
OF YOUR HEAD
ARE ALL NUMBERED

(From Matthew, Chapter 10, Verse 30.)

21094 Gunner
George Walter FERRY, *MM*
'A' Battery, 75th Brigade, Royal Field Artillery
Died 7 September 1917, aged 21

TO SAVE HIS FLAG HE DIED

212461 Gunner
William Henry George GOUGE
460th Battery, 15th Brigade, Royal Field Artillery
Died 20 September 1917, aged 19

OUR ONLY BOY
GOD BE WITH YOU
TILL WE MEET AGAIN

(The 460th Battery had served in the Gallipoli
campaign in 1915, which would undoubtedly be
why Gunner Gouge's parents named their Dorset
home 'Suvla'.)

65108 Driver
Albert James KENT
13th Battery, 17th Brigade, Royal Field Artillery
Died 23 July 1917, aged 21

TWO MEN
SHALL BE IN THE FIELD
THE ONE SHALL BE TAKEN
AND THE OTHER LEFT

(A quote from Luke, Chapter 17, Verse 36.)

W/5513 Gunner
Thomas VICARAGE
'A' Battery, 121st Brigade, Royal Field Artillery
Died 27 July 1917, aged 23

VICTOR, YET IN HIS GRAVE
ALL THAT HE HAD HE GAVE

Cement House Cemetery

330973 Private
George BARRETT
11th Battalion, Royal Scots
Died 15 October 1918, aged 19

A TOKEN OF HIS LOVE HE GAVE
A PLEDGE OF LIBERTY

16708 Corporal
William Richard BRIGGS
'D' Company, 7th Battalion,
Somerset Light Infantry
Died 16 August 1917, aged 25

SOON, SOON
TO FAITHFUL WARRIORS
COMES THEIR REST

(From William Walsham How's hymn For All
The Saints.)

35821 Private
Christopher Cecil CLARK
21st (Tyneside Scottish) Battalion,
Northumberland Fusiliers
Died 19 October 1917, aged 22

MY DEAR LAD
WAS A WALL UNTO ME
C. CLARK

(Private Clark's father, also Christopher, was a
widower.)

Lieutenant
Sir Robert George Vivian DUFF, *Baronet*
2nd Life Guards
Died 16 October 1914, aged 37

"NOTHING IS HERE FOR TEARS:
NOTHING BUT WELL AND FAIR"

(From John Milton's poem Samson Agonistes.*)*

945086 Gunner
Cecil John Francis FRANKLIN
'C' Battery, 291st Brigade, Royal Field Artillery
Died 16 December 1917, aged 19

AS CHRIST DIED
TO MAKE MEN HOLY
SO THEY DIED
TO MAKE MEN FREE

46446 Private
Robert HALL
17th Battalion, Lancashire Fusiliers
Died 21 November 1917, aged 19

ANSWERED HIS COUNTRY'S CALL
OCT. 1914. AT THE AGE OF 16

12447 Lance Sergeant
Alfred Albert HEAVEN
'C' Company, 6th Battalion,
Oxfordshire & Buckinghamshire Light Infantry
Died 20 September 1917, aged 21

HIS LIFE'S PLEASURE WAS SHORT
HIS SACRIFICE NOBLE

215042 Gunner
Thomas Ellis JONES
'B' Battery, 76th Brigade, Royal Field Artillery
Died 4 October 1917, aged 24

FAR AWAY IS THE GRAVE
WHERE OUR LOVED ONE SLEEPS
OH MAY THE SUMMER SUN
SHINE KINDLY O'ER HIS GRAVE

Captain
Owen Robert LLOYD, *MC*
3rd Battalion, attached 7th Battalion,
King's Shropshire Light Infantry
Died 20 September 1917, age 25

FORGET ME NOT DEAR LAND
FOR WHICH I FELL

S/21750 Rifleman
Charles Henry PROBERT
12th Battalion, The Rifle Brigade
Died 20 September 1917, aged 32

ALL THAT HE HAD HE GAVE
AND HE WILL NOT RETURN

Cérisy-Gailly Military Cemetery

Captain
Dudley Fletcher GOODWIN
157th Brigade, Royal Field Artillery
Died 7 March 1917, aged 24

THE HUMAN-HEARTED MAN I LOVED
A SPIRIT
NOT A BREATHING VOICE
MOTHER

670203 Private
William Gilbert Raymond McGREER
47th Battalion, Canadian Infantry
(Western Ontario Regiment)
Died 11 August 1918, aged 24

"YOUNG MEN …
YE HAVE OVERCOME
THE WICKED ONE"
1 JOHN 2. 13

Chambrecy British Cemetery

242838 Private
Herbert Nelson BENNETT
11th Battalion, Cheshire Regiment
Died 26 May 1918, aged 31

THE ONLY WAY

Chapelle-d'Armentières Old Military Cemetery

Second Lieutenant
Robert Percy HARKER
1st Battalion, North Staffordshire Regiment
Died 20 March 1915, aged 42

'TISN'T LIFE THAT MATTERS
'TIS THE COURAGE
YOU BRING TO IT

(Before being commissioned, Second Lieutenant
Harker had enlisted in the Honourable Artillery
Company right at the start of the War.)

Chester Farm Cemetery

448179 Private
James Duncan Montgomery
MacGILLIVRAY
14th Battalion, Canadian Infantry
(Quebec Regiment)
Died 25 April 1916, aged 40

A DIRECT DESCENDANT
OF THE YOUNG CHIEF
THAT FELL ON CULLODEN FIELD

(Private McGillivray's age appears incorrectly on
the headstone as 41. The ancestor was Alexander
MacGillivray of Dunmaglass.)

151198 Private
George RILEY
13th Battalion, Canadian Infantry
(Quebec Regiment)
Died 8 August 1916, aged 41

LET BROTHERLY LOVE CONTINUE

132179 Private
Roy Novello RILEY
13th Battalion, Canadian Infantry
(Quebec Regiment)
Died 8 August 1916, aged 18

HE LIKE A SOLDIER FELL
FOR KING & COUNTRY
ON 18TH BIRTHDAY

(Despite the fact that they served in the same
battalion, died on the same day and are buried
adjacent graves, it appears that this Private Riley,
the only son of London parents, was not related to
the Ireland-born Private George Riley [above].)

Chocques Military Cemetery

12581 Private
Joseph BERRY
7th Battalion, Loyal North Lancashire Regiment
Died 27 October 1915, aged 19

HE THAT IN THE BATTLE DIES
LIVETH FOR EVER IN THE SKIES
FOR EVER WITH THE LORD

3533 Private
Vernon Aubrey BODY
1st/4th Battalion, Leicestershire Regiment
Died 18 October 1915, aged 17

A YOUNG LIFE
GLORIOUSLY COMPLETED
AT THE POST OF DUTY

Captain
Henry Mason BOUCHER, *MC*
3rd Battalion, attached 1st Battalion,
Somerset Light Infantry
Died 23 April 1918, aged 27

SPLENDIDO

13600 Sapper
John Martin BROMILOW
54th Field Company, Royal Engineers
Died 9 October 1915, aged 31

THE FITTEST PLACE
WHERE MAN CAN DIE
IS WHERE HE DIES FOR MAN

1333 Private
Samuel Henry DOVEY
3rd Battalion, London Regiment (Royal Fusiliers)
Died 25 April 1915, aged 21

FAREWELL BELOVED AND BRAVE
THY LAST MARCH PAST IS O'ER

Second Lieutenant
Warren Kemp FENN-SMITH
20th Squadron, Royal Flying Corps
Died 18 January 1918, aged 18

ALAS, THAT SPRING
SHOULD VANISH WITH THE ROSE
THAT YOUTH'S SWEET, SCENTED
MANUSCRIPT SHOULD CLOSE

(From Edward Fitzgerald's translation of The
Rubaiyyat of Omar Khayyam.*)*

12622 Sergeant
John Othic HOLROYD
7th Battalion, Norfolk Regiment
Died 11 October 1915, aged 28

ALSO IN MEMORY OF
SERJT. WILFRID H. HOLROYD
NORFOLK REGIMENT
MISSING OCT. 13TH 1915

(The death of this Birmingham University graduate
was followed by that of his younger brother, of the
same battalion, only two days later. Wilfrid has no
known grave and is commemorated on the Loos
Memorial to the Missing.)

1426 Lance Sergeant
Percy Henry HUNT
1st/21st Battalion, London Regiment
(1st Surrey Rifles)
Died 28 May 1915, aged 23

GONE FROM THE FIELDS OF WAR
TO THOSE OF PEACE
MOTHER AND NIN.
R.I.P.

6256 Company Quarter Master Sergeant
Thomas Douglas Benjamin JACKSON
1st Battalion, Gordon Highlanders
Died 20 April 1918, aged 38

SPRINGS OF LIFE
IN DESERT PLACES

(A holder of the London Service & Good Conduct
Medal, Company Quarter Master Sergeant
Jackson was a Boer War veteran.)

Lieutenant
Walter Anderson PORKESS
Nottinghamshire Yeomanry (Sherwood Rangers),
attached 10th Squadron, Royal Flying Corps
Died 10 February 1917, aged 29

HE WAS AN ENGLISHMAN
A KNIGHT OF WAR
WITHOUT FEAR
WITHOUT REPROACH

S/43290 Private
Donald Robert Ross THOMSON
2nd Battalion, Seaforth Highlanders
Died 18 April 1918, aged 19

OH BERTIE DARLING
HOW WE MISS YOU

Citadel New Military Cemetery

8779 Private
Christopher DONOVAN
2nd Battalion, Royal Irish Regiment
Died 8 June 1916, aged 32

ONLY THOSE
WHO HAVE LOVED AND LOST
CAN TELL
WHAT THAT GREAT WAR COST

Lieutenant
Harold Llewellyn TWITE
9th Battery, 1st/3rd (London) Brigade,
Royal Field Artillery,
attached 183rd Tunnelling Company,
Royal Engineers
Died 1 December 1915, aged 36

THEY DIE NOT
WHO LEAVE THE WORLD
RICHER BY A GREAT THOUGHT
OR ACT

Cité Bonjean Military Cemetery

2031 Private
Arthur Henry AUSTIN
36th Battalion, Australian Infantry
Died 17 March 1917, aged 19

MAN'S INHUMANITY TO MAN
CAUSED COUNTLESS THOUSANDS
TO MOURN

(From the poem Man Was Made To Mourn, *by*
Robert Burns.)

---

400 Sergeant
John McDonald BAILLIE
39th Battalion, Australian Infantry
Died 8 January 1917, aged 48

A BRITISH GENTLEMAN

(Sergeant Bailey was born in Scotland, but left a
widow in Australia.)

1622 Private
Norman Samuel Andrew BRIGHT
35th Battalion, Australian Infantry
Died 14 March 1917, aged 28

NOBLY HE LIVED
NOBLY HE DIED
MY SON – MY SON

(One of countless tributes from widowed mothers, in
this case Mrs Elizabeth Alma Bright of
Auckland, New Zealand.)

---

728 Private
Edward DOYNE
37th Battalion, Australian Infantry
Died 23 April 1917, aged 19

WHO GAVE HIS LIFE
FOR THE EMPIRE, IN FRANCE

576 Private
Howard Otis IRISH
38th Battalion, Australian Infantry
Died 29 December 1916, aged 23

THE LARKS YE HEARD
THEY SING OF THE CAUSE
WHICH MADE THEE DIE

---

69 Private
Karl Maynard Delahunt MATTHEWS
9th Company, Australian Machine Gun Corps
Died 22 January 1917, aged 26

FAR FROM HOME HE PERISHED
BUT A SOLDIER
AND FOR HIS COUNTRY

---

180 Private
William Lionel STALKER
36th Battalion, Australian Infantry
Died 22 January 1917, aged 23

NOT OF FLOWERS
THAT FADE AWAY
WEAVE WE THIS
THY CROWN TO-DAY

THEIR NAME LIVETH
FOR EVERMORE

Lieutenant
Harry TAYLOR
98th Field Company, Royal Engineers
Died 27 February 1916, aged 27

REST FROM MIRTH
WHITE IN YOUR YOUTH
STRETCHED UPON FOREIGN EARTH

Combles Communal Cemetery
Extension

21910 Private
Arthur TORODE
7th Battalion, Royal Irish Fusiliers
Died 5 September 1916, aged 19

THERE IS A VICTORY
IN DYING FOR FREEDOM
AND YOU HAVE NOT DIED
IN VAIN

4877 Rifleman
Leonard Alfred Robert WHEATLEY
16th Battalion, London Regiment
(Queen's Westminster Rifles)
Died 10 September 1916, aged 20

THEY GAVE US PEACE
BY THEIR WARFARE
AND LIFE BY THEIR DEATH

Connaught Cemetery

26694 Private
Richard FOWLER
9th Battalion, Royal Inniskilling Fusiliers
Died 1 July 1916, aged 19

HE DIED FOR ULSTER
GAVE OUR BEST

22524 Private
Samuel Peter HUTCHINGS
9th Battalion, Royal Inniskilling Fusiliers
Died 1 July 1916, aged 33

"REDEEMED"
TO MEET THE FOE
WITH HEART OF GRACE
DEATH - IS IT, I AM READY

G/9057 Private
William Stephen ROWING
'A' Company, 7th Battalion,
The Queen's Own (Royal West Kent Regiment)
Died 27 September 1916, aged 18

GONE BEFORE US
NE'ER TO BE FORGOTTEN
IN THE HAVEN OF PEACE

Captain
Charles Owen SLACKE
14th Battalion, Royal Irish Rifles
Died 1 July 1916, aged 44

I HAVE FOUGHT A GOOD FIGHT
II TIMOTHY 4.7

(The son of a knight of the realm, Captain Slacke
had joined the Ulster Division as a volunteer on the
outbreak of war.)

44696 Private
Fred STANDRING
147th Company, Machine Gun Corps (Infantry)
Died 3 September 1916, aged 29

FOR ENGLAND'S GLORY
WHAT GREATER SACRIFICE

Contalmaison Château Cemetery

15889 Private
Francis Edgell BELL
13th Battalion, Durham Light Infantry
Died 25 September 1916, aged 22

SUDDEN DEATH
IS SUDDEN GLORY

3208 Gunner
Thomas HUDSON
250th Brigade, Royal Field Artillery
Died 22 October 1916, aged 24

THE UNDONE YEARS
THE CRUELTY OF WARS
SADLY MISSED
BY WIDOW, DAUGHTER AND FATHER

123 Gunner
Arthur George PRATT
36th Group, Australian Heavy Artillery
Died 10 November 1916, aged 31

THE LAST POST HAS SOUNDED
YOU HAVE LAID ASIDE YOUR GUN
CALLED HOME

(Gunner Pratt's precise age is the subject of some
confusion. His widow said 33, his headstone says
32, but at the time of his enlistment in 1915 he
gave his date of birth as 2 August 1885, which
would make him 31 when he died. There are many
instances of lies being told about ages on enlistment,
but not by men of around 30.)

Contay British Cemetery

23760 Bombardier
Charles Henry CALE
'B' Battery, 83rd Brigade, Royal Field Artillery
Died 2 November 1916, aged 27

HE LEFT FOR THE FRONT
IN SADNESS O'ERCAST
BUT DUTY WAS DUTY
WITH HIM TILL THE LAST

Second Lieutenant
Felix Ramon Arthur DANSEY
7th Battalion, London Regiment
Died 25 July 1918, aged 27

YOUR MOTHER
DOES NOT CEASE
TO THINK OF YOU
FOR A SINGLE MOMENT

(Argentinian by birth and nationality, this
subaltern left his native land to fight for the country
of his father.)

84120 Driver
Andrew DONALDSON
6th Brigade, Canadian Field Artillery
Died 2 November 1916, aged 21

MORE BRAVE FOR THIS
THAT HE HAD MUCH TO LOVE

43274 Private
Leslie Doughty KILLENS
10th Battalion, Essex Regiment
Died 4 November 1916, aged 21

AN ENGLISH FLOWER
IN A FRENCH GARDEN

47904 Corporal
Hugh Gordon MUNRO
15th Battalion, Canadian Infantry
(Central Ontario Regiment)
Died 9 October 1916, aged 19

THIS CORNER
OF A FOREIGN FIELD
SHALL BE FOREVER CANADA

(This epitaph takes up the theme of Rupert
Brooke's poem The Soldier, *and adapts it to*
reflect Corporal Munro's nationality.)

3962 Private
James Stephen REID
7th Field Ambulance,
Australian Army Medical Corps
Died 31 August 1916, age 26

IT'S JIST OOR JEEMES
BUT HE'LL NEVER BE FORGOTTEN

(Although serving in an Australian unit, Private
Reid was born in Aberdeen, where his parents still
lived.)

488293 Private
James Edward STICKELS
Royal Canadian Regiment
Died 9 October 1916, aged 18

HE FELL AT THE SOMME
IT IS IMMORTAL HONOR

36486 Private
Wilfred Henry TEW
6th Battalion, Royal Berkshire Regiment
Died 14 November 1916, aged 18

DIED ON
HIS EIGHTEENTH BIRTHDAY

Corbie Communal Cemetery

15277 Private
Reginald John BROWN
6th Battalion, Northamptonshire Regiment
Died 31 December 1915, aged 19

'TIS STRANGE BUT TRUE
I WONDER WHY
THE GOOD ARE ALWAYS
FIRST TO DIE

Corbie Communal Cemetery Extension

Lieutenant Colonel
Humphrey Francis William BIRCHAM, *DSO*
Commanding 2nd Battalion,
King's Royal Rifle Corps
Died 23 July 1916, aged 41

HE DIED WITH HIS MEN
HE LIVES WITH THOSE
HE LEFT BEHIND

2605 Sergeant
Robert John CALLANDER
'V' Company, 10th Battalion,
The King's (Liverpool Regiment)
Died 11 August 1916, aged 23

DEAR OLD JACK

Second Lieutenant
Edward Cotnam FIELDS
27th (Tyneside Irish) Battalion,
Northumberland Fusiliers
Died 22 June 1916, aged 34

IT IS GOOD TO DIE
THAT ENGLAND MAY LIVE

(Before being commissioned, this only son of a
widowed mother fought at Festubert and Loos in
the ranks.)

S/1278 Rifleman
Charles Abraham GENDERS
11th Battalion, The Rifle Brigade
Died 2 September 1916, aged 21

WHAT'S BRAVE, WHAT'S NOBLE
LET'S DO IT AND MAKE DEATH
PROUD TO TAKE US

(From Shakespeare's Antony and Cleopatra,
Act 4, Scene 13.)

Lieutenant
Gilbert LYE
4th Battalion, attached 23rd Battalion,
Manchester Regiment
Died 21 July 1916, aged 23

HE DIED A HERO
MANY A TIME THAT DAY

Captain
Charles Surtees ROBINSON
9th Battalion, Norfolk Regiment
Died 13 September 1916. aged 42

BON TRES BON

(Translation from the French: 'Good, very good'.)

Courcelles-au-Bois Communal Cemetery Extension

1377 Sapper
Albert Edward CLEMENT
1st/1st (Cheshire) Field Company,
Royal Engineers
Died 4 November 1916, aged 43

SOMETHING ATTEMPTED
SOMETHING DONE.

55003 Private
Norman Vivian WILLIAMS
2nd Battalion, Wellington Regiment,
New Zealand Infantry
Died 6 April 1918, aged 24

BELOVED SON OF
GEORGE & RUTH WILLIAMS
BRISTOL ENG.
HE DIED FOR YOU AND ME

(The New Zealand authorities refused to allow the graves of their soldiers to carry personal inscriptions. This one, nevertheless, does, and it seems to be the only such instance. The explanation is unknown.)

Coxyde Military Cemetery

Lieutenant
Robert ANGUS
Royal Naval Reserve,
HM Coastal Motorboat 33A
Died 12 April 1918, aged 35

SUNSET AND EVENING STAR
AND ONE CLEAR CALL FOR ME

(From Tennyson's poem Crossing the Bar.*)*

440197 Sapper
Frederick BLACKBURN
431st Field Company, Royal Engineers
Died 26 July 1917, aged 36

THE DEARLY BELOVED HUSBAND
OF ELEANOR H. BLACKBURN
LIFE'S GOLDEN DREAM IS O'ER

121391 Gunner
Alfred Ernest FERGUS
325th Siege Battery, Royal Garrison Artillery
Died 26 July 1917, aged 20

HERE RESTS IN GLORIOUS HOPE
A DEVOTED AND GREATLY LOVED
SON OF GREAT BRITAIN

282510 Sergeant
James FRANKLIN
1st/7th Battalion, Lancashire Fusiliers
Died 16th October 1917, aged 37

THE BLOOD OF OUR HEROES
IS THE SEED OF FREEDOM

L/11991 Shoeing Smith Corporal
George HALTON
'C' Battery, 168th Brigade, Royal Field Artillery
Died 30 July 1917, aged 22

I KNOW
WHERE YOU ARE DEAR LAD
BUT HARD TO SAY
YOUR BROTHER IS MISSING

(The missing brother, who is commemorated on the
Nieuport Memorial to the Missing, was L/11992
Gunner Richard Halton, Royal Field Artillery.
The consecutive service numbers indicate that the
pair enlisted together.)

202555 Private
John William HUTTON
1st/4th Battalion,
King's Own Yorkshire Light Infantry
Died 25 July 1917, aged 35

THOU THEREFORE
ENDURED HARDNESS
AS A GOOD SOLDIER
OF JESUS CHRIST

(From II Timothy, *Chapter 2, Verse 3.)*

710315 Driver
Sidney KENT
'A' Battery, 211th Brigade, Royal Field Artillery
Died 25 October 1917, aged 23

ALL LIFE FOR LIFE
IS SACRIFICE

68268 Private
Joseph Franklin KERSHAW
126th Company, Machine Gun Corps (Infantry)
Died 14 October 1917, aged 33

ARTIST. OLDHAM. LANCASHIRE

Midshipman
John Dermot Angell LANE
Royal Naval Reserve,
Coastal Motorboat 71A
Died 15 October 1918, aged 19

UNTIL WE MEET AGAIN
AND BE TOGETHER ALL WAYS
HIS POSTHUMOUS LETTER

11329 Private
David John MACLEOD
2nd Battalion, Argyll & Sutherland Highlanders
Died 27 August 1917, aged 29

VOLUNTEER FROM
COLONIA COSME, PARAGUAY

(Expatriates such as Private Macleod returned
from many parts of the world in order to enlist.)

Captain
Leslie OLDERSHAW
Royal Army Medical Corps,
attached 1st/8th Battalion, Manchester Regiment
Died 2 October 1917, aged 24

THE DAUNTLESS HEART
THAT FEARED NO HUMAN PRIDE

Crouy British Cemetery

306998 Private
George BARTY
1st Battalion, Tank Corps
Died 23 August 1918, aged 31

OUR HERO
HE WAS ONLY ONE
BUT HE WAS OUR ONE

390653 Sergeant Bandmaster
Cecil Frederick Gottlieb COLES
9th Battalion, London Regiment
(Queen Victoria's Rifles)
Died 26 April 1918, aged 29

HE WAS A GENIUS
BEFORE ANYTHING ELSE
AND A HERO
OF THE FIRST WATER

(Cecil Coles was a musician and composer, one of
whose works was used as the title music for the
Channel 4 television series The First World
War.*)*

ERRATUM – The appearance of a Victoria Cross
image beside the C.F.G.Coles portrait is an error.

6932 Private
Peter CROSSAN
26th Battalion, Australian Infantry
Died 8 June 1918, aged 19

A FLOWER OF THE FOREST
IS WEEDED AWAY

Captain
Austin Kirk SHENTON, *MC*
12th Signal Company, Royal Engineers
Died 26 July 1918, aged 22

LOOS – 1915. LYS-VIMY 1916.
ARRAS – 1917. CAMBRAI – 1917.
MONTDIDIER – 1918.

Lieutenant
Peter Robert SWANN, *MM*
20th Battalion, Canadian Infantry
(Central Ontario Regiment)
Died 8 August 1918, aged 23

HE TOOK THE ONLY WAY
& FOLLOWED IT
TO A GLORIOUS END

Dantzig Alley British Cemetery

12208 Private
Robert Stanley ELKINGTON
10th Battalion,
West Yorkshire Regiment (Prince of Wales's Own)
Died 1 July 1916, aged 21

THERE'S NOT A JOY
THE WORLD CAN GIVE
LIKE THAT IT TAKES AWAY

Captain
Walter Vincent Thomas GRIPPER
3rd Battalion, attached 1st Battalion,
East Surrey Regiment
Died 24 July 1916, aged 27

EAGER AT HIS COUNTRY'S CALL
STRONG, UNDISMAYED
SURRENDERED ALL

17927 Lance Corporal
Edward Holt HOLME
20th Battalion, Manchester Regiment
Died 1 July 1916, aged 28

FULL LASTING IS THE SONG
THOUGH HE, THE SINGER, PASSES

Second Lieutenant
Ralph HOSEGOOD
12th Battalion, Gloucestershire Regiment
Died 23 July 1916, aged 23

SECOND & TWIN SON
OF HENRY & HELEN HOSEGOOD
BRISTOL

*(The other twin had already been killed 17 months
earlier, and the war was to claim a third brother
seven weeks later. They are all buried in France, in
three different cemeteries.)*

16400 Private
Albert LAPPIN
20th Battalion, Royal Fusiliers
Died 1 July 1916, aged 19

FELL IN A RIGHTEOUS CAUSE
AS AN ENGLISHMAN AND A JEW

1214 Private
Sidney Percy ROSE
102nd Field Ambulance,
Royal Army Medical Corps
Died 10 August 1916, aged 26

HIS NAME SHALL BE
IN THEIR FOREHEADS
REV. XXII. 4

42391 Private
Arthur SMITH
1st Field Ambulance, Royal Army Medical Corps
Died 22 September 1916, aged 26

OF BOLTON, LANCS.
HE DIED NOBLY
RELIEVING THE SUFFERING
AND PAIN OF HIS COMRADES.

17539 Private
Harold WORTH
20th Battalion, Manchester Regiment
Died 1 July 1916, aged 19

GLORY OF YOUTH
GLOWED IN HIS VEINS
WHERE IS THAT GLORY NOW?

(Adapted from Sing Me a Song of a Lad That
is Gone, *a poem by Robert Louis Stevenson.)*

Daours Communal Cemetery Extension

5312 Lance Corporal
John Harold COTTERILL
21st Battalion, Australian Infantry
Died 2 September 1918, aged 30

AS A CHILD
HE PLAYED BEING A SOLDIER
AS A SOLDIER
HE PLAYED THE MAN

*(This lance corporal was a holder of the French
Medaille Militaire.)*

Lieutenant
George DUNDAS, *MC & Bar*
'A' Battery, 61st Brigade, Royal Field Artillery
Died 2 September 1918, aged 25

METHODIST LOCAL PREACHER
UNIVERSITY STUDENT, TORONTO
MY BEST BOY

4480 Private
Richard FORREST
58th Battalion, Australian Infantry
Died 24 April 1918, aged 24

GIVE A KIND THOUGHT
TO THE SORROWING ONES
WHOSE BOYS FOUGHT & DIED

6746 Private
William George Miller FORSYTH
3rd Battalion, Australian Infantry
Died 11 August 1918, aged 31

FAR AWAY
FROM THE LAND OF THE WATTLE
HE LIES IN A HERO'S GRAVE

391974 Lance Corporal
Christopher John FOXWELL
2nd/9th Battalion, London Regiment
(Queen Victoria's Rifles)
Died 1 September 1918, aged 22

DIED A SPORT

---

798 Private
Rupert GREGG
44th Battalion, Australian Infantry
Died 26 August 1918, aged 29

HE LEFT HIS LITTLE ONE
IN AUSTRALIA
TO OBEY THE EMPIRE'S CALL

Lieutenant
Constant Clifford William MEYER
2nd Battalion, Lincolnshire Regiment
Died 3 July 1916, aged 20

I PLUCKED IT
IN ALL ITS FRESH BEAUTY
BEFORE THE SCORCHING BREEZE
HAD TARNISHED ITS PURITY

3900 Private
John OTTERSPOOR
4th Battalion, Australian Pioneers
Died 22 May 1918, aged 25

"THE MEASURE OF A MAN'S LIFE
IS THE WELL SPENDING OF IT
NOT THE LENGTH"
PLUTARCH

Dartmoor Cemetery

Second Lieutenant
Henry BYRON
1st/5th Battalion, South Lancashire Regiment
Died 8 September 1916, aged 22

HE LIVED A GLORIOUS LIFE
HE DIED A GLORIOUS DEATH
THY WILL BE DONE

6029 Sergeant
George LEE
'A' Battery, 156th Brigade, Royal Field Artillery
Died 5 September 1916, aged 44

THY WILL BE DONE

*(Could any First World War wife and mother have
suffered a more grievous single blow than Mrs Lee
of Peckham Road, London? Her husband,
Sergeant Lee, and their 19-year-old son, Corporal
Robert Frederick Lee, serving in the same unit,
were killed in the same incident, are buried in
adjacent graves, and have the same epitaph.)*

3168 Private
Thomas Edwin PARSONS
52nd Battalion, Australian Infantry
Died 11 January 1917, aged 30

WE SHALL KNOW HIM AGAIN
THOUGH TEN THOUSAND
SURROUND HIM

Major
Randolph Albert SHAW
'A' Battery, 62nd Brigade, Royal Field Artillery
Died 14 November 1916, aged 35

WITHOUT FEAR OF REPROACH
WTHOUT HOPE OF REWARD

Lieutenant
Henry WEBBER
7th Battalion, South Lancashire Regiment
Died 21 July 1916, aged 67

OF HORLEY, SURREY
DULCE ET DECORUM EST
PRO PATRIA MORI

(The oldest known battle-death of the Great War, widely and erroneously said to have been at the age of 68. From early in the war Lieutenant Webber had made strenuous efforts to be accepted for military service, and eventually lied about his age, post-dating his birth by exactly ten years. Having been given a commission, and when serving as transport officer for his battalion, he was killed by a shell. His Latin epitaph, a popular one among the families of dead soldiers, is by Horace and translates as 'It is sweet and glorious to die for one's country'.)

Delville Wood Cemetery

Second Lieutenant
Herbert FLOWERS
8th Battalion,
The Queen's Own (Royal West Kent Regiment)
Died 1 September 1916, aged 36

DOWN TO THE
GATES OF DEATH LOYAL
GOD REST HIM

24444 Private
James RATHBAND
9th Battalion, Royal Dublin Fusiliers
Died 9 September 1916, aged 16

O SO YOUNG & YET SO BRAVE

Second Lieutenant
Thomas McCreary SCOTT
9th Battalion, attached 2nd Battalion,
King's Own Scottish Borderers
Died 3 September 1916, aged 21

GOD MOVES
IN A MYSTERIOUS WAY

2512 Private
Leslie Andrew SHEFFIELD
17th Battalion, Australian Infantry
Died 26 July 1916, aged 17

ADIEU DEAR LAD
WHAT NEED OF TEARS
OR FEARS FOR YOU

33353 Private
Sydney TAYLOR
1st Battalion, The King's (Liverpool Regiment)
Died 8 August 1916, aged 24

TO SERVE THE PRESENT AGE

22243 Private
Bernard Victor WHITTINGHAM
98th Battalion, Machine Gun Corps (Infantry)
Died 23 July 1916, aged 17

MOTHER'S BABY SON
SORELY MISSED

Dernancourt Communal Cemetery Extension

49036 Bombardier
Gerald Mitchell BEANLAND
37th Siege Battery, Royal Garrison Artillery
Died 9 November 1916, aged 24

THE DEVICES OF MAN
MAY DESTROY THE BODY
BUT THE SOUL THAT IS HIS
NEVER

2032 Private
Arthur Lethero JAMES
2nd Australian Light Trench Mortar Battery
Died 2 February 1917, aged 23

HE FELL
THE REST MARCHED ON
TO VICTORY
AH GOD MY LITTLE SON

Second Lieutenant
Francis Bedford MARSH
4th Battalion,
The Queen's (Royal West Surrey Regiment),
and Machine Gun Corps
Died 5 October 1916, aged 19

LET DEEDS NOT WORDS EXPRESS
THINE EXCEEDING LOVELINESS

2147 Private
Percy William MARTIN
1st Battalion, Australian Pioneers
Died 22 February 1917, aged 23

AUSTRALIA IS PROUD
OF HER HERO
WHO WAS ONLY A PRIVATE
THAT'S ALL

6332 Private
Charles Henry Harold PARKER
5th Battalion, Australian Infantry
Died 11 March 1917, aged 31

STRIVING TO CROWN
OUR LAND WITH FREEDOM'S BAYS
DEATH HE DISDAINED

2203 Private
Lake Launcelot REID
9th Battalion, Australian Infantry
Died 3 March 1917, aged 23

LORD HAVE MERCY
LET THE LIGHT OF AUSTRALIA
SHINE ON HIM FOR EVER

Dickebusch New Military Cemetery

951306 Gunner
Alfred William GOODWIN
'A' Battery, 235th Brigade, Royal Field Artillery
Died 16 January 1917, aged 21

NUMBERED AMONG
THE VALIANT DEAR
HIS SPIRIT SPED
TO REALMS ABOVE

Captain
Charles Robert Forbes HAY-WEBB
'B' Battery, 235th Brigade, Royal Field Artillery
Died 28 December 1916, aged 22

"LOOKING AFTER HIS MEN"

Second Lieutenant
Dudley HURST-BROWN
129th Battery, 30th Brigade, Royal Field Artillery
Died 15 June 1915, aged 18

DARLING DUDLEY
LAST YEAR BUT A BOY
BUT ENGLAND'S MARTYR NOW
MOTHER

Lieutenant
John Selby Chadwick PEILE
'C' Battery, 190th Brigade, Royal Field Artillery
Died 2 June 1917, aged 21

HE HAS OUTSOARED
THE SHADOW OF OUR NIGHT

(This is the title of a 1st-century work of Latin
verse by Publius Papinius Statius.)

1239 Rifleman
Frank Poole RIVERS
1st/5th Battalion, London Regiment
(London Rifle Brigade)
Died 3 January 1916, aged 20

AGE SHALL NOT WEARY THEM
NOR THE YEARS CONDEMN

(These words are of course from a very familiar verse
of Laurence Binyon's poem For the Fallen, *which*
is universally recited at Armistice Day and
Remembrance Sunday commemorations every year.)

G/6982 Private
Ernest Albert SELMES
11th Battalion,
The Queen's (Royal West Surrey Regiment)
Died 5 March 1917, aged 27

ONLY A BRITISH SOLDIER
ONLY A MOTHER'S SON
BURIED ON FIELD OF BATTLE
YOU KNOW MY DUTY I'VE DONE

14669 Private
Reuben SKEELS
12th Battalion, East Surrey Regiment
Died 21 February 1917, aged 21

SUMMON'D HOME
THE CALL HAS SOUNDED
BIDDING A SOLDIER
HIS WARFARE CEASE

Second Lieutenant
Charles Victor TOWNSEND
7th Battalion, King's Shropshire Light Infantry
Died 21 March 1916, aged 27

"ONE OF THE BRAVEST MEN
I HAVE EVER MET"
HIS COMMANDING OFFICER

44164 Private
George Albert TURNER
23rd Battalion, Middlesex Regiment
Died 1 April 1917, aged 27

BRIEF, BRAVE AND GLORIOUS
WAS HIS YOUNG CAREER

Dickebusch New Military Cemetery Extension

3833 Corporal
Henry ARMITAGE
2nd Battalion, Army Cyclist Corps
Died 2 August 1917, aged 39

ALSO IN MEMORY OF HIS
SON JAMES KILLED SOMEWHERE
IN FRANCE SEPT. 2ND 1918
AGE 19. UNTIL WE MEET AGAIN

(Mrs Armitage of Longsight, Manchester, was by
no means unique in having lost both a husband and
a son on the battlefields. James has no known grave
and is commemorated on the Vis-en-Artois
Memorial to the Missing.)

L/31651 Corporal
Henry Joseph BINSTED
'C' Battery, 119th Brigade, Royal Field Artillery
Died 20 June 1917, aged 23

HE DIED IN WAR
BUT RESTS IN PEACE

40875 Private
Vincent Corbet ELLIS
6th (Pioneer) Battalion, South Wales Borderers
Died 19 July 1917, aged 23

EVER REMEMBERED
BY WHAT WE HAVE DONE

Second Lieutenant
Trice MARTIN
11th Battalion,
The Queen's (Royal West Surrey Regiment)
Died 7 June 1917, aged 36

ATTIRED IN SUDDEN BRIGHTNESS
LIKE A MAN INSPIRED

(From Wordsworth's poem Character of the
Happy Warrior.*)*

Lieutenant
James Allanson PICTON, *MC*
'B' Company, 9th Battalion,
East Surrey Regiment
Died 23 July 1917, aged 23

YOUR GLORIOUS DEATH
SHALL SHINE LIKE BEACON STARS
OF SACRIFICE

533387 Private
Frank Wilson SMITH
1st/15th Battalion, London Regiment
(Prince of Wales's Own Civil Service Rifles)
Died 7 June 1917, aged 31

NOT FOR MYSELF
BUT MY COUNTRY

T2/015650 Driver
Harry SWEETLAND
193rd Company, Royal Army Service Corps,
attached 70th Infantry Brigade Headquarters
Died 2 July 1917, aged 19

DEAR SAVIOUR TELL MY MOTHER
I'LL BE THERE

Dickebusch Old Military Cemetery

Lieutenant
John Dutton CALVERT
4th Battalion, The Rifle Brigade
Died 15 February 1915, aged 23

IN THEIR LOVE OF LIFE
THEY FEARED NOT DEATH

Dive Copse British Cemetery

Second Lieutenant
Rowland Tallis EAGAR
9th Battalion, Royal Fusiliers
Died 8 August 1918, aged 24

FORTIFIED IN ENGLAND'S GLORY
HE FELL A HERO
CHERISHED IS HIS MEMORY

Y/1536 Rifleman
Samuel GUNN
1st Battalion, King's Royal Rifle Corps
Died 27 July 1916, aged 20

WELL PLAYED! LAD

Second Lieutenant
George Helliwell HARDING
79th Squadron, Royal Flying Corps
Died 27 March 1918, aged 24

THAT THEIR DUST
MAY REBUILD A NATION
AND THEIR SOULS
RELIGHT A STAR

(From Songs Before Sunrise *by*
A.C.Swinburne.)

---

160 Driver
Hector MACMILLAN
9th Divisional Ammunition Column,
Royal Field Artillery
Died 16 July 1916, aged 26

FAR DISTANT, FAR DISTANT
LIES SCOTIA THE BRAVE
HERE LIES A TRUE HIGHLANDER

(Driver Macmillan was born at Campbeltown,
Kintyre. The first two lines are from Jamie
Foyers, *a song based on a traditional Perthshire*
bothy song.)

4224 Sergeant
Jack Percival PERRY
18th Battalion, Australian Infantry
Died 19 May 1918, aged 23

GONE WEST IN ALL THE GLORY
OF THE SETTING SUN
THY WILL BE DONE

6895 Sergeant
John Edward SMEETON
22nd Battalion, Australian Infantry
Died 14 May 1918, aged 23

OUR DEAR JACK
IN THE DAWN
OF SPLENDID MANHOOD

Divisional Cemetery

2148 Private
Leslie BARNES
2nd Battalion, London Regiment (Royal Fusiliers)
Died 23 August 1915, aged 20

ONE MOMENT
THE ROAR OF BATTLE
THE NEXT
PERFECT PEACE WITH GOD

Lieutenant
John Philip BENINGFIELD
59th Battery, Royal Field Artillery
Died 27 April 1915, aged 23

ALSO TO
2ND LT MAURICE VICTOR BENINGFIELD
AGE 17
1ST WORCESTERSHIRE REGT.
KILLED 10TH MARCH 1915
NEUVE CHAPELLE
ONLY SONS OF THE LATE
COLONEL J.W. BENINGFIELD
ESSEX REGIMENT
"EVER GLORIOUS"

(This personal inscription runs to nearly three times
the stipulated maximum number of characters. The
younger of the Beningfield brothers, who were killed
within six weeks of each other, has no known grave
and is commemorated on the Le Touret Memorial
to the Missing.)

Divisional Collecting Post Cemetery & Extension

25034 Sapper
Nigel Everard BLAKE
2nd Field Squadron, Royal Engineers
Died 3 May 1915, aged 23

WOULD TO GOD
I HAD DIED FOR THEE
O NIGEL MY SON, MY SON

(Adapted from II Samuel, *Chapter 18, Verse 33.)*

Dochy Farm New British Cemetery

29190 Lance Corporal
John Arthur MORGAN
1st/6th Battalion, Royal Warwickshire Regiment
Died 4 October 1917, aged 34

BETTER DEATH THAN DISHONOUR
HE FELL OBEYING DUTY'S CALL

Doingt Communal Cemetery Extension

62104 Private
Edwin Arthur Montague BISHOP
11th Battalion, Royal Fusiliers
Died 3 October 1918, aged 27

FOR HIM, PEACE WAS DECLARED

Second Lieutenant
Thomas Edward LAWRENCE
7th Battalion, Royal Sussex Regiment
Died 22 September 1918, aged 19

WE ARE YOURS
ENGLAND, MY OWN!

Lieutenant
Arthur Duncan SWALE
6th Battalion, attached 11th Battalion,
Sherwood Foresters
(Nottinghamshire & Derbyshire Regiment)
Died 5 October 1918, aged 21

WE GAVE HIM PROUDLY
NOW ONLY PRIDE REMAINS

39100 Private
Herbert Walter WRIGHT
8th Battalion, East Surrey Regiment
Died 26 September 1918, aged 20

ALL IS OVER AND DONE
RENDER THANKS TO THE GIVER
ENGLAND, FOR THY SON

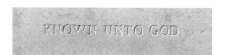

Dozinghem Military Cemetery

38801 Private
John Noel ARKLE
2nd Battalion,
King's Own Yorkshire Light Infantry
Died 9 March 1918, aged 19

HIS SPIRIT
SAVED HIS COUNTRY

172955 Gunner
Arthur James BIRD
128th Battery, Royal Field Artillery
Died 15 September 1917, aged 33

HE GREATLY LOVED
HE GREATLY LIVED
AND DIED RIGHT MIGHTILY

(From John Oxenham's poem Livingstone.*)*

46214 Private
Albert Evan BISHTON
15th Battalion, Sherwood Foresters
(Nottinghamshire & Derbyshire Regiment)
Died 29 October 1917, aged 19

TILL CHILD AND MOTHER
MEET AGAIN

26391 Guardsman
Wilfred CALLOWAY
2nd Company, 1st Battalion, Grenadier Guards
Died 18 July 1917, aged 22

HE WAS ONE OF GOD'S
GENTLEMEN
AND HE DIED FOR FREEDOM
AND LIBERTY

78307 Gunner
Joseph HATCHER
144th Siege Battery, Royal Garrison Artillery
Died 6 November 1917, aged 26

WE DO NOT KNOW
WHAT PAIN HE BORE
WE ONLY KNOW HE NOBLY FELL
AND COULD NOT SAY GOODBYE

S/40617 Lance Corporal
John McAndrew JOHNSTONE
6th Battalion, Cameron Highlanders
Died 17 July 1917, aged 26

WHAT HERE IS FAITHFULLY BEGUN
SHALL BE COMPLETED NOT UNDONE

2089 Trooper
Leonard LAWTON
1st Household Battalion
Died 3 October 1917, aged 19

HE SOUGHT THE GLORY
OF HIS COUNTRY
AND FOUND THE GLORY
OF HIS GOD

15/23314 Private
William LEAHY
15th Battalion, Cheshire Regiment
Died 19 October 1917, aged 17

A BOY THAT WAS
NEVER FORGOTTEN
BY MR. & MRS. TRAYNOR
57 PARK ST., LIVERPOOL

(The Traynors were foster-parents.)

13062 Lance Sergeant
James McDOWELL
3rd Battalion, Grenadier Guards
Died 22 July 1917, aged 28

AT REST
ALSO IN MEMORY OF
HIS LITTLE SON
GONE TO DADDY

Second Lieutenant
Thomas MALCOLM
3rd Battalion, Highland Light Infantry
Died 23 October 1917, aged 31

AT REST
WITH HIS BROTHER WILLIAM
EVEN DEATH
COULD NOT PART THEM

(William is buried in Amara War Cemetery, Iraq.
They had both returned to Scotland from America
in April 1915 to serve in the War.)

15482 Corporal
Hubert William NEWBURY
'A' Company, 4th Battalion,
Worcestershire Regiment
Died 12 August 1917, aged 41

SERVED DARDANELLES, EGYPT
TWICE IN FRANCE
DIED 5TH WOUND
A SOLDIER

S/16432 Private
Stanley PLUMPTON
1st/4th Battalion, Seaforth Highlanders
Died 21 September 1917, aged 27

HE HAS GONE TO A LAND
WHERE THERE IS
NO FIGHTING OR SORROW
AMEN

214066 Driver
Herbert SANDERSON
11th Divisional Ammunition Company,
Royal Field Artillery
Died 12 August 1917, aged 37

THE BLOOD OF HEROES
IS THE SEED OF FREEDOM

390229 Private
Frank Willard STEPHENSON
3rd (Northumbrian) Field Ambulance,
Royal Army Medical Corps
Died 30 October 1917, aged 22

FREEDOM LIVES ON EARTH TO-DAY
BECAUSE HE DIED

9304 Private
William Arthur TERRETT
'D' Company, 10th Battalion,
Gloucestershire Regiment
Died 11 November 1917, age 26

HE SLEEPS
BESIDES HIS COMRADES
IN A GRAVE ACROSS THE FOAM

(Armistice Day commemorations would have an
extra poignancy for Private Terrett's family, for
whom 11 November had become a significant date
a year before the war ended.)

200071 Gunner
Joseph WENLOCK
'C' Battery, 75th Brigade, Royal Field Artillery
Died 5 September 1917, aged 19

HE WAS A BOY
IN HEART AND MIND
BUT A GOLDEN MEMORY
HE LEFT BEHIND

Dranouter Churchyard

Captain
Robert John Charles OTTER
2nd Battalion, attached 1st Battalion,
Norfolk Regiment
Died 15 February 1915, aged 34

A GALLANT ENGLISHMAN
AND A GOOD SPORTSMAN

(Captain Otter had served in the Boer War.)

Dranoutre Military Cemetery

Second Lieutenant
Thomas Hanson AVERILL
17th Battalion, The King's (Liverpool Regiment)
Died 30 August 1917, aged 24

THERE IS NO DEATH
CLOSER IS HE THAN BREATHING
NEARER THAN HANDS AND FEET

(From Tennyson's poem Closer Is He Than
Breathing.*)*

G/6795 Private
Arthur Clifford Joy BAXTER
8th Battalion,
The Queen's Own (Royal West Kent Regiment)
Died 29 July 1916, aged 21

TO ANOTHER GOD GIVETH
THE LAURELLED BROW
ME HE GRANTED TO FIGHT

Dud Corner Cemetery

Lieutenant
Robert Leslie CARPENTER
1st/17th (County of London) Battalion,
London Regiment
Died 26 October 1915, aged 20

AN ONLY SON
"TO WHAT PURPOSE
IS THIS WASTE?"
S. MATT. 26.8.

21616 Private
Frederick Dalton GILES
'C' Company, 8th Battalion, Royal Irish Fusiliers
Died 3 April 1916, aged 24

MY HERO STANDS
AT THE BEAUTIFUL GATE
WAITING AND WATCHING FOR ME

2064 Lance Sergeant
Charles Edgar HARRISON
1st/8th Battalion, Sherwood Foresters
(Nottinghamshire & Derbyshire Regiment)
Died 5 October 1915, aged 36

IS IT NOTHING TO YOU
ALL YE THAT PASS BY?

(From Lamentations, *Chapter 1, Verse 12.)*

2746 Rifleman
Leonard HEARNE
1st/18th Battalion, London Regiment
(London Irish Rifles)
Died 21 October 1915, aged 19

"TO HAVE LIVED
HOW SWEET IT IS
TO KNOW HOW TO DIE
HOW GLORIOUS". HANS ANDERSEN

9204 Private
Simon McGUINNESS
6th Battalion, Connaught Rangers
Died 26 May 1916, aged 29

HIS MOTHER
BRIDGET MCGUINNESS
DIED 29TH JULY 1898
AGE 29 YEARS

(Attention is drawn here to the added poignancy of
Private McGuinness's early death at precisely the
same age as his mother's.)

S/6531 Lance Corporal
Donald Robert MACLEAN
'A' Company, 8th Battalion, Seaforth Highlanders
Died 25 September 1915, aged 21

DUTIES ARE OURS
EVENTS ARE GOD'S

3077 Rifleman
Frederick William SHERRING
17th (County of London) Battalion,
London Regiment
Died 30 October 1915, aged 19

A PLUCKY BOY
GOD REST HIS SOUL

S/10145 Private
Arthur Allison SMITH
1st Battalion,
The Black Watch (Royal Highlanders)
Died 22 December 1915, aged 29

'TIS NOT OUR WISH
TO REAP REWARD
BUT SEE OUR EFFORTS
ARE NOT IN VAIN

2280 Corporal
Walter George WISE
'C' Company, 2nd/8th Battalion,
London Regiment
(Post Office Rifles)
Died 12 November 1915, aged 25

A WARRIOR'S GRAVE
MODEST, MAJESTIC

Duhallow ADS Cemetery

704012 Private
William Henry ANGEL
3rd Battalion, Canadian Labour Corps
Died 1 August 1917, aged 44

BILLY DEAR WE MISS YOU
BUT IT'S HONOUR ON YOUR NAME
REST IN PEACE TILL
WE MEET AGAIN. EMMA & BOYS

(Like many other war-widows who were left with
children and no breadwinner, Emma had remarried
by the time she provided details for the headstone.
She was a year out with the US-born Private
Angel's age, which consequently is inscribed as 45.)

Captain
Matthew Henry GIBSON, *MC & Bar*
12th Battalion, Royal Irish Rifles
Died 29 October 1918, aged 28

GREATER LOVE HATH NO MAN
HE CAME FROM MEXICO
TO SERVE IN 1915

285 Sergeant
Ernest Joseph GOODWIN
14th Company, Australian Machine Gun Corps
Died 29 September 1917, aged 20

WHAT MORE CAN A MAN DO
THAN DIE FIGHTING
FOR THOSE HE LOVED

5669 Sapper
George Rewcastle GRIEVE
1st Divisional Signal Company,
Canadian Engineers
Died 26 April 1915, aged 30

THE PATRIOT'S BLOOD'S THE SEED
OF FREEDOM'S TREE

(A quote by the Scottish poet Thomas Campbell.)

276890 Gunner
William JOINER
212th Siege Battery, Royal Garrison Artillery
Died 18 November 1917, aged 34

THAT HOWSOE'ER
THE BATTLE WENT FOR HIM
TWAS VICTORY THAT DAY
NELLIE AND SONNIE

117822 Gunner
William JONES
460th Battery, 15th Brigade, Royal Field Artillery
Died 17 August 1917, aged 25

I WAITED AND WAITED
BUT ALL IN VAIN
FOR THE DAY OF LEAVE
THAT NEVER CAME

926423 Gunner
Leonard Charles VINCE
'C' Battery, 290th Brigade, Royal Field Artillery
Died 10 October 1917, aged 19

ALSO IN MEMORY OF
935588 GNR. WILLIAM F. VINCE
ROYAL FIELD ARTILLERY
CALLED HOME OCT. 10TH 1917

(Serving in the same battery, the Vince brothers
were killed on the same day. William has no
known grave and is commemorated on the Tyne Cot
Memorial to the Missing.)

Ebblinghem Military Cemetery

2160 Private
Gerald Patrick HEAVEY
1st Battalion, Australian Infantry
Died 17 April 1918, aged 17

GREAT GRAND NEPHEW
TO MICHAEL DWYER
THE FAMOUS WICKLOW CHIEFTAIN

(Michael Dwyer was a United Irish leader who
fought a guerrilla campaign against the British
army in the Wicklow Mountains from 1798 to
1803.)

Lieutenant Colonel
Edward Thesiger Frankland HOOD, *DSO*
Royal Field Artillery, commanding 38th Brigade
Died 15 May 1918, aged 36

"IN MEMORY
OF A GREAT COLONEL"
TRIBUTE OF BRIGADE
ON HIS CROSS

(Before the inscribed headstones were erected after
the war, grave-markers were simple wooden crosses.
This senior officer was a holder of the Croix de
Guerre.)

5273A Lance Corporal
Frank JAMES
10th Battalion, Australian Infantry
Died 24 April 1918, aged 27

OUR SUNNY BOY

Ecoivres Military Cemetery

541 Private
Frederick BRESLIN
13th Battalion, Cheshire Regiment
Died 13 May 1916, aged 25

YOU FOR ENGLAND LIVE
I FOR ENGLAND DIED

10/14047 Private
William Arthur DUTTON
10th Battalion, Cheshire Regiment
Died 20 May 1916, aged 29

HE KNEW BEFORE HE WENT
THAT HIS FATE WOULD BE
DEATH IN BATTLE

2425 Private
Eric John EASTON
8th Battalion, Sherwood Foresters
(Nottinghamshire & Derbyshire Regiment)
Died 4 April 1916, aged 19

HE SOUGHT THE GLORY
OF HIS COUNTRY
HE FOUND
THE GLORY OF GOD

13857 Lance Corporal
James HOLLAND
10th Battalion, Cheshire Regiment
Died 30 May 1916, aged 31

HIS DUTY NOBLY DONE

(Lance Corporal Holland was executed for cowardice.)

S/3199 Sergeant
Albert William KIMBERLEY
8th Battalion, The Rifle Brigade
Died 25 May 1916, aged 29

'TWAS SUCH AS HE
THAT SAVED ENGLAND

Second Lieutenant
Walter Richard MAYBROOK
1st Battalion, Wiltshire Regiment
Died 24 April 1916, aged 22

GENTLEMAN UNAFRAID

Second Lieutenant
Eric Lionel STEPHENSON
4th Battalion, Lincolnshire Regiment
Died 18 March 1916, aged 24

ONE OF SEVEN BROTHERS
WHO SERVED
THREE OF WHOM
REST IN FRANCE

19565 Private
George Frederick TANNER
2nd Battalion, South Lancashire Regiment
Died 25 May 1916, aged 20

MAY THE HEAVENLY WINDS
BLOW SOFTLY O'ER
THIS SWEET AND HALLOWED SPOT

Erquingham-Lys Churchyard Extension

73524 Private
Ernest BUCHAN
'A' Company, 16th Battalion,
Royal Welsh Fusiliers
Died 15 March 1918, aged 19

VICTORIOUS HIS FALL
FOR HE ROSE AS HE FELL

1625 Private
Harry PAYNE
17th Battalion, Australian Infantry
Died 15 April 1916, aged 22

MY LIFE I GAVE
FOR MY COUNTRY'S GOOD
& THEY TOOK IT FROM ME
WHERE I STOOD

29086 Driver
Fred RICHARDS
17th Company, Royal Engineers
Died 20 July 1915, aged 21

SLEEP ON, SLEEP ON MY SON
YOUR NOBLE WORK IS DONE

358135 Private
Forbes Macbean ROLLO
2nd/10th Battalion,
The King's (Liverpool Regiment)
Died 19 March 1917, aged 26

BUT AH WE GRUDGED HIM SAIR
TO THE LAND OF THE LEAL

(An extract from The Land O' The Leal, *a*
poem by Carolina, Lady Nairne. The Land o' the
Leal is the home of the blessed after death
(Heaven), and 'sair' is Scots dialect for 'sore'.)

Esquelbecq Military Cemetery

82264 Private
Hyman Herbert FARBER
'B' Company, 20th Battalion,
Durham Light Infantry
Died 14 September 1918, aged 19

BENEATH
IN AN UNTIMELY GRAVE
A LOVING SON
A WARRIOR BRAVE

781755 Gunner
Robert Douglas LAW
'C' Battery, 246th Brigade, Royal Field Artillery
Died 21 May 1918, aged 21

ONE SUNNY SPOT IN FRANCE
WHICH IS FOR EVER ENGLAND

Second Lieutenant
William John MILLS
20th (Tyneside Scottish) Battalion,
Northumberland Fusiliers,
attached Royal Air Force
Died 4 September 1918, aged 23

HE GREATLY LOVED
HE GREATLY LIVED
AND DIED RIGHT MIGHTILY

(From the poem Livingstone, *by John Oxenham.)*

16501 Corporal
George MORGAN, *MM*
9th Battalion,
King's Own Yorkshire Light Infantry
Died 27 April 1918, aged 23

HIS BATTLES ARE O'ER
AND GOD THOUGHT IT BEST
TO TAKE HIM TO
A BEAUTIFUL HOME OF REST

70183 Private
William Shadrach OWEN
9th Battalion, Royal Welsh Fusiliers
Died 9 May 1918, aged 19

CHRISTIANS
NEVER SEE EACH OTHER
FOR THE LAST TIME

110906 Gunner
William Wilson THOMSON
241st Siege Battery, Royal Garrison Artillery
Died 5 May 1918, aged 24

HOW BRIGHT
THESE GLORIOUS SPIRITS SHINE

(The title of a hymn by Isaac Watts.)

Essex Farm Cemetery

8566 Guardsman
William Charles COLLINS
No 1 Company, 2nd Battalion,
Coldstream Guards
Died 27 July 1916, aged 28

NOT A DRUM WAS HEARD
NOT A FUNERAL NOTE

Second Lieutenant
James Oswald HALDANE
6th Battalion, The Rifle Brigade
Died 9 August 1916, aged 37

SPEED, FIGHT ON
FARE EVER THERE AS HERE

(Second Lieutenant Haldane was a district
commissioner in the Uganda Protectorate Civil
Service and as a young man had served in the Boer
War. His epitaph is from Robert Browning's
Epilogue to Alosando.)

Lieutenant
Alec Leith JOHNSTON
1st Battalion, King's Shropshire Light Infantry
Died 22 April 1916, aged 26

ABOVE AND STRONGER
THAN HIS WISH TO LIVE
HIS WISH TO DO HIS DUTY

16527 Lance Corporal
William JONES
13th Battalion, Royal Welsh Fusiliers
Died 23 September 1916, aged 35

WHOSE SILVER CHORD
WAS BROKEN
ERE THE MORN
HAD BRIGHTENED INTO DAY

87379 Sapper
Victor Leonard LEGGETT
39th Divisional Signal Company, Royal Engineers
Died 12 June 1917, aged 19

STATELY IS SERVICE ACCEPTED
BUT LOVELIER IS SERVICE
RENDERED

(From The Bothie of Tober-Na-Vuolich, *a*
poem by Arthur Hugh Clough.)

56731 Private
Olaf Stanley OLSON
'D' Company, 14th Battalion, Welsh Regiment
Died 15 September 1916, aged 20

IN FREEDOM'S NAME HE SUFFERED
FOR RIGHTEOUSNESS HE DIED
HIS NOT TO SEE THE VICTORY
AND WELCOME IT WITH PRIDE

Étaples Military Cemetery

C/1415 Rifleman
Alfred Herbert BURTT
16th Battalion, King's Royal Rifle Corps
Died 6 August 1916, aged 30

FOR GOD
RIGHT AND LIBERTY

(Rifleman Burtt was wounded at High Wood when
a bullet struck him in the thigh, causing five of his
own cartridges to explode. Accompanied by her
sister (grandmother of this book's author), Mrs

Burtt was with her husband when he died in a base hospital at Camiers, family visits being allowed in the case of soldiers on the Dangerously Ill List.)

1596 Private
William Herbert HICKS
53rd Battalion, Australian Infantry
Died 8 December 1916, aged 25

MY ONLY CHILD DIES
THE EMPIRE LIVES
A LONELY MOTHER MOURNS

2158 Private
Kenneth David HYAM
18th Battalion, Australian Infantry
Died 17 August 1916, aged 23

TAKE COMFORT
YE WHO MOURN A LOVED ONE
LOST UPON THE BATTLEFIELD

Etreux British Cemetery

Lieutenant
Chaloner Francis Trevor CHUTE
2nd Battalion, Royal Munster Fusiliers
Died 27 August 1914, aged 29

IF LOVE COULD HAVE SAVED HIM
HE WOULD NOT HAVE BEEN KILLED

Second Lieutenant
Philip Hamilton SULIVAN
'B' Company, 2nd Battalion,
Royal Munster Fusiliers
Died 27 August 1914, aged 20

DIED ON HIS 20TH BIRTHDAY
FAULTLESS BEFORE THEE
WITH EXCEEDING JOY

(Adapted from Jude, *Chapter 1, Verse 24.)*

Etreux Communal Cemetery

9968 Private
George LAY
1st Battalion, Royal Berkshire Regiment
Died 28 April 1915, aged 22

MAY HIS SOUL
REST IN THE LORD

(This soldier was one of a number who lost their way on the retreat from Mons, stayed in the area, and were later captured by the Germans, who executed them in the alleged belief that they were spies.)

Euston Road Cemetery

26487 Private
Alexander Arthur ASTLE
14th Battalion, Hampshire Regiment
Died 16 September 1916, aged 41

HE VOLUNTARILY LENT
A HELPING HAND

15907 Sergeant
Rupert D'Arcy HYDE
1st Battalion, Norfolk Regiment
Died 2 September 1918, aged 25

GO STRANGER
TELL OUR PEOPLE WE LIE HERE
HAVING OBEYED THEIR WORD

1575 Private
Frederick PEARCE
23rd (City of London) Battalion,
London Regiment (Royal Fusiliers)
Died 1 November 1916, aged 27

HIS GALLANT SHARE

Believed to be buried in this cemetery
12/525 Sergeant
John William STREETS
12th Battalion, York & Lancaster Regiment
Died 1 July 1916, aged 31

I FELL; BUT YIELDED NOT
MY ENGLISH SOUL
THAT LIVES OUT HERE
BENEATH THE BATTLE'S ROLL

(Will Streets gave up the opportunity of going to a grammar school and became a miner, because of the need to support his younger brothers. He wrote a book about mining and a volume of war poems, from one of which his epitaph is taken. He was killed while attempting to rescue one of his men from no-man's-land.)

Faubourg d'Amiens Cemetery

365591 Gunner
John McLaughlan ALCORN
100th Siege Battery, Royal Garrison Artillery
Died 21 March 1917, aged 20

THAT LOVE MIGHT REIGN
ENTHRONED BY PEACE
'TWAS TO THIS END HE DIED

15911 Private
Alec BAILEY
11th Battalion, Suffolk Regiment
Died 24 March 1917, aged 22

FOR BRITAIN'S HONOUR
AND A MOTHER'S LOVE

R/4281 Rifleman
Ernest Richard James BAILEY
13th Battalion, King's Royal Rifle Corps
Died 9 April 1917, aged 21

IN BOTH OUR HEARTS
HE IS STILL LIVING

Lieutenant
William George BANNISTER
405th Siege Battery, Royal Garrison Artillery
Died 28 March 1918, aged 32

MY HERO
TOPSY

(It is probably safe to guess that 'Topsy' had been the deceased's pet name for the widowed Nellie Maria Bannister, grieving at home in Southsea.)

Second Lieutenant
Roger Mortimer BASKETT
14th Battalion, attached 16th Battalion,
Cheshire Regiment
Died 14 November 1916, aged 21

NOT UNWEPT
NOT UNHONOURED
MY BOY
ONLY UNSUNG

(The epitaph is based on the last line of Sir Walter Scott's poem Patriotism.*)*

Second Lieutenant
Ernest James BLIGHT
27th (Tyneside Irish) Battalion,
Northumberland Fusiliers
Died 11 March 1917, aged 31

THERE REMAINS A HERITAGE
OF HEROIC EXAMPLE
AND NOBLE OBLIGATION

200425 Lance Corporal
Harry Roy BOSUSTOW
1st Battalion, London Regiment (Royal Fusiliers)
Died 1 May 1917, aged 23

FOR HIM
'TWAS VICTORY THAT DAY

A SOLDIER
OF THE GREAT WAR

639891 Private
Ward BURKE
9th Battalion, Canadian Infantry
Died 29 March 1918, aged 21

OUR DEAR WARD
HE GAVE UP ALL
FOR VICTORY AND GOD
FATHER AND MOTHER

52905 Lance Corporal
Richard Douglas EVANS
9th Battalion, Royal Fusiliers
Died 1 May 1917, aged 24

FOR PEACE
HIS SOUL WAS YEARNING
AND NOW PEACE
LAPS HIM ROUND

Captain
Douglas Marsden EWART, *MC*
7th Battalion, Canadian Engineers
Died 26 August 1918, aged 28

WHO DIES FOR THEE AND THINE
WINS THEE AT LAST

(Very soon after hearing of Captain Ewart's death,
his parents learned that the official status of their
other son, Second Lieutenant K.P.Ewart, had been
changed from 'Missing' to 'Killed in Action' – see
under Niergnies Communal Cemetery.)

Major
John Campbell FISHER
1st Battalion, Royal Scots Fusiliers
Died 6 May 1917, aged 23

BY CHANCE A REAL SCOT
FROM THE ISLAND OF BUTE
RESTS HERE
IN HOPE

90201 Sergeant
John FORSTER
'B' Battery, 51st Brigade, Royal Field Artillery
Died 29 April 1917, aged 20

IN BLOOM OF LIFE
DEATH CLAIMED HIM
IN THE PRIDE
OF HIS MANHOOD DAYS

529064 Private
Paul Evan GILLESPIE
9th Canadian Field Ambulance,
Canadian Army Medical Corps
Died 7 September 1918, aged 19

OVER HIM NOW
THE RED POPPIES GROW
NODDING A LULLABY OF REST
TO OUR BOY

15/1200 Private
Walter William GOSSAGE
15th Battalion, Royal Warwickshire Regiment
Died 4 June 1916, aged 21

OUR ONLY CHILD
GOD KNOWETH OUR HEARTS

152662 Gunner
Charles Leonard HOSKIN
59th Siege Battery, Royal Garrison Artillery
Died 2 September 1918, aged 19

GREAT IS THE SORROW FOR YOU
MY GOOD AND GLORIOUS BOY

12494 Private
George Frederick JAMES
6th Battalion,
The Queen's (Royal West Surrey Regiment)
Died 5 April 1917, aged 20

HE WAS THE LOVED OF ALL
YET NONE O'ER HIS LOW BED
MAY WEEP

Captain
Nelson Gordon JOHNSTONE, *MC*
9th Battalion,
The Black Watch (Royal Highlanders)
Died 30 December 1917, aged 30

ONE CROWDED HOUR
OF GLORIOUS LIFE
IS WORTH AN AGE
WITHOUT A NAME

15722 Private
John William KILBY
27th Company, Labour Corps
Died 24 September 1917, aged 40

ONLY ONE IN THOUSANDS
BUT ALL THE WORLD TO ME
ONE OF THE BEST

2657104 Gunner
Hugh Christopher LACKEN
3rd Brigade, Canadian Garrison Artillery
Died 11 September 1918, aged 22

WELL DONE
GOOD AND FAITHFUL BROTHER

88501 Gunner
Herbert LOVE
50th Brigade, Royal Field Artillery
Died 27 March 1917, aged 21

WE QUESTION
AND WAIT TILL THE MORNING

15/902 Private
John Edwin LUDLOW
15th Battalion, Royal Warwickshire Regiment
Died 4 June 1916, aged 17

LET'S DO WHAT'S RIGHT & NOBLE
AND SO MAKE DEATH
PROUD TO TAKE US

Lieutenant
Alan Stewart MACLAUCHLAN
405th Siege Battery, Royal Garrison Artillery
Died 28 March 1918, aged 32

OUT OF THE DIN OF THE DOING
INTO THE PEACE OF THE DONE

Second Lieutenant
Alastair James MORLEY-BROWN
9th Battalion, King's Own Scottish Borderers
Died 29 April 1916, aged 18

I CONSIDER IT AN HONOUR
TO DIE FOR MY COUNTRY

Second Lieutenant
Sydney Vernon PHILLIPS
'B' Company, 10th Battalion,
attached 7th Battalion,
Leicestershire Regiment
Died 14 August 1916, aged 28

"PROMOTED"

Lieutenant
Fred ROBERTS
11th Battalion, attached 6th Battalion,
King's Own Yorkshire Light Infantry
Died 23 July 1916, aged 24

M.A. MANCHESTER UNIVERSITY
THE MAGNITUDE
OF HIS SACRIFICE
KNOWN ONLY UNTO GOD

3/2859 Private
Robert ROBERTSON
9th Battalion,
The Black Watch (Royal Highlanders)
Died 7 April 1917, aged 25

MY RACE IS RUN
MY WARFARE'S O'ER

1011 Private
Raymond George SALMON
'D' Company, 16th Battalion,
Royal Warwickshire Regiment
Died 10 April 1916, aged 22

LOOKING THIS WAY

Second Lieutenant
Charles Vaughan SANDEMAN
184th Tunnelling Company, Royal Engineers
Died 4 July 1916, aged 33

THE MEN WE LOVED
WERE NOT FOUND WANTING
AND TURNED NOT BACK
IN THE DAY OF BATTLE

192829 Gunner
John Douglas SCOTT
38th Battery, 158th Brigade, Royal Field Artillery
Died 5 April 1918, aged 18

SPLENDID YOU PASSED
INTO THE LIGHT
THAT NEVERMORE SHALL FADE

(The words are from Sir John Arkwright's hymn
O Valiant Hearts.*)*

301355 Gunner
James William STANWAY
10th Battery, Canadian Field Artillery
Died 29 August 1918, aged 27

AS HIS MAKER BEFORE
HE GAVE HIS LIFE
TO SAVE OTHERS

116308 Gunner
Samuel WAINWRIGHT
29th Battery, 42nd Brigade, Royal Field Artillery
Died 5 April 1917, aged 20

THE SOUL
WOULD HAVE NO RAINBOW
HAD THE EYE NO TEARS

(This is a North American Indian proverb.)

42128 Corporal
Alfred William WARD
61st Field Company, Royal Engineers
Died 23 July 1916, aged 28

THAT TWILIGHT
OF ENCHANTED DAYS
THE IMPERISHABLE PAST
HIS LOVING WIFE ROSE

Ferme Olivier British Cemetery

76362 Gunner
William John BROWN
207th Siege Battery, Royal Garrison Artillery
Died 23 June 1917, aged 22

THE SACRIFICE
IS OFFERED STILL
IN SECRET AND ALONE

20955 Corporal
Percy GRANT
10th Battalion, South Wales Borderers
Died 3 March 1917, aged 31

THE STRIFE IS O'ER
THE BATTLE DONE
NOW IS THE VICTOR'S
TRIUMPH WON. ALLELUIA

(From The Strife is O'er: Hymns fitted to
the Order of Common Prayer, *by Francis
Pott.)*

12360 Guardsman
Gordon SMITH
2nd Battalion, Scots Guards
Died 2 July 1916, aged 30

HIS DEATH
WAS THAT WHICH HEROES
LOVE TO DIE

Feuchy Chapel British Cemetery

Lieutenant
Juan Manuel ALDANA
12th Battalion, Worcestershire Regiment
Died 21 April 1917, aged 21

THE CONVICTION OF DUTY
IS A DIVINE INSPIRATION

33862 Private
Harry BAILEY
57th Company, Labour Corps
Died 23 July 1917, aged 24

WHO PLUCKED THIS FLOWER
I SAID THE MASTER
AND THE GARDENER WAS SILENT

19881 Lance Corporal
Percy JOBBINS
2nd Battalion, South Wales Borderers
Died 14 April 1917, aged 33

A BIRTH OF LOVE
AND A DEATH OF HONOUR

Second Lieutenant
Ernest Albert LANE
*3rd Battalion, attached 2nd Battalion,
Essex Regiment*
Died 1 September 1918, aged 27

YOU WENT DEAR
YOUR DUTY PLAIN
YOU FELL DEAR
BROKEN HEARTED I REMAIN

Five Points Cemetery

75076 Private
Hubert Leslie HICKS
12th/13th Battalion, Northumberland Fusiliers
Died 18 September 1918, aged 19

A GRIEF TOO GREAT FOR WORDS

Fouilloy Communal Cemetery

778132 Sergeant
Donald Ross MACKENZIE
2nd Battalion, Canadian Railway Troops
Died 30 March 1918, aged 30

HE SLEEPS NOT HERE
BUT IN THE HEARTS
ACROSS THE SEAS

Franvillers Communal Cemetery Extension

1215 Lance Sergeant
Thomas Arthur GOGGIN
20th Battalion, Australian Infantry
Died 14 May 1918, aged 23

NOT OUR LOSS ONLY
BUT THAT OF A NATION

2397 Lance Corporal
Alfred Henry HUISH
17th Battalion, Australian Infantry
Died 9 May 1918, aged 30

THERE IS NO FIRESIDE
HOWEVER DEFENDED
BUT HAS ONE VACANT CHAIR

2709 Lance Corporal
George Easton PAPE
54th Battalion, Australian Infantry
Died 25 July 1918, aged 21

BEYOND EARTH'S
FARTHEST HILLS HE FARES
SONG-CROWNED IMMORTAL

(Adapted from a poem by Wilfrid Wilson Gibson entitled Rupert Brooke.*)*

Fréchencourt Communal Cemetery

18948 Gunner
Harry Twyford TRUMAN
5th Brigade, Australian Field Artillery
Died 19 April 1918, aged 20

THE GUNNER SMILED
AS HE WENT OUT WEST

Godewaersvelde British Cemetery

93202 Lance Bombardier
Harry Reginald BASFORD
23rd Heavy Battery, Royal Garrison Artillery
Died 20 October 1917, aged 29

SADLY MISSED
BY HIS LONELY WIFE MARIE

2134 Driver
John Ernest Macquarie DUGAN
17th Battalion, Australian Infantry
Died 31 March 1918, aged 24

IT IS SWEET AND GLORIOUS
TO DIE FOR ONE'S COUNTRY

(This epitaph appears much more frequently in Horace's original Latin – 'Dulce et decorum est pro patria mori'.)

18342 Private
John Henry ELY
'C' Company, 11th Battalion,
The Queen's Own (Royal West Kent Regiment)
Died 1 August 1917, aged 20

A FAITH IN CHRIST
AND GOD IN LIFE
PASSION FOR ART
ABHORRING STRIFE

184645 Gunner
William Roy FOUNTAIN
410th Battery, 96th Brigade, Royal Field Artillery
Died 1 August 1918, aged 27

YE THAT LIVE ON,
REMEMBER US AND THINK,
"WHAT MIGHT HAVE BEEN"

Lieutenant
William Reginald HARVEY
'B' Battery, 95th Brigade, Royal Field Artillery
Died 23 September 1917, aged 31

ENSHRINED HEREIN
RESTS PART OF ENGLAND

53072 Gunner
Thomas William George JOHNSON
'B' Battery, 95th Brigade, Royal Field Artillery
Died 7 October 1917, aged 26

YIELDED HIS ALL
IN UTMOST SACRIFICE

Gommecourt British Cemetery No 2

6586 Lance Corporal
William Tunnage ABBOTT
2nd Battalion, Honourable Artillery Company
Died 15 March 1917, aged 24

STAUNCH TO THE END
AGAINST ODDS UNCOUNTED

230790 Corporal
Leonard Edward ROWE
2nd Battalion, London Regiment (Royal Fusiliers)
Died 1 July 1916, aged 20

A MERE BOY
BUT A GREAT SPORTSMAN

241048 Lance Corporal
Frederick James TAYLOR
'C' Company, 1st/5th Battalion,
East Lancashire Regiment
Died 19 April 1918, aged 22

DUTY AND HONOUR FIRST
PLEASURE AFTERWARDS

Captain
Edward Henry Courtenay THORP
1st Battalion, Devonshire Regiment
Died 21 August 1918, aged 20

HERE A BOY
HE DWELT THROUGH ALL
THE SINGING SEASON

29558 Private
Hugh WALMSLEY
8th Battalion, Somerset Light Infantry
Died 1 May 1918, aged 19

HIS RIGHT HAND
AND HIS HOLY ARM
HATH GOTTEN HIM THE VICTORY

(From Psalms, Chapter 98, Verse 1.)

Gordon Dump Cemetery

23931 Private
Edric James COUZENS
1st Battalion, Worcestershire Regiment
Died 8 July 1916, aged 23

WAS IT IN VAIN

11612 Gunner
Frank CROMMELIN
6th Brigade, Australian Field Artillery
Died 7 August 1916, aged 20

PEACE TO THE ASHES
OF A SINGULARLY GOOD BOY

Captain
Octavius Ralph Featherstone JOHNSTON
4th Battalion, Middlesex Regiment
Died 1 July 1916, aged 25

THE GAME IS DEEP
BUT I MUST PLAY IT OUT
I CAN NO OTHER
SO AWAY WITH FEAR

8428 Gunner
Allan MERCER
6th Brigade, Australian Field Artillery
Died 7 August 1916, aged 20

DEAD ERE HIS PRIME
FAME IS NO PLANT
THAT GROWS ON MORTAL SOIL

(From Lycidas *by John Milton.)*

---

955 Gunner
Albert Roy TEMPANY
103rd Howitzer Battery, 3rd Brigade,
Australian Field Artillery
Died 8 August 1916, aged 18

A HERO GONE
TO CLAIM HIS JUST REWARD
SO MOTE IT BE

('Mote' is an archaic word meaning 'may'.)

12891 Private
James WORSLEY
7th Battalion,
The King's Own (Royal Lancaster Regiment)
Died 4 July 1916, aged 37

IN GLORIOUS MEMORY
COURAGEOUS AND CHEERFUL
IN THE DARKEST HOUR

Gorre British & Indian Cemetery

G.49393 Lance Corporal
John Paul Spencer BORASTON
'B' Company, 22nd Battalion, Royal Fusiliers
Died 13 September 1917, aged 26

THAT WAR MAY CEASE
IN THE EARTH
AND THE NATIONS
MAY HAVE PEACE

280997 Private
Joseph BUTLER
2nd/7th Battalion, Lancashire Fusiliers
Died 17 March 1917, aged 19

A SHORT
BUT TROUBLED LIFE
NIPPED IN THE BUD
SADLY MISSED

THEIR NAME LIVETH
FOR EVERMORE

4666 Private
William HENDERSON
'B' Company, 1st/6th Battalion,
Argyll & Sutherland Highlanders
Died 29 December 1916, aged 19

HE DIED
TO SAVE OUR LIBERTIES
FROM AGGRESSION

18/1325 Lance Corporal
James Thomas STENHOUSE
'D' Company, 18th Battalion,
West Yorkshire Regiment (Prince of Wales's Own)
Died 27 September 1916, aged 22

ONE OF KITCHENER'S VOLUNTEERS
WHO DIED FOR ENGLAND'S HONOUR

Grootebeek British Cemetery

Captain
George Alan Campbell SMITH, *MC*
14th Battalion, Argyll & Sutherland Highlanders
Died 28 September 1918, aged 22

ONCE MORE ON MY ADVENTURE
BRAVE AND NEW

Grove Town Cemetery

27814 Lance Corporal
Ernest Edward ATKINSON
12th Battalion, The King's (Liverpool Regiment)
Died 9 October 1916, aged 20

OH HOW WE MISS HIM
ONE OF THE BEST
IT WAS FOR HIS COUNTRY'S
GOOD, HE WAS SLAIN

Second Lieutenant
Guy Cheselden Reuell ATKINSON
12th Battalion, attached 2nd Battalion,
East Lancashire Regiment
Died 30 October 1916, aged 26

O QUIET HEART
CAN YOU HEAR US TELL
HOW PEACE WAS WON
BY THE MEN WHO FELL

44665 Corporal
Thomas Harold BALSHAW
'B' Company, 12th Battalion,
Manchester Regiment
Died 14 February 1917, aged 28

GOOD OLD YAL
HIS FRIENDS DO SAY
WHO SADLY MISS HIM
DAY BY DAY

33977 Private
Robert BOUCH
12th Battalion, Manchester Regiment
Died 13 November 1916, aged 25

MY ONE, MY ALL.
MOTHER.
RACHEL BOUCH

Captain
Hugh Henry BURN, *MC*
2nd Battalion, Coldstream Guards
Died 16 September 1916, aged 20

O SOLDIER SAINT
NO WORK BEGUN
SHALL EVER PAUSE FOR DEATH

2150 Private
Percival John CHILDS
1st/3rd Battalion, London Regiment
(Royal Fusiliers)
Died 23 September 1916, aged 18

HIS COUNTRY CALLED
HE HASTENED TO OBEY
WE MOURN BUT DO NOT MURMUR

11117 Private
George Leonard EDWARDS
11th Battalion, Essex Regiment
Died 24 September 1916, aged 15

QUEEN'S BEST BOY, 1915.
DO GOOD & BE GOOD

(This very young London boy, born in Hackney
and educated at Fortescue House, Twickenham,
was mourned by a widowed father.)

15510 Pioneer
Edgar Harold GARDNER
4th Company, Special Brigade, Royal Engineers
Died 22 October 1916, aged 32

THIS WE KNOW DEAR LAD
ALL'S WELL.

10165 Guardsman
James GREEN
1st Battalion, Coldstream Guards
Died 6 March 1917, aged 21

SMILE AND WAIT

36647 Private
Frank HITCHIN
59th Battalion, Machine Gun Corps
Died 22 September 1916, aged 18

IF THIS IS VICTORY, THEN
LET GOD STOP ALL WARS
HIS LOVING MOTHER

48841 Sapper
Albert Edward HOWARD
83rd Field Company, Royal Engineers
Died 9 October 1916, aged 29

HE FOUGHT
FOR THE CAUSE OF JUSTICE
AND DIED
NEATH THE UNION JACK

S/2989 Rifleman
Thomas Sell MILLER
11th Battalion, The Rifle Brigade
Died 29 September 1916, aged 45

PASS NOT THIS STONE
IN SORROW BUT IN PRIDE
& MAY YOU LIVE
AS NOBLY AS HE DIED

(Rifleman Miller was a veteran of the Punjab
Frontier campaign of 1897-1898 and the Boer
War.)

27287 Private
Leo William RIPPIN
1st Battalion,
The King's Own (Royal Lancaster Regiment)
Died 27 October 1916, aged 24

RECORD HIS NAME
IT IS HIS DUE
REMEMBER THAT
HE DIED FOR YOU

Second Lieutenant
Alfred Cecil SKOULDING
6th Battalion,
Oxfordshire & Buckinghamshire Light Infantry
Died 21 February 1917, aged 33

AN OLD WOODBRIDGIAN.
GOOD SHOT, KEEN CRICKETER
A DEVOTED SON
R.I.P.

6473 Corporal
Patrick SULLIVAN
2nd Battalion, King's Own Scottish Borderers
Died 28 September 1916, aged 22

DEAR SON
YOU LAY WITH THE BRAVE
WHERE NO TEAR OF YOUR MOTHER
CAN FALL ON YOUR GRAVE

Second Lieutenant
Reginald Cyrus TOKELY
2nd Battalion, Essex Regiment
Died 23 December 1916, aged 20

MILITANTS WHO FOUGHT
THY VALOUR BEST
ANGELS IN HEAVEN
KNOW THE REST

Guards' Cemetery, Les Bœufs

Second Lieutenant
Thomas Percy Arthur HERVEY
21st Battalion, King's Royal Rifle Corps
Died between 15 and 17 September 1916, aged 29

IN FAR FIJI
HE HEARD HIS COUNTRY'S CALL
AND CAME AND DIED

Second Lieutenant
Charles Dean PRANGLEY
1st Battalion, Lincolnshire Regiment
Died 25 September 1916, aged 19

HE GAVE THEE
HE TOOK THEE
AND HE WILL RESTORE THEE

*(A book which was dedicated to the memory of this
young officer, who was the son of a vicar, is now
kept in St George's Memorial Church, Ypres
[Ieper]. Designed in the style of a medieval
illustrated manuscript, the book has covers made
from a lime tree in the family garden, a gold cross on
the front which was made from the wedding ring of
Second Lieutenant Prangley's mother, and pages at
the back which were made from her wedding dress.)*

7794 Private
Walter Stephen SPRINGETT
13th (Kensington) Battalion, London Regiment
Died 5 October 1916, aged 23

HIS WAS NOT TO KNOW
THE REASON WHY
BUT TO GO AND DIE

Guards Cemetery, Windy Corner

Second Lieutenant
Frederick Walter BATTLEY
11th Battalion, Royal Sussex Regiment
Died 21 April 1916, aged 21

THEY SHALL GROW NOT OLD
AS WE THAT ARE LEFT GROW OLD

(Laurence Binyon's lines from For the Fallen *are
among the most familiar in the English language.
The poem first appeared in print in* The Times *as
early as September 1914.)*

26182 Private
Harry BEARDSMORE
*16th Battalion, Sherwood Foresters
(Nottinghamshire & Derbyshire Regiment)*
Died 4 June 1916, aged 19

HE WEARS THE ROSE
OF YOUTH UPON HIM

(The epitaph is from Shakespeare's Antony and
Cleopatra, *Act 3, Scene 11. Private Beardsmore's
brother William also fell and is buried in the
similarly named Guards' Cemetery, Les Bœufs, but
has no epitaph.)*

P/11 Rifleman
George David DAVIES
16th Battalion, The Rifle Brigade
Died 29 May 1916, aged 18

"HATRED STIRRETH UP STRIFES"

(From Proverbs, *Chapter 10, Verse 12.)*

24317 Pioneer
Frederick William DUNSTAN
26th Field Company, Royal Engineers
Died 21 January 1915, aged 20

TRANSLATED FROM
THE WARFARE OF THE WORLD
INTO THE PEACE OF GOD

Lieutenant
Geoffrey Montagu Mason FLEMING
Royal Army Medical Corps,
attached 2nd Battalion, Bedfordshire Regiment
Died 16 June 1915, aged 25

KILLED WHILE ATTENDING
TO THE WOUNDED
WITH CHRIST
TILL HE COME

19599 Private
Roland Alex Llewylen GALLEN
16th Battalion, Royal Welsh Fusiliers
Died 10 April 1916, aged 21

SWIFT AS AN ARROW
LIGHT AS A SWALLOW
SO MAY WE FIND YOU
BOY, WHEN WE FOLLOW

Tombes de Guerre du Commonwealth
Commonwealth War Graves

Second Lieutenant
Reginald Moon GOODMAN
2nd Battalion, Border Regiment
Died 16 May 1915, aged 26

"HE FOUGHT FOR ENGLAND
AND FOR ENGLAND DIED"
R.H. FORSTER

2903 Private
James KERR
9th (Glasgow Highland) Battalion,
Highland Light Infantry,
Died 9 July 1915, aged 19

BUT OH! FELL DEATH'S
UNTIMELY FROST
THAT NIPT MY FLOWER
SAE EARLY

(One of the early volunteers, Private Kerr enlisted in September 1914 and went out to France with his battalion on 4 November. His epitaph is from Burns's poem Highland Mary.*)*

Lieutenant
Albert William LANE-JOYNT
Dorsetshire Regiment,
attached Machine Gun Corps
Died 26 February 1916, aged 18

HEAVEN IS BY THE YOUNG
INVADED
THEIR LAUGHTER'S IN
THE HOUSE OF GOD

(From Katharine Tynan's poem Flower of Youth.*)*

Second Lieutenant
Edward Charles MORGAN
1st Battalion, attached 5th Battalion,
Royal Berkshire Regiment
Died 18 December 1915, aged 17

IF IT HAD NOT BEEN THE LORD
WHO WAS ON OUR SIDE
PS. CXXIV

19656 Private
Frank Adams SHENTON
15th Battalion, Cheshire Regiment
Died 2 March 1916, aged 19

THE AMBASSADORS OF PEACE
SHALL WEEP BITTERLY

(From Isaiah, *Chapter 33, Verse 7.)*

93

Guillemont Road Cemetery

Lieutenant
Raymond ASQUITH
3rd Battalion, Grenadier Guards
Died 15 September 1916, aged 37

SMALL TIME, BUT IN THAT SMALL
MOST GREATLY LIVED
THIS STAR OF ENGLAND

(This officer was a son of the Prime Minister, a barrister, a noted scholar and orator, and – like his brother Herbert – one of the war poets. His brother-in-law, Edward Horner, is buried in Rocquigny-Équancourt Road British Cemetery and has the same epitaph, which is from Shakespeare's Henry V, Act 5, Scene 2.)

15652 Corporal
Robert Henry CLARKE
17th Battalion, The King's (Liverpool Regiment)
Died 30 July 1916, aged 21

THEY WERE A WALL UNTO US
BOTH BY DAY AND NIGHT
AND WE WERE NOT HURT

(This is a combination of two separate passages from I Samuel, Chapter 25.)

Second Lieutenant
William Alexander Stanhope FORBES
3rd Battalion, attached 1st Battalion,
Duke of Cornwall's Light Infantry
Died 3 September 1916, aged 23

HE SAW BEYOND THE FILTH
OF BATTLE, AND THOUGHT DEATH
A FAIR PRICE TO PAY
TO BELONG TO THE COMPANY
OF THESE FELLOWS

(This strikingly upbeat epitaph extends well beyond the stipulated maximum length.)

25349 Private
Arthur Kenrick LLOYD
19th Battalion, The King's (Liverpool Regiment)
Died 30 July 1916, aged 20

GOOD-NIGHT BELOVED
GOOD-NIGHT, GOOD-NIGHT

HAC Cemetery

786502 Sergeant
Charles Harold BULLIVANT
'C' Battery, 312th Brigade, Royal Field Artillery
Died 13 April 1917, aged 19

A MAN IN DEEDS
A BOY IN YEARS
CISSIE AND MARK

Captain
Christopher George FOWLER
1st/6th Battalion, Norfolk Regiment
Died 6 April 1917, aged 21

SECURE FROM CHANGE
IN THEIR HIGH-HEARTED WAYS
BEAUTIFUL EVERMORE

(From Ode Recited at the Harvard Convention, 21st July 1865, by James Russell Lowell.)

4870 Private
Cleve Hartley PACKHAM
13th Battalion, Australian Infantry
Died 11 April 1917, aged 22

FOR YOUR TOMORROW
WE GAVE OUR TODAY

(This epitaph is from a collection of inscriptions for war memorials published by John Maxwell Edmonds in 1919. A variation of the verse from which the words are taken is famously inscribed on a Second World War divisional memorial in Kohima, India.)

Hagle Dump Cemetery

359136 Pioneer
Arthur Henry Ebeneezer BROWN
4th Foreway Company, Royal Engineers
Died 15 September 1918, aged 20

HE SPENT HIS BOY'S DEAR LIFE
FOR ENGLAND
SO WE MUST TRY TO BE CONTENT

Second Lieutenant
Alfred Charles RANSDALE
15th Battalion, Loyal North Lancashire Regiment
Died 1 September 1918, aged 23

HE CAME FROM THE ARGENTINE
AT HIS NATION'S CALL FOR HELP

470448 Sapper
Andrew SMITH
4th Tramway Company, Royal Engineers
Died 15 July 1918, aged 29

OUR BODIES MAY BE
FAR REMOVED
BUT STILL OUR HEARTS ARE ONE

Hamel Military Cemetery

906 Gunner
William Henry RUSSELL
'X' 39th Trench Mortar Battery,
Royal Field Artillery
Died 29 September 1916, aged 18

AGE WILL NOT WEARY HIM

(Adapted from a phrase in Laurence Binyon's
poem For the Fallen.)

2401 Private
John THOMAS
'B' Company, 12th Battalion,
Royal Sussex Regiment
Died 3 September 1916, aged 22

HE FELL
UPON THE FIELD OF BATTLE
THANK GOD
HE DID HIS DUTY WELL

Hangard Wood British Cemetery

445312 Private
John Bernard CROAK, *VC*
13th Battalion, Canadian Infantry
(Quebec Regiment)
Died 8 August 1918, aged 26

DO YOU WISH
TO SHOW YOUR GRATITUDE?
KNEEL DOWN AND PRAY
FOR MY SOUL

(A posthumous VC was awarded to Private
Croak for a succession of incidents at Amiens which
culminated in his death.)

322267 Corporal
Walter Bernard Frank GILES, *MM*
2nd/6th Battalion, London Regiment
(City of London Rifles)
Died 4 April 1918, aged 24

A BROKEN-HEARTED
CHILD AND WIFE
WILL EVER MOURN
HIS PRECIOUS LIFE

553954 Rifleman
Arthur RENTON
*16th Battalion, London Regiment
(Queen's Westminster Rifles)
Died 5 April 1918, aged 21*

WAR LOVES
TO SEEK ITS VICTIMS
IN THE YOUNG

Hargicourt British Cemetery

116354 Private
William Henry FOSTER
*72nd Company, Machine Gun Corps (Infantry)
Died 20 November 1917, aged 19*

THE BLOOD OF HEROES
NEVER DIES

Second Lieutenant
William FYVIE
*3rd Battalion, Royal Scots
Died 26 August 1917, aged 32*

HE CAME FROM FIJI ISLANDS
TO HELP HIS NATIVE LAND

270214 Private
Benjamin HOWARD
*5th/6th Battalion, Royal Scots
Died 26 August 1917, aged 19*

HIS MOTHER'S JOY
AND
HIS FATHER'S BOY

5720 Private
Reginald Percy PAKES
*3rd Battalion, Australian Infantry
Died 18 September 1918, aged 19*

FAREWELL MY DEAR REG.
WE ARE ONLY PARTED
FOR LITTLE WHILE
MUM & YOU

Haringhe (Bandaghem) Military Cemetery

14803 Private
Ernest Leonard KERLY
*49th Battalion, Machine Gun Corps (Infantry)
Died 16 April 1918, aged 21*

I FOUGHT OUT HERE
I DIED OUT HERE
BUT WHAT IS THAT
TO THOSE SO DEAR

30990 Private
Joseph Bertram LANCELOTTE
*16th Battalion, Lancashire Fusiliers
Died 16 March 1918, aged 19*

ALL HONOUR TO HIM
WHO NOBLY STRIVING
NOBLY FELL
THAT WE MIGHT LIVE

Harlebeke New British Cemetery

99044 Airman 1st Class
John Stanley CLARKE
*57th Squadron, Royal Flying Corps
Died 10 October 1917, aged 18*

SUNSHINE AND YOUTH
AND LAUGHTER
ALL HE GAVE IN SACRIFICE

THERE'S A COTTAGE HOME IN ENGLAND
WHERE HIS MOTHER SITS AND WEEPS
A powerful example of the grieving-mother theme.
(Rifleman P.T.Redmond, Bedford House Cemetery)

LOVE THAT HATH US IN THE NET
CAN HE PASS AND WE FORGET? DEAR WIFE
Not only mothers; young wives too were left to grieve.
(Guardsman E.J.Lewis, Solferino Farm Cemetery)

GOODNIGHT THOUGH LIFE AND ALL TAKE FLIGHT
NEVER GOOD BYE
Roland Leighton's correspondence with Vera Brittain
is immortalized in Letters from a Lost Generation.
(Lt R.A.Leighton, Louvencourt Military Cemetery)

A GRAVE IN FRANCE WHERE A BRAVE HERO SLEEPS
A HOME IN ENGLAND WHERE LOVED ONES WEEP
It's hard to understand how the fundamental error
here was left uncorrected: the grave is in Belgium.
(Guardsman R.Smith, Brandhoek Military Cemetery)

THE MIDNIGHT STARS ARE GLEAMING
OVER THE GRAVE WE MAY NEVER SEE
*Commonplace today, a visit to northern France was
beyond aspiration for many British families then.
(Pte F.Burden, Awoingt British Cemetery)*

HE WAS THE LOVED OF ALL
YET NONE O'ER HIS LOW BED MAY WEEP
*If a grave in France was beyond the reach of British
families, how much more so for Australians.
(Sapper J.A.Stirling, Adelaide Cemetery)*

GOOD OLD YAL HIS FRIENDS DO SAY
WHO SADLY MISS HIM DAY BY DAY
*This fond and cheery greeting is typical of the
homespun approach often adopted by next-of-kin .
(Cpl T.H.Balshaw, Grove Town Cemetery)*

THERE WAS A MAN SENT FROM GOD
WHOSE NAME WAS JOHN
*Could any Christian tribute surpass this as a moving
blend of simplicity and powerful eloquence?
(Major J.G.Griffith, Ypres Town Cemetery)*

IT IS NOT CHAOS AND DEATH
IT IS ETERNAL LIFE
Paying tribute through expressions of a deeply-held
Christian faith was a popular approach.
(Lt Col B.H.Charlton, Roisel Communal Cemetery
Extension)

HERE LIES A PORTSMOUTH MAN
WHO DIED IN FREEDOM'S CAUSE R.I.P.
Patriotism is a prominent theme throughout the
cemeteries – and occasionally <u>local</u> pride, too.
(Pte W.R.Donohue, La Chapelle-d'Armentières
Communal Cemetery)

"GREATER LOVE HATH NO MAN THAN THIS
THAT A MAN LAY DOWN HIS LIFE FOR HIS FRIENDS"
The most common epitaph of all - but a unique
headstone nonetheless.
(Capt N.G.Chavasse, Brandhoek New Military Cemetery)

WHO STANDS IF FREEDOM FALL?
WHO DIES IF ENGLAND LIVE?
The words are by Rudyard Kipling, who himself
lost a son in the Great War.
(Capt P.S.Banning, Ypres Town Cemetery)

HIS LIFE FOR THE LIFE FRANCE GAVE US
OFF USHANT, 6TH OCT. 1779
*An incident long ago, but not forgotten by the
Crawfords. The headstones in this cemetery lie flat,
owing to the instability of the soil.
(Lt E.Crawford, Wimereux Communal Cemetery)*

R.I.P.   JUBE ME VENIRE AD TE
GOD KEEP THEE, BELOVED
*They weren't all young. Lady Theodora Davidson
lost not only a son on the Western Front, but also
this 65-year-old husband.
(Col W.L.Davidson, St Sever Cemetery)*

SHOT AT DAWN   ONE OF THE FIRST TO ENLIST
A WORTHY SON OF HIS FATHER
*No other Great War epitaph refers to an execution,
which in this case was for desertion.
(Pte A.Ingham, Bailleulmont Communal Cemetery)*

NO LONGER DOES THE HELMET PRESS THY BROW
OFT WEARY WITH ITS
SURGING THOUGHTS OF BATTLE
*By request, there's no Christian cross inscribed here.
(Sgt W.McEwan, Puchevillers British Cemetery)*

108177 Private
William Nicol CROSS
'D' Company, 1st Canadian Mounted Rifles
(Saskatchewan Regiment)
Died 11 June 1916, aged 23

THEY FLUNG THEIR GLORY
TO THE GRAVE
THAT THE FUTURE
MIGHT BE WHOLE

Lieutenant
Edward Thomas Hills HEARN
Royal Field Artillery
and 57th Squadron, Royal Flying Corps
Died 11 September 1917, aged 27

HEARD THE CALL
IN FAR OFF INDIA
AND NOBLY RESPONDED

Hawthorn Ridge Cemetery No 2

22774 Private
Michael GIBBONS
1st Battalion, Royal Dublin Fusiliers
Died 8 July 1916, aged 28

ALL YOU WHO PASS
PRAY FOR HIS SOUL

---

616 Private
Eric Shannon MARTIN
1st Battalion, Royal Newfoundland Regiment
Died 1 July 1916, aged 23

UNTIL GOD
RECKONS UP YOUR TALENTS
SOLDIER SLEEP, THY DUTY'S DONE

Hazebrouck Communal Cemetery

9813 Private
Leonard GREGG
2nd Battalion, Lancashire Fusiliers
Died 23 October 1914, aged 26

ALSO IN MEMORY OF
4399 DRUMMER ROBERT GREGG
KILLED IN BOER WAR
AT SPION KOP

(The Greggs were a military family, Leonard's
father having served as a colour sergeant in his
time.)

37820 Sergeant
James William LEMMON
18th Battery, Royal Field Artillery
Died 10 May 1915, aged 27

A SUDDEN CHANGE
HE IN A MOMENT FELL
HE HAD NOT TIME
TO BID FAREWELL

Second Lieutenant
Robert Clifford LOVELL
101st Squadron, Royal Flying Corps
Died 26 January 1918, aged 26

BRIEF, BRAVE AND GLORIOUS
WAS HIS YOUNG CAREER
AND NOW HE RESTS

56799 Acting Bombardier
Henry Cecil SIMMONS, *DCM*
123rd Heavy Battery, Royal Garrison Artillery
Died 7 May 1915, aged 22

IN MEMORY OF AN ONLY SON
WHO FELL EAST OF YPRES
FLANDERS
R I P

(This soldier was born in Constantinople, where his
widowed father continued to live, and he resigned his
contract abroad as an electrical engineer in order to
enlist in 1914.)

Heath Cemetery

2787 Sergeant
Roy Henry BRUCE
4th Battalion, Australian Infantry
Died 23 August 1918, aged 27

THE EMPIRE CALLED FOR MEN
NEARER MY GOD TO THEE

Second Lieutenant
Edmund Jasper Shalcrass CAVE
8th Squadron, Royal Air Force
Died 14 August 1918, aged 23

ONE MOMENT STOOD HE
AS THE ANGELS STAND
HIGH IN THE IMMANENCE OF AIR
THE NEXT – HE WAS NOT
TO THE FATHERLAND
DEPARTED UNAWARE

60193 Private
Matthew CONNELL
5th/6th Battalion, Royal Scots
Died 27 August 1918, aged 19

WE MAY BE HERE
BUT OUR HEARTS
ARE WHERE OUR GALLANT
BRITISH SOLDIER LIES

Lieutenant
Harold Charles DYER, *MM*
8th Battalion, Australian Infantry
Died 9 August 1918, aged 25

OUR DEAR BOY
GOD LOVED HIM
& TOOK HIM HOME
FOUR YEARS NOBLE SERVICE

5389 Private
John James GAUL
6th Battalion, Australian Infantry
Died 23 August 1918, aged 24

AMID THE DIN OF SHOT & SHELL
HE FOUND A SOLDIER'S GRAVE

256 Private
David Henry HERD
29th Battalion, Australian Infantry
Died 9 August 1918, aged 25

O SON & BROTHER DEAR
WELL HAST THOU PLAYED
THY PART
AFAR IN FRANCE

6340 Lance Corporal
Stephen Joseph KITCHENER, *MM*
18th Battalion, Australian Infantry
Died 9 August 1918, aged 28

HE WENT TO UPHOLD
THE FLAG OF HIS FOREFATHERS

3803 Private
Davitt Jack SCHWIND
46th Battalion, Australian Infantry
Died 8 August 1918, aged 19

KIND READER
PRAY FOR AN ONLY SON
OF A WIDOWED MOTHER
DEEPLY MOURNED

Lieutenant
Richard STONE
201st Squadron, Royal Air Force
Died 9 August 1918, aged 19

SHOT DOWN AT DAWN
OVER THE GERMAN LINES
FAITHFUL UNTO DEATH

7837 Private
John Campbell Dale WARREN
16th Battalion, Australian Infantry
Died 16 August 1918, aged 21

OF DYLIABING, W.A.
O DAUGHTERS OF FRANCE
LET IT NOT BE IN VAIN

6842 Private
Alexander George WHITE
11th Battalion, Australian Infantry
Died 10 August 1918, aged 22

MY SON, MY SON
HOW HARD OH GOD TO SAY
THY WILL BE DONE

62939 Private
Victor Arthur WIGHTMAN
'A' Company, 7th Battalion,
The Queen's (Royal West Surrey Regiment)
Died 30 April 1918, aged 19

PASSED BEYOND
THE CANNON'S ROAR
BUT NOT BEYOND LOVE

Hébuterne Military Cemetery

2782 Private
Arthur James BUTLER
1st/4th Battalion, Royal Berkshire Regiment
Died 25 August 1915, aged 18

HE WAS YOUNG BUT DUTY CALLED

Lieutenant
Philip Denys DOYNE
4th Battalion,
Oxfordshire & Buckinghamshire Light Infantry
Died 28 December 1915, aged 24

"WE ARE ABLE"

4764 Gunner
Albert Brindley PARRY
56th Divisional Ammunition Column,
attached 'Y' 56th Trench Mortar Battery,
Royal Field Artillery
Died 1 July 1916, aged 20

AMONG THE REST
"MY BOY"

(Gunner Parry was buried in a mass grave of 61,
all killed on the first day of the Battle of the
Somme. There is room for only 21 shared
headstones, and he shares one of them with three
other soldiers.)

Heestert Military Cemetery

93300 Private
George Edward BUTTERWORTH
20th Battalion, Durham Light Infantry
Died 25 October 1918, aged 19

HE SERVES HIS COUNTRY BEST
WHO JOINS THE TIDE
THAT LIFTS HER NOBLY ON

89971 Corporal
Richard Whitaker Leith PEMELL
'A' Company, 26th Battalion, Royal Fusiliers,
Died 25 October 1918, aged 36

ENLISTED AUGUST 1914
LIVE THOU FOR ENGLAND
I FOR ENGLAND DIED

Heilly Station Cemetery

43451 Private
William Harold BRUNTON
12th Battalion, Highland Light Infantry
Died 23 September 1916, aged 19

FOR ALL WHO NOBLY STRIVING
NOBLY FELL
PRAISE WITHOUT CEASING
PRAISE

16103 Private
Alfred BURDEN
20th Battalion, Royal Fusiliers
Died 29 July 1916, aged 18

"IT IS FINISHED"

F/99 Private
Sidney Bartholomew BUTLER
17th Battalion, Middlesex Regiment
Died 12 August 1916, aged 19

WHO JOINED THE ARMY
LED BY GOD
WHOSE SWEET WATCHWORD
IS PEACE

2342 Lance Corporal
Hilton John CHESHAM
18th Battalion, Australian Infantry
Died 14 May 1918, aged 27

THEY LAID OUR HERO
DOWN TO REST
IN THE FLAG
WITH THE SOUTHERN CROSS

46661 Gunner
Reymond Ligonier DE MONTMORENCY
'D' Battery, 94th Brigade, Royal Field Artillery
Died 3 October 1916, aged 24

THE LORD IS MY SHEPHERD
I FEAR NO EVIL
IT IS WELL WITH THE LAD

(Adaptations of two biblical sources are used here:
Psalms, *Chapter 23, and* II Kings, *Chapter 4,*
Verse 26.)

Major
Montague ELPHINSTONE
Royal Army Service Corps and
Royal Flying Corps
Died 22 March 1917, aged 36

HE HAS CAST OFF THE ARMOUR
OF DARKNESS AND PUT ON THE
ARMOUR OF LIGHT
YOUR WIFE NORAH

(Adapted from Romans, *Chapter 13, Verse 12.)*

548040 Private
Ernest Walter Henry ENGLAND
15th Battalion, London Regiment
(Prince of Wales's Own Civil Service Rifles)
Died 4 September 1918, aged 19

ENGLAND'S SACRIFICE
FOR BRITAIN'S HONOUR

1094 Lance Corporal
John Edward GILFORD
27th Battalion, Australian Infantry
Died 11 November 1916, aged 22

NOT MY WILL OH GOD BUT THINE

*(*Luke, *Chapter 22, Verse 42, is the source of a*
great many epitaphs, often slightly varied, as is this
one. Armistice Day would not have been an
occasion of wild celebration in at least one South
Australian household, it coinciding with the
anniversary of Lance Corporal Gilford's death.)

Brigadier General
Duncan John GLASFURD
Commanding 12th Brigade, Australian Infantry
Died 12 November 1916, aged 43

A BRAVE MAN
AND A GALLANT SOLDIER

Lieutenant
Thomas Seaman GREEN
3rd Squadron, Royal Flying Corps
Died 13 February 1917, aged 22

EVER REMEMBERED
THE LAST FLIGHT
OF A "LAD WITH WINGS"

Second Lieutenant
James Douglas HODDING
'A' Company, 10th Battalion, Royal Fusiliers
Died 10 July 1916, aged 17

DEAR HAPPY BOY

(The Southsea-born Second Lieutenant Hodding's
family emigrated to Canada, whence he returned in
order to volunteer for military service. He was
commissioned at the age of 16.)

Lieutenant
Albert KING
Royal Field Artillery
Died 23 August 1916, aged 38

HE ONLY KNOWS
THAT NOT THROUGH HIM
SHALL ENGLAND COME TO SHAME

25037 Private
John McKEEN
16th Battalion, Royal Scots
Died 21 June 1916, aged 40

REST THEE
WE HAVE NO PROUDER GRAVE

11732 Gunner
Andrew Armour Burns MACKIE
2nd Brigade, Australian Field Artillery
Died 7 November 1916, aged 21

MY LADDIE
'TIS BUT THE CASKET BURIED
THE GEM IS SPARKLING YET

S/15376 Private
William McRAE
'C' Company, 14th Battalion,
Argyll & Sutherland Highlanders
Died 7 September 1916, aged 26

HE FELL
WHERE'S MANHOOD'S MORNING
ALMOST TOUCHES NOON

Major
Statham Broadbent MAUFE
11th Battalion,
West Yorkshire Regiment (Prince of Wales's Own)
Died 5 May 1916, aged 29

GARRY

---

576 Private
Coldron Slater SINGLETON
10th Battalion, Lincolnshire Regiment
Died 3 July 1916, aged 21

A VOLUNTEER
MAY THE WORLD REMEMBER THEE
AND ALL THY COMRADES
FOR THIS HUMAN CAUSE

Second Lieutenant
Harry SKELTON
8th Battalion, Royal Fusiliers
Died 12 October 1916, aged 28

HE LAID DOWN DEAR LIFE
FOR THE SAKE OF A LAND
MORE DEAR

2239 Rifleman
William Harold THOMAS
6th Battalion, The King's (Liverpool Regiment)
Died 12 September 1916, aged 22

HE DIED AS FEW MEN
GET THE CHANCE TO DIE
FIGHTING TO SAVE
A WORLD'S MORALITY

(Is 'few' quite the right word here? ..... Rifleman
Thomas has the same epitaph as his younger
brother, Private A.S.Thomas, who died in 1918.)

Hem Farm Military Cemetery

Second Lieutenant
George Edward CATES, *VC*
2nd Battalion, The Rifle Brigade
Died 9 March 1917, aged 24

"I CAN DO ALL THINGS
THROUGH CHRIST
WHICH STRENGTHENETH ME"
PHIL. 4.13

(In order to protect his men, Second Lieutenant
Cates placed his foot on a burning grenade, which
exploded and killed him. A posthumous VC was
awarded.)

Second Lieutenant
Winter NICHOLSON
224th Field Company, Royal Engineers
Died 16 March 1917, aged 34

THE HEART OF HONOUR
THE TONGUE OF TRUTH

3391 Private
Abell Abraham SHIRES
40th Battalion, Australian Infantry
Died 30 August 1918, aged 29

THY DRESS
WAS LIKE THE LILIES
AND THY HEART
AS PURE AS THEY

(From Longfellow's poem A Gleam of
Sunshine.*)*

Héninel-Croisilles Road Cemetery

G/53233 Private
William Richard GARDINER
20th Battalion, Royal Fusiliers
Died 16 April 1917, aged 20

AND DUTY MARKED
EACH STEP HE TROD
AND LOVE TO MAN
AND LOVE TO GOD

(From Ye Fair Green Hills of Galilee, *a hymn*
by Eustace R. Conder)

Second Lieutenant
Arthur Richard HENRY
5th Battalion, attached 1st Battalion,
Middlesex Regiment
Died 23 April 1917, aged 33

HE DIED A HERO
ADMIRED BY HIS OFFICERS
ADORED BY HIS MEN

G/53254 Private
William Charles PAYNE
20th Battalion, Royal Fusiliers
Died 16 April 1917, aged 24

HE LIKE OUR SAVIOUR
DIED OF WOUNDS
THAT OTHERS MIGHT BE SAVED
MOTHER

Hersin Communal Cemetery Extension

31613 Sergeant
Francis Albert HAWES
Headquarters IV Corps Heavy Artillery,
Royal Garrison Artillery
Died 11 July 1916, aged 25

I HAVE FELT
WITH MY NATIVE LAND
I AM ONE WITH MY KIND

505225 Lance Corporal
Bernard RICHARDSON
13th (Kensington) Battalion, London Regiment
Died 22 October 1918, aged 21

SOMEBODY FELL
AS THE CHOSEN FALL
SOMEBODY'S ONE-AND-ONLY

KNOWN UNTO GOD

Highland Cemetery

Second Lieutenant
Charles Tolme BROWN
5th Battalion, Argyll & Sutherland Highlanders
Died 17 March 1917, aged 19

SWEET FLOW'RET
OF THE MARTYR BAND

506333 Lance Corporal
Arthur Savours Gould RICHARDS
Canadian Railway Troops
Died 4 April 1917, aged 24

WHAT SEEMS TO BE DEATH
IS BUT A HUMAN EXPERIENCE
GOD IS ETERNAL

Hooge Crater Cemetery

3755 Lance Corporal
Frank ABBOTT
25th Battalion, Australian Infantry
Died 31 October 1917, aged 21

ONE OF AUSTRALIA'S BEST
SLEEP DEAR FRANK
IN FAR OFF GRAVE

47873 Sapper
Frank AINDOW
89th Field Company, Royal Engineers
Died 28 June 1915, aged 18

THEY DIED THE NOBLEST DEATH
A MAN MAY DIE
FIGHTING FOR GOD
AND LIBERTY

33152 Gunner
Laurence BUTLER
4th Divisional Ammunition Column,
Australian Field Artillery
Died 12 October 1917, aged 28

ONE OF
AUSTRALIA'S NIGHTINGALES
LIES BURIED HERE

Second Lieutenant
George William FRANKLYN
'C' Company, 23rd Battalion, London Regiment
Died 7 June 1917, aged 32

ENGLAND HAD NEED OF HIM

Second Lieutenant
Alexander Howard Parker FYFE
8th Company, Australian Machine Gun Corps
Died 26 September 1917, aged 24

FOND MEMORY
IS THE ONLY FRIEND
THAT GRIEF CAN CALL ITS OWN

3707 Private
Horace HIGGS
10th Battalion, Australian Infantry
Died 7 October 1917, aged 33

HE HEARD HIS EMPIRE CALLING
AND HIS EAGER FOOTSTEPS CAME

18552 Private
John Henry HOPKINS
6th Battalion, Duke of Cornwall's Light Infantry
Died 23 August 1917, aged 20

A NOTABLE EXAMPLE
TO SUCH AS BE YOUNG
TO DIE WILLINGLY
AND COURAGEOUSLY R.I.P.

406740 Private
Albert George HUGHES
1st Battalion, Canadian Infantry
(Western Ontario Regiment)
Died 26 April 1916, aged 20

GOOD SON

2668 Private
Thomas HUGHES
32nd Battalion, Australian Infantry
Died 14 October 1917, aged 22

HE SLEEPS WITH THE DEAD
WHO IN BLOOD
SIGNED THE CHARTER
OF FREEDOM

Captain
John Llewelyn Thomas JONES
'D' Company, 3rd Battalion,
London Regiment (Royal Fusiliers)
Died 16 August 1917, aged 22

"OUR NEVER TO BE FORGOTTEN
CAPTAIN AND LEADER"
COMPANY MESSAGE

5587 Private
William Jacob JUSTIN
19th Battalion, Australian Infantry
Died 9 October 1917, aged 25

A DUTY NOBLY DONE
FRANCE WILL NOT FORGET

Lieutenant
Alfred Ernest George LEWIS
195th Battalion, Machine Gun Corps (Infantry)
Died 6 September 1917, aged 40

SUDDEN DEATH
SUDDEN GLORY

4568 Private
Clarence Hurtle McGUINNESS
32nd Battalion, Australian Infantry
Died 28 September 1917, aged 25

THEY LAID MY HERO
DOWN TO REST
IN THE FLAG
WITH A SOUTHERN CROSS

327235 Private
William John George Richard MAXTED
1st Battalion, Cambridgeshire Regiment
Died 15 November 1917, aged 21

THE CHERISHED FLOWERS
OF FRANCE MAY FALL
BUT HONOUR
WILL OUTLIVE THEM ALL

22891 Private
Walter McClean MURRAY
9th Battalion, Royal Irish Fusiliers
Died 30 September 1918, aged 21

RELIGION CHURCH OF IRELAND
AN IRISHMAN LOYAL TO DEATH
TO KING AND COUNTRY

16417 Private
Abraham NATHAN
8th Battalion, Devonshire Regiment
Died 26 October 1917, aged 24

A JEW WHO GAVE HIS LIFE
FOR THE FREEDOM OF THE WORLD

---

540 Private
Hereward William RAY
22nd Battalion, Australian Infantry
Died 18 September 1917, aged 24

MY FIRST PRIDE
MY FIRST JOY
MY BRAVE SOLDIER BOY

G/15777 Corporal
Herbert Henry RENSHAW, *MM*
'B' Company, 11th Battalion,
Royal Sussex Regiment
Died 25 September 1917, aged 38

HE DIED FOR US
IN OUR HEARTS
AND THE VALHALLA OF HEROES

404445 Private
John Cameron ROBERTSON
14th Battalion, Canadian Infantry
(Quebec Regiment)
Died 3 June 1916, aged 29

OUR DEAD
ARE NEVER DEAD TO US
UNTIL WE HAVE FORGOTTEN
THEM

265642 Private
Walter Norbury ROWBOTHAM
1st/6th Battalion, Cheshire Regiment
Died 20 November 1917, aged 31

THESE POURED OUT
THE RED SWEET WINE OF YOUTH
GAVE UP THE YEARS TO BE

(An extract from Rupert Brooke's poem The
Dead.*)*

Second Lieutenant
Anthony Darley RUSSEL RENDLE
9th Battalion, Devonshire Regiment
Died 10 October 1917, aged 21

HE FOUGHT AS ONE
WHO FAIN WOULD DIE
AND DYING CONQUER DEATH

(Like so many young subalterns, Second Lieutenant
Russel Rendle had been in the Officers' Training
Corps at his public school – in his case, Blundell's
– in the years leading up to the war. He went on to
serve in the New Zealand Expeditionary Force
[2nd Canterbury Regiment] at Gallipoli before
reaching France.)

229758 Private
Harry James STAMMERS
1st Battalion, London Regiment (Royal Fusiliers),
attached 13th Battalion, Royal Fusiliers
Died 8 March 1918, aged 29

MINE FOR A WHILE,
NOW GOD'S
TO SERVE
IN THE HEAVENLY ARMY
ALICE

1937 Gunner
John Willie WOLSTENHULME
19th Battalion, Machine Gun Corps (Motors)
Died 8 October 1917, aged 25

THE SEARCH HAS ENDED
I KNEW NOT WHERE YOU LAY
REST IN PEACE DEAR FATHER
EDITH 8TH OCTOBER 1993

(After Gunner Wolstenhulme's daughter had
contacted the Commonwealth War Graves
Commission to draw attention to factual errors on
the original headstone, a new one was erected
bearing the correct details. In view of this, and the
fact that there had been no previous contact with the
family, Edith was allowed to choose a personal
inscription.)

Hop Store Cemetery

22792 Gunner
John GALLAGHER
'D' Battery, 78th Brigade, Royal Field Artillery
Died 16 November 1915, aged 22

THIS LITTLE SPOT
I'D LIKE TO SEE.
IT WAS DEARLY BOUGHT,
BY A NEAR FRIEND TO ME

Hospital Farm British Cemetery

751347 Sergeant
George BELL
223rd Brigade, Royal Field Artillery
Died 22 October 1917, aged 28

THE DAYS ARE DARK
FRIENDS ARE FEW
DEAR SON
HOW WE THINK OF YOU

620337 Corporal
Arthur Griffiths MOOTZ
'C' Battery, 223rd Brigade, Royal Field Artillery
Died 1 November 1917, aged 31

ONE OF THAT
BRAVE AND GLORIOUS BAND
WHO GAVE HIS ALL
FOR THE MOTHERLAND

Houchin British Cemetery

24652 Lance Corporal
Thomas DUNBEBIN
1st/4th Battalion,
The King's Own (Royal Lancaster Regiment)
Died 26 April 1918, aged 28

HE DIED FOR ALL
THAT THEY WHO LIVE
SHOULD NOT LIVE
UNTO THEMSELVES

(An abbreviated version of II Corinthians,
Chapter 6, Verse 15.)

200123 Sergeant
Arthur HARLING, *MM*
2nd/5th Battalion, Lancashire Fusiliers
Died 21 September 1918, aged 23

THE SETTING IS BROKEN
BUT THE GEM IS SAFE

57764 Private
Albert Edward MANLEY
'D' Company, 2nd/5th Battalion,
Lancashire Fusiliers
Died 6 September 1918, aged 18

ENOUGH!
THEY MURMUR O'ER MY GRAVE
HE LIKE A SOLDIER FELL

19386 Private
Henry SAMPLES
1st Battalion, Northamptonshire Regiment
Died 13 June 1918, aged 41

FOUR YEARS HAVE PASSED
OUR HEARTS ARE SORE
BUT STILL WE MISS HIM
MORE AND MORE

Hyde Park Corner (Royal Berks) Cemetery

Lieutenant
Ronald William POULTON PALMER
1st/4th Battalion, Royal Berkshire Regiment
Died 4 May 1915, aged 25

"HIS WAS THE JOY
THAT MADE PEOPLE SMILE
WHEN THEY MET HIM"
LT. S.L. REISS

(This officer, better known as Ronnie Poulton, was the most glamorous rugby union star of his time. He scored a famous try against South Africa, four in one game against France, and captained England. He was killed by a sniper's bullet. Lieutenant Reiss, a fellow-officer in the Royal Berkshire Regiment, met his own death five months later and has the bizarre and poignant distinction of having his name inscribed on this headstone, but not on one of his own – he is commemorated on the Loos Memorial to the Missing.)

Jonchery-sur-Vesle British Cemetery

Captain
John Hamon MASSEY, *MC*
45th Brigade, Royal Field Artillery
Died 27 May 1918, aged 24

GREAT WAS HIS SOUL
IN ITS STAY
GREATER STILL
IN ITS GOING AWAY

(The New Zealand-born Captain Massey was a Cambridge graduate and a holder of the Croix de Guerre.)

Kandahar Farm Cemetery

B/203715 Rifleman
Ernest Albert PHIPPS
7th Battalion, Rifle Brigade
Died 11 September 1917, aged 34

NOT BORN FOR A SOLDIER
YET WHAT HE DID
HE DID WELL
R.I.P.

Second Lieutenant
Ronald Howorth STOTT
3rd Battalion, Loyal North Lancashire Regiment
Died 20 September 1917, age 21

A BRAVE, BRIGHT SPIRIT
HIS LAST WORDS WERE
"CARRY ON"

118710 Pioneer
Ephraim TAYLOR
7th (Labour) Battalion, Royal Engineers
Died 21 July 1917, aged 61

HE IS NOT DEAD
BUT OVER WAR'S LOUD SWELL
HE HEARD HIS CAPTAIN'S CALL
AND ALL IS WELL

(In a long military career, this veteran – still
soldiering in his seventh decade – had in his time
been awarded the Egyptian Medal, the Khedive's
Star, and King and Queen South African Medals.)

19153 Driver
George Nixon WILLIAMSON
110th Howitzer Battery, 10th Brigade,
Australian Field Artillery
Died 14 June 1917, aged 35

THE FLAMES
OF SACRIFICE ILLUME
AS WELL AS CONSUME

Kemmel Château Military Cemetery

678 Sergeant
Thomas William DOWSETT
1st Battalion, Honourable Artillery Company
Died 30 January 1915, aged 22

LIVE YOU FOR HONOUR
WE FOR HONOUR DIED

6591 Private
William George DRAY
15th Battalion, Australian Infantry
Died 15 August 1917, aged 27

HOLIER DEATH
CAN NO MAN SUFFER
DYING FOR THE RIGHT

73446 Private
Count Ove Krag Juel Vind FRIJS
28th Battalion, Canadian Infantry
(Saskatchewan Regiment),
Died 15 November 1915, aged 25

NU LUKKER SIG MIT ØJE
GUD FADER I DET HØJE
VARETÆGT MIG TAG

(Translation from the Danish: 'Now my eye is
closing, God on high take care of me'. When this
young Copenhagen-born aristocrat enlisted, he was
working as a bank clerk in Canada. Before leaving
his native land he had served in the Danish Royal
Life Guards.)

6310 Private
Thomas Wilkinson GAMBLE
1st Battalion, Duke of Cornwall's Light Infantry
Died 28 March 1915, aged 30

A HERO BRAVE
WHO NOBLY GAVE
HIS LIFE FOR EMPIRE'S GLORY

Second Lieutenant
George Frederick Whitby HARRISON
3rd Reserve Regiment of Cavalry,
attached 6th (Wiltshire Yeomanry) Battalion,
Wiltshire Regiment
Died 30 September 1917, aged 23

STRAIGHT OF LIMB
TRUE OF EYE
STEADY AND AGLOW

(These words are from one of the less familiar verses
of Laurence Binyon's For the Fallen.*)*

Captain
Cuthbert Hayward KIRKUS
283rd Siege Battery, Royal Garrison Artillery
Died 31 July 1917, aged 37

THEIR GLORY SHALL NOT
BE BLOTTED OUT
THEY URGE THE WORLD'S BEST
THOUGHT TO SOMETHING HIGHER

Knightsbridge Cemetery

1115 Private
Robert John WILLIAMS
1st Battalion, Royal Newfoundland Regiment
Died 1 July 1916, aged 21

OH FRANCE BE KIND
AND KEEP GREEN FOR ME
MY SOLDIER'S GRAVE
R.I.P MOTHER

La Belle Alliance Cemetery

29780 Private
Henry George HAYWOOD
7th Battalion, South Staffordshire Regiment
Died 27 July 1917, aged 19

HIS LIFE WAS TAKEN AWAY
FIGHTING FOR HIS MOTHER
FATHER, SISTERS, BROTHER AND
FOR HIS COUNTRY. GOD BLESS HIM

La Brique Military Cemetery No 2

S/107 Corporal
Alfred George DRAKE, *VC*
8th Battalion, The Rifle Brigade
Died 23 November 1915, aged 21

THERE IS A LINK
DEATH CANNOT SEVER
LOVE & REMEMBRANCE
LIVE FOR EVER

(Corporal Drake's VC was awarded posthumously. While facing heavy rifle and machine-gun fire close to enemy lines – not in France, as the citation states, but in the Ypres Salient – he stopped to bandage the wounds of an officer. A rescue party later found the officer unconscious but alive, with Corporal Drake beside him, dead and riddled with bullets. Although his headstone says 22, he was actually 17 days short of that age.)

G/12022 Private
Abel FLITNEY
13th Battalion, Royal Sussex Regiment
Died 2 August 1917, aged 39

FLING OPEN WIDE
THE GOLDEN GATES
AND LET THE VICTORS IN

(From Ten Thousand Times Ten Thousand,
a hymn by Henry Alford.)

80630 Gunner
Eric Brandon FOTHERBY
'C' Battery, 91st Brigade, Royal Field Artillery
Died 19 April 1915, aged 18

MY MOTHER

3/8789 Private
Arthur SMITH
1st Battalion,
West Yorkshire Regiment (Prince of Wales's Own)
Died 28 June 1915, aged 23

THE LOSS IS OURS
ITS MEASURE
WHO SHALL DARE
PRESUME OF GAUGE?

Lieutenant
Frederick Alfred TRENCHARD
86th Battery, Royal Field Artillery
Died 24 May 1915, aged 27

FOR ENGLAND'S NEEDS
A SOLDIER'S DEATH
GOD GIVETH HIM
THE VICTOR'S WREATH

La Chapelette British & Indian Cemetery

242439 Private
Arthur Harold EDLIN
2nd/6th Battalion, South Staffordshire Regiment
Died 14 May 1917, aged 19

THEY HAVE BROUGHT
GLORY AND HONOUR
TO THE NATION

375165 Private
Ernest KENYON
1st/10th Battalion, Manchester Regiment
Died 23 May 1917, aged 24

HE GAVE HIS LIFE
A RANSOM FOR MANY

A SOLDIER
OF THE GREAT WAR

La Chapelle-d'Armentières Communal Cemetery

10105 Private
William Richard DONOHUE
1st Battalion, Royal Fusiliers
Died 29 January 1915, aged 28

HERE LIES A PORTSMOUTH MAN
WHO DIED IN FREEDOM'S CAUSE
R.I.P.

(The family settled on the south coast, but Private
Donohue had actually been born in Reading.)

La Chaudière Military Cemetery

208026 Corporal
John James BURKE
Royal Canadian Regiment
Died 9 April 1917, aged 29

A MAN

141087 Private
James Winning CHAPMAN
8th Company, Canadian Machine Gun Corps
Died 9 April 1917, aged 26

ALAS! WHAT LINKS
OF LOVE THAT MORN
HAS WAR'S RUDE HAND
ASUNDER TORN

234106 Private
Arthur GAMBLE
44th Battalion, Canadian Infantry
(New Brunswick Regiment)
Died 3 June 1917, aged 31

HIS DEATH
IS A WOUND UNTIL DEATH
TO THOSE WHO LOVED HIM

La Clytte Military Cemetery

97325 Acting Bombardier
John FAZACKERLEY
180th Siege Battery, Royal Garrison Artillery
Died 27 May 1917, aged 36

SALUTE THE SACRED DEAD
WHO WENT AND WHO RETURN
NOT

L/22957 Gunner
Charley Wilfred FUGGLE
'D' Battery, 242nd Brigade, Royal Field Artillery
Died 14 March 1918, aged 23

HE DIED AND NEVER KNEW
ENGLAND HE DIED FOR YOU

4424 Private
Charles GOODWIN
2nd Battalion, Royal Scots
Died 10 May 1916, aged 18

FAITHFUL UNTIL DEATH
WHEN THE ROLL
IS CALLED UP YONDER
HE'LL BE THERE

44756 Bombardier
Douglas HEPWORTH
'A' Battery, 103rd Brigade, Royal Field Artillery
Died 21 October 1917, aged 24

MAY THE HEAVENLY WINDS
BLOW SOFTLY O'ER
THIS SWEET AND HALLOWED SPOT

5/14881 Private
Albert HILLIER
5th Battalion, South Wales Borderers
Died 24 August 1916, aged 24

SOMEWHERE IN FRANCE
AMONG THE BRAVE
LIES OUR DEAR BOY
IN A HERO'S GRAVE

(Actually somewhere in Belgium, not France.)

Captain
Matthew Struan ROBERTSON
1st Battalion, Gordon Highlanders
Died 2 March 1916, aged 23

WE MISS YOU SONNY BOY

S/6825 Private
John Charles Park WILLOX
1st Battalion, Gordon Highlanders
Died 19 December 1915, aged 22

YOUTH AND WORTH
AND HOPE ARE GONE
SORROW SITS IN TEARS ALONE

La Kreule Military Cemetery

Lieutenant
Joseph Jackson BROWN
'C' Company, 2nd Battalion, Royal Scots Fusiliers
Died 5 August 1918, aged 24

HE GAVE HIS SWEET YOUNG LIFE
WHAT FOR?

12327 Private
James Thomas BROWN
4th Regiment, South African Infantry
Died 18 August 1918, aged 38

THO' FAR IN A LONELY LAND
EVER GREEN IN MY MEMORY
LIES MY DEAR HUSBAND

200396 Corporal
William Arthur FEILING
5th Battalion, Cameron Highlanders
Died 19 August 1918, aged 33

STEEL TRUE
AND BLADE STRAIGHT
THE GREAT ARTIFICER
MADE MY MATE

(From a Robert Louis Stevenson poem, My Wife.
Corporal Feiling's mate was his widow, Elsie, of
Muswell Hill, north London.)

Second Lieutenant
Douglas Lionel FIGGURES, *MM*
'C' Battery, 46th Brigade, Royal Field Artillery
Died 15 October 1918, aged 29

1914-1918
SPLENDID

17172 Private
William Edward GIBBONS
4th Regiment, South African Infantry
Died 3 June 1918, aged 24

HE SLEEPS
BESIDES HIS COMRADES
IN A HALLOWED GRAVE
UNKNOWN
FATHER

3669 Lance Corporal
Harold GILKES
2nd Battalion, Australian Infantry
Died 24 June 1918, aged 22

AN ONLY SON
KILLED IN ACTION
ON HIS WAY TO
HIS LEAVE AND WEDDING

Captain
William Douglas KENYON
1st/7th Battalion, Cheshire Regiment
Died 16 September 1918, aged 27

HE WAS A MAN
TAKE HIM FOR ALL IN ALL
I SHALL NOT LOOK
UPON HIS LIKE AGAIN

(From Shakespeare's Hamlet, *Act I, Scene 2.)*

Second Lieutenant
Douglas Cecil MACKIE, *MC*
'A' Company, 1st Regiment,
South African Infantry
Died 19 July 1918, aged 28

FOR KIN, HOME AND LOVE
SEERS OF COSMOS MOURN NOT
THE SCHEME OF THINGS

7551 Private
Percy James Arnold SMITH
10th Battalion, Australian Infantry
Died 22 July 1918, aged 21

SLEEP ON
DEAR SOLDIER PERCY
TILL THE BUGLE SOUNDS AGAIN

Lapugnoy Military Cemetery

265539 Private
Harold James BARSTED
1st Battalion, Somerset Light Infantry
Died 4 June 1918, aged 25

ONLY SON
IVY YIELDS TO NO WEATHER
NOR OUR LOVE
TO THE CATACLYSM OF DEATH

19049 Private
William BENNETT
1st Battalion, Somerset Light Infantry
Died 16 April 1918, aged 20

SOMEONE'S DARLING
LIES SLUMBERING HERE

Deal/763(S) Sapper
James BENNETTON
Royal Marine Engineers, Royal Naval Division
Died 28 June 1916, aged 20

A MOTHER'S IDOL
A FATHER'S PRIDE
A COUNTRY'S HERO
SO HE DIED

328 Sapper
Gordon Harper BOWIE
5th Battalion, Canadian Railway Troops
Died 31 August 1918, aged 22

BORN AT OTTAWA, ONTARIO
THE ROSE STILL GROWS
BEYOND THE WALL

S/15938 Private
John GRAHAM
'B' Company, 6th Battalion,
Cameron Highlanders
Died 30 September 1915, aged 21

A MOTHER'S TRIBUTE
THE GLORIOUS SACRIFICE
HE MADE
GROWN NOBLER WITH THE YEARS

4237 Private
Leslie John HODGES
15th Battalion, London Regiment
(Prince of Wales's Own Civil Service Rifles)
Died 27 July 1916, aged 22

HE GAVE UP THE YEARS TO BE
OF WORK AND JOY

358315 Private
Robert Henry KIDDLE
'Y' Company, 1st/10th Battalion,
The King's (Liverpool Regiment)
Died 15 March 1918, aged 20

"... DEAD ERE HIS PRIME
YOUNG LYCIDAS
AND HATH NOT LEFT HIS PEER"

(From Milton's Lycidas.*)*

2649 Private
Ernest Victor Albert RUMBLE
'B' Company, 20th Battalion, London Regiment
Died 28 January 1916, aged 18

WILL GLORY O' ENGLAND
EVER DIE
SO LONG
AS WE'VE LADS LIKE HIM?

342015 Gunner
Lambert TAYLOR
1st Brigade, Canadian Field Artillery
Died 26 August 1917, aged 34

LOVED ONES HE LEFT
AND BABE UNBORN
SLEEP ON
TILL THE RESURRECTION MORN

(Gunner Taylor was the only son of Yorkshire parents and left a widow in the United States of America.)

Lieutenant
Frank Ewart TIPLADY
5th Battalion, Middlesex Regiment,
attached 'B' Company, 7th Battalion,
London Regiment
Died 27 September 1915, aged 22

"SATISFIED"

94167 Bombardier
Harold William Tate WEBBER
'A' Battery, 65th Brigade, Royal Field Artillery
Died 14 October 1915, aged 21

HE WAS SO BRIGHT
AND EVEN ON HIS DYING DAY
HE CHEERED HIS COMRADES

Larch Wood (Railway Cutting) Cemetery

9355 Private
Robert Gordon ALDERMAN
23rd Field Ambulance,
Royal Army Medical Corps
Died 24 October 1917, aged 34

HE IS DEAD
OUR BEAUTIFUL BOB
HE WAS THE LIFE
AND LIGHT OF OUR HOME

2566 Sergeant
Harley James BARON
3rd Battalion, Australian Infantry
Died 2 September 1916, aged 22

A MOST DEVOTED ONLY SON
WHO FULLY JUSTIFIED
HIS MANHOOD

Tombes de Guerre du Commonwealth
Commonwealth War Graves

12840 Lance Corporal
Henry CHILTON
'B' Company, 5th Battalion, Canadian Infantry
(Saskatchewan Regiment)
Died 3 June 1916, aged 34

ENLISTED AUG. 12. 1914
MOOSOMIN. SASK. CAN.

8109 Private
Matthew Clough SWINDLE
23rd Field Ambulance,
Royal Army Medical Corps
Died 8 October 1917, aged 21

I GAVE MY LIFE FOR THEE
WHAT HAST THOU DONE FOR ME?

La Targette British Cemetery

Lieutenant Colonel
Russel Hubert BRITTON, *DSO*
5th Brigade, Canadian Field Artillery
Died 2 May 1917, aged 36

AS GOLD IN THE FURNACE
HATH HE TRIED THEM
AND RECEIVED THEM
AS A BURNT OFFERING

(From Wisdom *[a book of* Apocrypha*],*
Chapter 3, Verse 6.)

---

367 Gunner
Norman BURGESS
2nd Divisional Ammunition Column,
Canadian Field Artillery
Died 22 September 1917, aged 34

TO-DAY AND YESTERDAY
BUT LESS THAN TOMORROW

Major
Samuel Henry DOAKE, *DSO*
52nd Army Brigade, Royal Field Artillery
Died 30 March 1918, aged 25

STRONG, BRAVE, GENTLE,
BELOVED
IN FRANCE FROM AUGUST 1914
FOUGHT IN TWENTY BATTLES

(Major Doake served continuously at the Front for
three-and-a-half years.)

14344 Private
William Josiah EADES
16th Battalion,
West Yorkshire Regiment (Prince of Wales's Own)
Died 19 August 1917, aged 19

WE ARE PROUD OF THE BRAVE
WHEN BOY STANDS AS MAN

203112 Private
John HUTTON
1st Battalion, Worcestershire Regiment
Died 27 August 1918, aged 37

A DAY'S MARCH NEARER HOME

94511 Lance Bombardier
Robert Frederick Thomas MORRISON
52nd Brigade, Royal Field Artillery
Died 22 April 1918, aged 30

SORROW IS HUSHED INTO PEACE
IN OUR HEARTS
LIKE THE EVENING
AMONG THE SILENT TREES

89688 Private
Jabez Harry MOWLE
150th Company, Labour Corps
Died 23 May 1917, aged 30

HE WAS MOTHER'S COMFORT

439909 Private
William Samuel PECK
52nd Battalion, Canadian Infantry
(Manitoba Regiment)
Died 31 May 1917, aged 38

"THESE ARE MY JEWELS"
RUSKIN

424309 Private
Mostyn Scott SANDS
28th Battalion, Canadian Infantry
(Saskatchewan Regiment)
Died 8 May 1917, aged 21

I RAISED MY BOY
TO BE A SOLDIER
MOTHER

Laventie Military Cemetery

Second Lieutenant
Charles CECIL
2nd/4th Battalion, Royal Berkshire Regiment
Died 16 July 1916, aged 44

THIS IS THE VICTORY
THAT OVERCOMETH THE WORLD
EVEN OUR FAITH

Le Cateau Military Cemetery

240458 Rifleman
Harry Simpson ASHCROFT
'D' Company, 1st/5th Battalion,
South Lancashire Regiment
Died 1 December 1917, aged 27

THROUGH TRAVAIL
AND SACRIFICE
TO ETERNAL JOY AND PEACE

114624 Private
Frederick George BARRINGER
235th Company, Machine Gun Corps (Infantry)
Died 30 December 1917, aged 19

IN THE BEST OF HEALTH
HE LEFT US
TO ANSWER HIS COUNTRY'S CALL

Captain
Charles Hunter BROWNING
124th Battery, 28th Brigade,
Royal Field Artillery
Died 26 August 1914, aged 36

WE WILL GO FORWARD
AT WHATEVER COST
QUIETLY, UNTIRINGLY
UNALARMED

(Captain Browning survived the Boer War but lost
his life only three weeks after the declaration of war
on Germany.)

Le Grand Beaumart British Cemetery

45321 Private
Alfred BROMLEY
18th Battalion, Durham Light Infantry
Died 12 April 1918, aged 19

SLEEP ON THOU MIGHTY DEAD
A GLORIOUS TOMB
THEY FOUND THEE

Le Grand Hazard Military Cemetery

72897 Sergeant
Albert Henry ANDREWS
'A' Battery, 15th Brigade, Royal Field Artillery
Died 30 June 1918, aged 24

THE DYING SOLDIER
DIES UPON A KISS
THE VERY KISS OF CHRIST

133606 Private
Stephen Giuseppi CAMOCCIO
'D' Company, 29th Battalion,
Machine Gun Corps
Died 14 April 1918, aged 19

LORD FORGIVE THEM
FOR THEY KNOW NOT
WHAT THEY DO

(Adapted from Luke, *Chapter 23, Verse 34.)*

242723 Private
James William HALL
13th Battalion, York & Lancaster Regiment
Died 20 July 1918, aged 39

NATIVE OF SOUTH SHIELDS
HIS AIM "BE STRONG"
THE BEST IS YET TO COME

189107 Driver
Herbert Ralph HAMMOND
'D' Battery, 64th Brigade, Royal Field Artillery
Died 12 April 1918, aged 24

A MOTHER'S BABY
IS SLEEPING HERE
MIDGE FROM WOOLWICH
A VOLUNTEER

40515 Private
John Wilson HELON
12th Battalion, Royal Scots Fusiliers
Died 10 July 1918, aged 22

AMONG THE OTHER
BRITISH HEROES
IN THAT FAR OFF
BETTER LAND

30168 Private
Cyril Norman KELLY
10th Battalion, East Yorkshire Regiment
Died 2 August 1918, aged 20

MANY ARE THE ROADS
BY WHICH GOD CARRIES
HIS OWN TO HEAVEN

Le Peuplier Military Cemetery

3952A Private
James Arthur MEECH
1st Battalion, Australian Pioneers
Died 29 July 1918, aged 29

THE MEMORY OF THE BRAVE
WILL NEVER DIE
BESS AND BABY

Les Baraques Military Cemetery

200397 Private
John ELLIOTT
'B' Company, 1st/4th Battalion,
Royal Scots Fusiliers
Died 17 February 1919, aged 26

FOR BRITAIN'S HONOUR & CROWN
HE FOUGHT AND FELL
TO GAIN A RADIANT CROWN
HIMSEL'

41663 Private
James LALLY
732nd Company, Labour Corps
Died 7 June 1919, age 26

WHAT'S BRAVE
WHAT'S NOBLE
LET'S DO IT
REST IN PEACE

(From Shakespeare's Antony & Cleopatra, *Act
4, Scene 15.)*

Second Lieutenant
Charles Samuel MARSHALL
1st Garrison Battalion, Suffolk Regiment
Died 2 April 1918, age 33

HE HAS MOVED A LITTLE NEARER
TO THE MASTER OF ALL MUSIC

510689 Private
Frederick MAYNARD
1st Divisional Unit of Supply,
Canadian Army Service Corps
Died 17 December 1917, aged 28

THAT IN CALAIS' FATAL WALLS
GOD'S FINGER TOUCHED HIM
AND HE SLEPT

27502 Private
James MURRAY
9th Battalion, Royal Inniskilling Fusiliers
Died 11 November 1918, aged 36

THEY LOVED NOT THEIR LIVES

(Private Murray died of wounds on the final day of hostilities.)

295017 Corporal
Arthur PRICE, *MM*
'A' Company, 12th Battalion,
Royal Scots Fusiliers
Died 3 November 1918, aged 30

WE LINGER TO CARESS HIM
WHEN BREATHING EVENING
PRAYER

M2/082708 Lance Corporal
William Haddock ROBINSON
364th Mechanical Transport Company,
Royal Army Service Corps
Died 12 August 1918, aged 39

DUTY ACCOMPLISHED
HONOUR DEFENDED

Second Lieutenant
Malcolm Winser WAKEMAN
53rd Squadron, Royal Air Force
Died 18 October 1918, aged 19

REMEMBER THE LOVE OF THEM
WHO CAME NOT HOME
FROM THE WAR

Le Vertannoy British Cemetery

39358 Private
Thomas Patrick BOURKE
'D' Company, 1st Battalion, Hampshire Regiment
Died 22 May 1918, aged 24

WE MISS YOU, GOD KNOWS
AND MOURN YOU UNSEEN
AND DWELL ON THE MEMORIES
OF DAYS THAT HAVE BEEN

Lijssenthoek Military Cemetery

200917 Regimental Sergeant Major
Albert John ABRAHAMS, *MSM*
2nd/7th Battalion, Worcestershire Regiment
Died 10 September 1917, aged 28

HE ALWAYS MADE HOME HAPPY
WHAT A NOBLE RECORD LEFT

Lieutenant
John Percy Fitzherbert ADAMS
4th Battalion, Durham Light Infantry
attached 20th Squadron, Royal Flying Corps
Died 14 October 1917, aged 26

YE REJOICE
WITH JOY UNSPEAKABLE
FULL OF GLORY

(From I Peter, Chapter 1, Verse 8. A son of parents who lived in Exmouth, Devon, Lieutenant Adams was curate of St John's, Newfoundland.)

13252 Private
James Whitson Ainslie AGNEW
12th Field Ambulance,
Australian Army Medical Corps
Died 29 September 1917, aged 24

WE ARE MORE THAN CONQUERORS
THROUGH HIM THAT LOVED US

(From Romans, Chapter 8, Verse 37.)

10339 Private
Frederick ARBLASTER
9th Battalion, South Staffordshire Regiment
Died 25 September 1917, aged 33

ONLY A PRIVATE SOLDIER
ONE OF THE RANK & FILE
GIVING HIS LIFE FOR ENGLAND
THE HONOUR OF OUR RACE

KNOWN UNTO GOD

M2/100291 Sergeant
Thomas ARMSTRONG, *DCM*
Mechanical Transport Unit,
Royal Army Service Corps,
attached 85th Siege Battery,
Royal Garrison Artillery
Died 15 August 1918, aged 34

WE ARE PROUD OF YOU

4659 Sergeant
Stephen ATKINSON
26th Battalion, Australian Infantry
Died 7 October 1917, aged 30

A HERO
M.

('M' was the widowed Myrtle Atkinson in far-off
Brisbane.)

291468 Private
Clifford Waterworth BASKERVILLE
1st Canadian Mounted Rifles
(Saskatchewan Regiment)
Died 14 November 1917, aged 27

WORDS FAIL TO ADD ANYTHING
TO THE HONOR OF
OUR GLORIOUS DEAD

Major
Charles Elles Stuart BEATSON, *MC*
105th Battery, 22nd Brigade,
Royal Field Artillery
Died 3 October 1917, aged 26

…..
THROUGH THE DOOR
OF SACRIFICE AND VICTORY
THEY HAVE PASSED ON

493379 Private
George BELCHER
13th (Kensington) Battalion, London Regiment,
attached 8th Battalion, Royal Irish Rifles
Died 5 August 1917, aged 23

MUSIC WHEN SOFT VOICES DIE
VIBRATES IN THE MEMORY

S/17522 Lance Corporal
Charles Frederick BELL
12th Battalion, Rifle Brigade
Died 2 February 1918, aged 24

DADDY DEAR
I DID NOT SEE YOU
BUT MUMMY
HAS TAUGHT ME TO LOVE YOU

29395 Private
William BOGAN
8th Battalion, Royal Inniskilling Fusiliers
Died 29 August 1917, aged 20

YOUR BODY MAY MINGLE IN FOREIGN CLAY
BUT IN OUR THOUGHTS EVER YOU STAY

M2/079924 Private
Thomas George BRICKNELL
Mechanical Transport,
attached 2nd Motor Ambulance Convoy,
Royal Army Service Corps
Died 16 September 1918, aged 24

BRAVELY HE FOUGHT AND NOBLY HE FELL
DYING A HERO AMID SHOT AND SHELL

5838 Private
George Allan BUCHANAN
22nd Battalion, Australian Infantry
Died 6 October 1917, aged 34

HE SLEEPS BESIDE
THE NOBLE SLAIN
OUR GEORGIE
FAITHFUL UNTO DEATH

205774 Sergeant
Henry Lewis BURT
18th Company, 'F' Battalion, Tank Corps
Died 24 August 1917, aged 20

LADDIE IN KHAKI
WE ARE THINKING OF YOU
DAD, MUM, AND LITTLE NORA

12024 Private
George CLAYTON
7th Battalion,
King's Own Yorkshire Light Infantry
Died 16 March 1916, aged 28

SOME CORNER
OF A FOREIGN FIELD
THAT IS FOR EVER ENGLAND

(An unsurprisingly popular choice of epitaph from
Rupert Brooke's poem The Soldier.)

Captain
Ross Penner COTTON
19th Battalion, Canadian Infantry
(Central Ontario Regiment),
attached
3rd Canadian Infantry Brigade Headquarters
Died 13 June 1916, aged 23

IN THE BEAUTY & THE STRENGTH
OF EARLY MANHOOD

489199 Private
Louis d'HORSET
43rd Battalion, Canadian Infantry
(Manitoba Regiment)
Died 21 May 1916, aged 46

IL LAISSE POUR PLEURER
SON EPOUSE ET SON FILS

(This soldier had been born France and emigrated
to Canada. The epitaph from his widow in French-
speaking Montreal translates as: 'He left to weep
his wife and his son'.)

Lieutenant
John Cragg DUNN
3rd Battalion, Dorsetshire Regiment
attached 59th Trench Mortar Battery
Died 25 March 1916, aged 26

SOON
SOON TO FAITHFUL WARRIORS
COMES THEIR REST
ALLELUIA

(From William Walsham How's hymn, For All
The Saints.)

G/12821 Lance Corporal
William Winter EDWARDS
1st Battalion, The Buffs (East Kent Regiment)
Died 13 April 1918, aged 20

IN THE GLORY AND JOY
OF HIS YOUTH
FOR HIS COUNTRY
HE GAVE HIS ALL

RMA/1611(S) Gunner
Percy ELLIS
Howitzer Brigade, Royal Marine Artillery
Died 10 July 1918, aged 25

ONLY ONE OF THOUSANDS
BUT ALL THE WORLD TO US

5512 Private
Edwin Augustus ESDAILE
4th Field Ambulance,
Australian Army Medical Corps
Died 21 October 1917, aged 25

ONLY A STRETCHER BEARER

(This is a dignified understatement by Private
Esdaile's parents, who would have known full well
that there was no 'only' about the duties of
battlefield stretcher-bearers, which often involved
bringing in the wounded from exposed positions
when the bullets and shells were flying.)

476603 Driver
Leland Wingate FERNALD
5th Brigade, Canadian Field Artillery
Died 8 May 1916, aged 28

A VOLUNTEER FROM THE U.S.A.
TO AVENGE
THE LUSITANIA MURDER

(The loss of 1,198 lives when the liner Lusitania
was torpedoed by a German U-boat included those
of 124 US citizens, whereupon thousands of young
Americans crossed into Canada to join up. The
powerful effect on public and political opinion in
America caused by the incident contributed
significantly to her eventual entry into the war.)

187 Private
Arthur George William FOWLER
40th Battalion, Australian Infantry
Died 6 October 1917, aged 24

O FOR A TOUCH
OF A VANISHED HAND
& THE SOUND OF
A VOICE SO STILL

(From Tennyson's Break, Break, Break, *except*
that in the last line 'so' has been substituted for
'that is' – presumably to keep the inscription within
the stipulated limit of 66 characters and spaces.)

457059 Corporal
Isaac Philip GARLICK
'B' Company, 60th Battalion, Canadian Infantry
Died 29 May 1916, aged 39

GOD BLESS THEE
WHERE-EVER
IN HIS GREAT UNIVERSE
THOU ART TO-DAY

(Early in his 12 years' service as an able seaman in
the Royal Navy, Corporal Garlick had served in
the Ashanti and Benin Expeditions of 1896-
1897.)

41862 Private
William Alfred GODFREY
'C' Company, 16th Battalion,
Manchester Regiment
Died 26 November 1917, aged 29

THY SACRIFICE DOTH RING
THY MEMORY SHALL CLING
REST IN PEACE

2167 Private
Albert GOODACRE
1st Battalion, Australian Infantry
Died 6 October 1917, aged 20

HE DIED
THE HELPLESS TO DEFEND
AN AUSTRALIAN SOLDIER'S
NOBLE END

35155 Private
Thomas Sutton HAMBLY
9th Battalion, Loyal North Lancashire Regiment
Died 14 August 1917, aged 35

HIS LIFE
WITH ALL ITS MANLINESS
WILL NEVER PASS AWAY
SORROWING WIFE & CHILDREN

723476 Private
Francis Barnard HARPER
24th Battalion, London Regiment
Died 4 March 1917, aged 20

HIS LAST MESSAGE
FROM THE TRENCHES
"I HAVE ABSOLUTE SECURITY
IN GOD"

Second Lieutenant
William HAY
12th Battalion, The Cameronians (Scottish Rifles),
attached Royal Scots Fusiliers
Died 1 April 1916, aged 20

HIS LAST MESSAGE
"I AM ALL RIGHT
KEEP CHEERY AND BRIGHT"

3/6846 Private
Charles Henry HENMAN
1st Battalion, Devonshire Regiment
Died 9 August 1916, aged 19

FOR HIS VOICE WE LISTEN AND YEARN
BUT OUR BOY WILL NEVER RETURN

G/1659 Lance Corporal
George HERBERT
8th Battalion,
The Queen's Own (Royal West Kent Regiment)
Died 24 May 1917, aged 28

OUR BUSINESS IS
LIKE MEN TO FIGHT
AND HERO-LIKE TO DIE

Second Lieutenant
Reginald Maurice HERRON
13th Battalion, Royal Sussex Regiment
Died 12 June 1917, aged 31

ONE OF BRITAIN'S SONS

206116 Lance Corporal
George Sydney HOPKINS
'B' Battalion, Heavy Branch, Tank Corps
Died 2 August 1917, aged 23

WHO IN RADIANT YOUTH
UNGRUDGINGLY GAVE HIS LIFE
FOR HIS FELLOW MEN

Second Lieutenant
William Jackson HORNER
V39 Heavy Trench Mortar Battery,
Royal Field Artillery
Died 15 July 1917, aged 30

AFTER ALL IS TOLD
HIS WAS A GLORIOUS DEATH
AND HE STILL LIVES

45043 Bombardier
James John HUTT
114th Siege Battery, Royal Garrison Artillery
Died 5 October 1917, aged 22

TO OUR DEAR BOY
HIS BLOOD WAS SHED
OUR HEARTS HAVE BLED
MAY WE NOT FORGET

Lieutenant
Alexander KERR
10th Battalion, Canadian Infantry
(Alberta Regiment)
Died 16 November 1917, aged 21

THIS LOVELY BUD
YOUNG AND FAIR
WAS CALLED HOME
IN PARADISE TO BLOOM

120586 Corporal
Eric Wilkinson KNOWLES
'N' Special Company, Royal Engineers,
Died 14 July 1917, aged 21

OUR COUNTRY
IN THE STORM OF WAR
HAS FOUND HIM FIT
TO FIGHT AND DIE FOR HER

415584 Private
Charles LABRADOR
25th Battalion, Canadian Infantry
(Nova Scotia Regiment)
Died 27 July 1916, aged 20

O MOTHER OF SORROW
FOR THE LOVE OF THIS SON

400633 Private
Frederick Richard LIVERMORE
7th Battalion, Canadian Infantry
(British Columbia Regiment)
Died 11 November 1917, aged 21

GIVE HIM HIS SOLDIER'S CROWN
HE CANNOT WAIT FOR HIS HONOR

24407 Private
Charles Morgan LLOYD
8th Battalion, Gloucestershire Regiment
Died 12 June 1917, aged 20

HOW ARE THE MIGHTY FALLEN
AND THE WEAPONS OF WAR
PERISHED

(From II Samuel, *Chapter 1, Verse 27.)*

3224 Lance Corporal
George William LOMAS
1st/6th Battalion, Sherwood Foresters
(Nottinghamshire & Derbyshire Regiment)
Died 4 July 1915, aged 20

"WENT THE DAY WELL?
WE DIED AND NEVER KNEW
BUT WELL OR ILL – ENGLAND
WE DIED FOR YOU" 1914-1918

(One of the collection of epitaphs for war memorials
published by John Maxwell Edmonds in 1919.)

12956 Rifleman
Charles William LONG
20th Battalion, King's Royal Rifle Corps
Died 30 September 1917, aged 21

LAY DOWN THE SHIELD
AND GIRT THE SWORD
FOR NOW THY WORK IS DONE

S/13514 Private
Fred LORD
1st Battalion, Gordon Highlanders
Died 3 April 1916, aged 24

JUST A BRITISH HERO

612A Corporal
James Joseph McCAGUE
5th Battalion, Australian Infantry
Died 3 November 1917, aged 31

IN THE FULL TIDE OF LIFE
LIKE ONE DIVINE
HE DIED TO SET MEN FREE

421 Private
John Victor McCALLUM
13th Company, Australian Machine Gun Corps
Died 26 October 1917, aged 25

A LIFE GIVEN IN ITS MORNING
PART PURCHASE OF OUR FREEDOM

97409 Driver
Albert Jesse McDOWALL
7th Divisional Ammunition Column,
Royal Field Artillery
Died 2 October 1917, aged 20

'TIS NOT IN MORTALS
TO COMMAND SUCCESS
BUT HE HAS DONE MORE
DESERVES IT

(Adapted from Joseph Addison's Cato, *and*
abbreviated at the end – possibly in an attempt to
keep the inscription within the maximum length
permitted, although it actually exceeds it by five
characters.)

02892 Private
Charles McGEARY
Princess Patricia's Canadian Light Infantry
(Eastern Ontario Regiment)
Died 16 November 1917, aged 40

HE WAS A GALLANT GENTLEMAN
HIS SOUL GOES MARCHING ON

(The second line is an adaptation of a line of Julia
W.Howe's Battle Hymn of the Republic.)

350559 Private
Archie Allison McGILP
11th Battalion, Royal Scots
Died 13 April 1918, aged 20

HUGH, ELDER BROTHER
AT HOOGE, MAY 1915
JOHN, TWIN BROTHER
AT ARRAS, APRIL 1917

(Hugh is buried in Sanctuary Wood Cemetery and
John is commemorated on the Arras Memorial to
the Missing.)

R/5991 Rifleman
William Homewood MANGER
8th Battalion, King's Royal Rifle Corps
Died 9 September 1915, aged 19

SHAPE THE WORLD
FOR WHICH HE DIED
THAT WAR AND STRIFE
MAY CEASE

2430 Private
John George MASON
1st/5th Battalion, Durham Light Infantry
Died 13 February 1916, aged 23

ENOUGH THIS WAS A MAN
THE NOBLEST NAME ON EARTH

G/3368 Private
Nehemiah MILES
8th Battalion, The Buffs (East Kent Regiment)
Died 13 March 1916, aged 31

TO LIVE, TO FIGHT, OR DIE
DETERMINED IS
YOUR BROTHER MI
APRIL 11TH 1915

C/4039 Lance Sergeant
Arthur Morley MILLER
20th Battalion, King's Royal Rifle Corps
Died 30 September 1917, aged 27

STILL, STILL WITH THEE
YOUR KATHLEEN

607 Sapper
Charles Ross MORRISON
6th Field Company, Canadian Engineers
Died 21 March 1916, aged 25

FOR OUR TO-MORROW
HE GAVE HIS TO-DAY

(Adapted from one of John Maxwell Edmonds's
1919 collection of epitaphs for war memorials.)

Second Lieutenant
Terence Donough O'BRIEN
16th (The Queen's) Lancers,
attached 6th Squadron, Royal Flying Corps
Died 3 March 1916, aged 20

A VERY GALLANT OFFICER
AND GENTLEMAN
TRULY DEPICTED
IN PSALM XV

(The son of a brigadier general and educated at
Winchester and the Royal Military College, this
young officer, who had been in Flanders since 1914,
would have been proud of his epitaph. Psalm 15
lists a catalogue of noble virtues.)

373980 Rifleman
Frank OSBORNE
8th Battalion, London Regiment
(Post Office Rifles)
Died 3 April 1917, aged 19

TELL MOTHER I SENT HER
MY DEAREST LOVE

12842 Private
George PEACOCK
1st/6th Battalion,
Duke of Wellington's (West Riding Regiment)
Died 28 February 1918, aged 22

FAITHFUL AND HONEST
UPRIGHT AND TRUE
CALLED HOME AT THE AGE OF 22

Joseph Frank PEACOCK-NEWPORT
served as
3/7572 Private
Joseph Frank PEACOCK
2nd Battalion, Bedfordshire Regiment
Died 25 April 1918, aged 22

SOLDIER JOE 1914-1918
IN PROUD & GRATEFUL MEMORY

Second Lieutenant
Douglas St George PETTIGREW
14th Battalion, attached 17th Battalion,
Sherwood Foresters
(Nottinghamshire & Derbyshire Regiment)
Died 23 October 1917, aged 25

TRAMORE 1892, YPRES 1917
ONLY SURVIVING SON OF
R.W. AND ELLA PETTIGREW

(Second Lieutenant Pettigrew, a son of County
Waterford, had been severely wounded at Thiepval
12 months before losing his life in the Ypres
Salient.)

43822 Sapper
William John POYNTER
20th Divisional Signal Company, Royal Engineers
Died 22 July 1916, aged 24

ONWARD GO, THE VICTORY LIES
IN THE STRUGGLE, NOT THE PRIZE

Lieutenant
John Edward RAPHAEL
18th Battalion, King's Royal Rifle Corps
Died 11 June 1917, aged 35

CHARACTER IS DESTINY

(Lieutenant Raphael was an England rugby union
captain who also played first-class cricket. By what
seems pure coincidence, only four graves separate his
from that of another England rugby international,
Lieutenant Colonel G.E.B.Dobbs of the Royal
Engineers, who died six days later.)

3211 Private
Stanley Edgar Stephen RAVELL
19th Battalion, Australian Infantry
Died 29 October 1917, aged 28

THESE ARE DEEDS
WHICH SHOULD NOT PASS AWAY
NAMES THAT MUST NOT WITHER

8684 Private
James RAWLINGS
1st Battalion, North Staffordshire Regiment
Died 25 October 1915, aged 38

IN MEMORY OF
A SOLDIER'S SON
BORN A SOLDIER
DIED A SOLDIER

(This soldier's father had served in the same
regiment.)

Second Lieutenant
Percy Thomas RAYNER, *MC & Bar*
18th Battalion, King's Royal Rifle Corps
Died 25 August 1918, aged 26

OUT OF THE SNOW, THE
SNOWDROP
OUT OF DEATH COMES LIFE

5787 Private
William Henry RICKARD
28th Battalion, Australian Infantry
Died 4 October 1917, aged 25

IT IS MEN
OF MY AGE AND SINGLE
WHO ARE EXPECTED
TO DO THEIR DUTY

Second Lieutenant
William Keith SEABROOK
17th Battalion, Australian Infantry
Died 21 September 1917, aged 21

A WILLING SACRIFICE
FOR THE WORLD'S PEACE

Captain
James OGILVIE-GRANT,
The Right Honourable the Earl of SEAFIELD
3rd Battalion, attached 5th Battalion,
Cameron Highlanders
Died 12 November 1915, aged 39

CHIEF OF CLAN GRANT
TILL THE DAY DAWN
AND THE SHADOWS FLEE AWAY

340671 Gunner
Frederick SIPLING
256th Siege Battery, Royal Garrison Artillery
Died 19 September 1917, aged 39

AS TIME ROLLS ON
THE MORE I MISS YOU
YOUR SORROWING KATE

R/6022 Rifleman
Ernest Malcolm SMITH
8th Battalion, King's Royal Rifle Corps
Died 8 August 1915, aged 19

IT IS GREAT TO DIE
FOR FREEDOM

13769 Private
Matthew SMITH
'A' Company, 8th Battalion, Yorkshire Regiment
Died 24 September 1917, aged 20

HE LAID HIS RICHEST GIFT
HIS LIFE
ON THE ALTAR OF DUTY

4290 Corporal
Herbert George SPENCER
2nd Brigade, Australian Machine Gun Corps
Died 6 October 1917, aged 21

OUR HERO HERB
LOVED IN LIFE
HONOURED IN DEATH
TREASURED IN MEMORY

Major
Arthur SPRAY, *MC*
5th Battalion, Tank Corps
Died 5 May 1918, aged 33

BLESSED ARE
THE PURE IN HEART
MY DEAR, DEAR HUSBAND
DAISY

(The first two lines are taken from Matthew,
Chapter 5, Verse 8.)

355003 Quarter Master Sergeant
James STODDART
10th Battalion, The King's (Liverpool Regiment)
Died 2 August 1917, aged 49

A SOLDIER'S DEATH
MY BODY DIES
TO GLORY WED

63978 Private
Joseph Askins TAYLOR
20th Battalion, Royal Fusiliers
Died 28 November 1917, aged 25

WAR'S BITTER COST
A DEAR LIFE LOST

325184 Private
David James THOMSON
1st/8th Battalion, Royal Scots
Died 12 July 1917, aged 24

JUST MARKED BY A SIMPLE CROSS
'TIS THE MARK
OF A NATION'S HERO
THE SIGN OF A MOTHER'S LOSS

*(There's no longer "just ... a simple cross", of
course. It was replaced by the white headstone on
which the epitaph is inscribed.)*

7651 Sapper
Lewis THORNTON
*4th Divisional Signal Company,
Australian Engineers*
Died 28 September 1917, aged 27

OH MY SON
WOULD GOD
I HAD DIED FOR THEE
MY LOVED SON

(From II Samuel, *Chapter 18, Verse 33.)*

429608 Private
James TRAIN
*7th Battalion, Canadian Infantry
(British Columbia Regiment)*
Died 12 November 1917, aged 25

WITH CHEERY SMILE AND WAVE OF HAND
HE WANDERED TO AN UNKNOWN LAND

Captain
John Wilfrid Hugh TRENCHARD
122nd Heavy Battery, Royal Garrison Artillery
Died 3 October 1917, aged 20

AS A SON AND A SOLDIER
HE DID HIS DUTY

A/34894 Private
Charles TURNER
*10th Battalion, Canadian Infantry
(Alberta Regiment)*
Died 16 June 1916, aged 22

REJECTED FOUR TIMES
ACCEPTED THE FIFTH
REST AFTER LABOUR

203246 Private
Cyril George VINECOMBE
4th Battalion, Worcestershire Regiment
Died 17 April 1918, aged 22

IN MEMORY OF OUR BELOVED
AND ONLY BOY CYRIL
HE WAS THE LIFE & JOY
OF THE HOME. R.I.P.

Second Lieutenant
Thomas Frederick Henry WAKE
1st Battalion, attached 8th Battalion,
North Staffordshire Regiment
Died 10 April 1918, aged 19

WE THANK GOD FOR
19 YEARS OF HAPPINESS
WITH OUR ONLY CHILD

2255 Private
Alfred WALKER
45th Battalion, Australian Infantry
Died 29 September 1917, aged 24

HE NEVER SPOKE
OF WHAT HE DID
BUT KEPT IT TO HIMSELF
R.I.P.

30636 Lance Corporal
Joseph WEATHERHOGG
10th Battalion,
The Queen's Own (Royal West Kent Regiment)
Died 1 October 1918, aged 25

FOUGHT & DIED WITH THOUSANDS MORE
GOD GRANT WE MEET ON YONDER SHORE

47982 Gunner
Christopher WESTMORELAND
12th Siege Battery, Royal Garrison Artillery
Died 29 August 1915, aged 25

PASSED FROM THE SHELL SWEPT
FIELD OF EARTH
TO THE CALM AND PEACE
OF PARADISE

Second Lieutenant
Ralph Ernest WHITE
12th Battalion, East Surrey Regiment
Died 28 September 1917, aged 40

HE NOTHING COMMON DID
OR MEAN
UPON THAT MEMORABLE SCENE

(From Horatian Ode upon Cromwell's
Return from Ireland, *by Andrew Marvell.)*

Lieutenant
Harold Mackenzie WILSON
15th Battalion, Canadian Infantry
(Central Ontario Regiment)
Died 9 June 1916, aged 24

OUT OF WEAKNESS MADE STRONG
WAXED VALIANT IN FIGHT

Second Lieutenant
William Gerald WRIGHT
8th Battalion, Hampshire Regiment
Died 8 June 1917, aged 24

SUNSHINE AND YOUTH
AND LAUGHTER
ALL HE GAVE IN SACRIFICE

Lieutenant
Eric Hallman ZIEGLER
7th Brigade, Canadian Machine Gun Corps
Died 7 June 1916, aged 23

FOR LOVE OF THE EMPIRE
HE LIVES IN THE FREEDOM
HE DIED TO SAVE

Lillers Communal Cemetery

24617 Second Corporal
William Arthur BAILEY
55th Field Company, Royal Engineers
Died 2 November 1915, aged 21

QUIT YOU LIKE MEN, BE STRONG

(From I Corinthians, *Chapter 16, Verse 13.)*

SR/49 Private
George CLARK
2nd Battalion, Royal Sussex Regiment
Died 31 January 1915, aged 40

A SPLENDID SOLDIER
A LOVING DADDY
MAMA & NELLY

(Private Clark had served in the Royal Sussex
Regiment for 12 years, which encompassed the
Chitral, Punjab Frontier and Tirah campaigns.)

8623 Private
John GRENNAN
1st Battalion, The King's (Liverpool Regiment)
Died 23 May 1915, aged 29

PRAY FOR HIS SOUL
WHOSE GRAVE YOU SCAN
A BRITISH SOLDIER
AND A MAN

13621 Corporal
Wallace William GREY
10th Battalion, Gloucestershire Regiment
Died 27 September 1915, aged 21

A SOLDIER BOY
A BRAVE LAD TRUE
A MOTHER'S JOY
HE DIED FOR YOU

1301 Private
Fred LAND
2nd Battalion, Welsh Regiment
Died 15 January 1915, aged 18

GOOD-BYE FRED. YOU HAVE
NOBLY DONE YOUR DUTY
THOUGH YOUR MOTHER'S HEART
WAS BROKEN

10039 Guardsman
Archibald McLEAVER
1st Battalion, Scots Guards
Died 30 September 1915, aged 20

LIKE A MAN
HE FOUGHT HIS FIGHT
AND FIGHTING DIED

Captain
Rupert Auriol Conant MURRAY
1st Battalion, Seaforth Highlanders
Died 11 March 1915, aged 32

"HE TRIED TO DO HIS DUTY"
SIR HENRY LAWRENCE 1857

645208 Driver
Henry Richard PENGELLY
51st Divisional Ammunition Column,
Royal Field Artillery
Died 15 April 1918, aged 22

OUR GLORIOUS DEVONPORT LAD
DIED FOR HIS HOMELAND
A BITTER BLOW TO US ALL

3106 Guardsman
John Wilson SHUTTLEWORTH
2nd Battalion, Coldstream Guards
Died 30 December 1914, aged 34

THESE GAVE YOUR LIVES
THAT YOU WHO LIVE
MAY REAP A RICHER HARVEST
ERE YOU FALL ASLEEP

9907 Driver
Henry John SOUTH
'D' Battery, 71st Brigade, Royal Field Artillery
Died 21 January 1916, aged 21

HE HAD NO CHANCE
TO BID HIS FRIENDS FAREWELL

Lieutenant Colonel
Halford Claude Vaughan HARRISON
16th Divisional Ammunition Column,
Royal Field Artillery
Died 1 April 1916, aged 54

HERE HE LIES
WHERE HE LONGED TO BE
THE HUNTER
HOME FROM THE HILL

Loker Churchyard

24269 Sergeant
Sydney Thomas ATKINSON
'C' Battery, 160th Brigade, Royal Field Artillery
Died 4 January 1917, aged 22

OUR DEAR OLD SYD

72029 Private
Cyril George Michael BRIMBLE
27th Battalion, Canadian Infantry
(Manitoba Regiment)
Died 16 October 1915, aged 27

THOU THEREFORE
ENDURE HARDNESS
AS A GOOD SOLDIER
OF JESUS CHRIST

(From II Timothy, *Chapter 2, Verse 3.)*

Lieutenant
James Chester HUGHES
6th Field Company, Canadian Engineers
Died 15 November 1915, aged 27

HIS BODY LIES HERE
IN A HERO'S GRAVE
HE LIVES IN THE FREEDOM
HE DIED TO SAVE

146503 Lance Corporal
John Oliver NEVILLE
'O' Special Company, Royal Engineers
Died 4 June 1917, aged 22

"THE HOPELESS TANGLE
OF OUR AGE
THOU TOO HAST SCANNED IT WELL!"
ARNOLD

London Cemetery, Longueval

Captain
David HENDERSON
8th Battalion, Middlesex Regiment,
attached 19th Battalion, London Regiment
Died 15 September 1916, aged 27

"PEACE WAS THE PRIZE
OF ALL HIS TOIL AND CARE"

(This officer's father was The Right Honourable
Arthur Henderson, MP, Leader of the Labour
Party and a member of Prime Minister Asquith's
cabinet. The epitaph is from Heroic Stanzas on
the Death of Oliver Cromwell *by John*
Dryden.)

London Cemetery, Neuville-Vitasse

4756 Private
John EVANS
1st/13th (Kensington) Battalion,
London Regiment
Died 18 April 1917, aged 33

HIGH AND LOW
RICH AND POOR
ONE WITH ANOTHER

250749 Private
George Philip POPE
3rd Battalion, London Regiment (Royal Fusiliers)
Died 11 April 1917, aged 19

A BOY
HE SPENT HIS BOY'S DEAR LIFE
FOR ENGLAND

(Much had been packed into the last few years of
this short life. Private Pope enlisted in September
1914 and had served at Malta, Khartoum and
Gallipoli before reaching the Western Front.)

London Rifle Brigade Cemetery

1820 Private
Alfred Frederick DANIEL
41st Battalion, Australian Infantry
Died 23 March 1917, aged 33

KILLED AT THE FRONT
TRIUMPHANT DEATH

11503 Private
Eric Warton HENLEY
11th Battalion,
The Queen's (Royal West Surrey Regiment)
Died 9 August 1916, aged 24

HIS LIFE WAS GENTLE
BUT THE ELEMENTS
OF NATURE WOULD SAY
THIS WAS A MAN

(A condensed version of Shakespeare's words in
Julius Caesar, *Act 5, Scene 5.)*

S/10649 Private
Alexander STEWART
8th Battalion, Gordon Highlanders
Died 8 March 1916, aged 22

"HE COMETH FORTH
LIKE A FLOWER
AND IS CUT DOWN"
JOB 14.2

Longpré-les-Corps-Saints British Cemetery

391408 Rifleman
Arthur Edward WALES
2nd/9th Battalion, London Regiment
(Queen Victoria's Rifles)
Died 24 April 1918, aged 23

NOW THE BATTLE DAY IS PAST
ON HIS TOMB ARE LAURELS
WHICH WILL LAST

Longueau British Cemetery

5124 Private
Frederick Jacques OSWALD
27th Battalion, Australian Infantry
Died 8 August 1918, aged 26

YOU FOUGHT
FOR THE FINEST CAUSE
AND DIED
IN THE GREATEST OF WARS

2989 Private
Seth THOMAS
52nd Battalion, Australian Infantry
Died 12 May 1918, aged 21

WELL DONE COMRADE

Longuenesse (St Omer) Souvenir Cemetery

267115 Private
Arthur Ernest ABBOTT
1st/7th Battalion, Sherwood Foresters
(Nottinghamshire & Derbyshire Regiment)
Died 8 April 1917, aged 36

LO! THE PAIN OF LIFE IS PAST
ALL HIS WARFARE NOW IS O'ER

57060 Gunner
John Norfolk BEVAN
106th Siege Battery, Royal Garrison Artillery
Died 4 October 1916, aged 19

MY SON, MY SON
2 SAM. XVIII.33

6547 Private
Robert Hilton CAMPBELL
'D' Company, 1st Battalion, Canadian Infantry
(Western Ontario Regiment)
Died 14 March 1915, aged 24

HE RESTS IN PEACE
THIS SOLDIER TRUE

306802 Private
Haswell Harry CARTER
'B' Company, 1st/8th Battalion,
West Yorkshire Regiment (Prince of Wales's Own)
Died 28 July 1917, aged 19

GOD MOVES
IN A MYSTERIOUS WAY

7235 Private
Isaac Morgan DE LEACY
9th Battalion, Australian Infantry
Died 21 July 1918, aged 24

FOR HIS KING, COUNTRY & MATES
HE DIED
& LEFT A SPOTLESS NAME

(This Queenslander's age according to his headstone
was 25, but in fact he was killed by a shell three
days short of completing his twenty-fifth year, having
previously been gassed on four occasions. His brother
Walter was also killed in action, but has no known
grave and is commemorated on the Menin Gate
Memorial to the Missing, where his name is
incorrectly inscribed as De Lacey.)

Lieutenant
Arthur DUDGEON
Royal Garrison Artillery,
attached 4th Field Survey Company,
Royal Engineers
Died 19 November 1918, aged 31

THY LOVE TO ME WAS
WONDERFUL
SAMUEL 1.26
HIS WIFE

2376 Private
George James FISK
24th Battalion, London Regiment
Died 8 February 1916, aged 21

ONLY A PRIVATE SOLDIER
HIS PARENTS' ONLY SON

19187 Lance Corporal
James Wiseman GREENWELL
12th Battalion, Durham Light Infantry
Died 16 December 1915, aged 29

HE ANSWERED
HIS COUNTRY'S CALL
BUT LEFT ME TO MOURN

21/312 Private
Harry HAIL
21st Battalion,
West Yorkshire Regiment (Prince of Wales's Own)
Died 5 September 1918, aged 23

TRANQUIL YOU LIE
YOUR MEMORY HALLOWED
IN THE LAND YOU LOVED

(From Sir John Arkwright's hymn O Valiant
Hearts.*)*

Lieutenant
John Clarence HANSON
104th Battalion, Canadian Infantry
(New Brunswick Regiment),
attached 55th Squadron, Royal Flying Corps
Died 14 July 1917, aged 24

MY COUNTRY BEFORE EVEN YOU
MOTHER DEAR
(HIS PARTING WORDS
ON LEAVING HOME)

56016 Acting Bombardier
George Martin HARBOUR
47th Siege Battery, Royal Garrison Artillery
Died 27 November 1917, aged 20

HIS LAST ROLL CALL

71 Private
Thomas Herbert HEARD
1st Battalion,
The Queen's Own (Royal West Kent Regiment)
Died 15 March 1915, aged 41

NO PRICE IS YET TOO GREAT
WHEN HONOUR AND DUTY
ARE AT STAKE

Second Lieutenant
Charles Frederick HEATLY
16th Battalion, Royal Welsh Fusiliers,
and 38th Divisional Sniping Company
Died 17 April 1918, aged 23

A LOVING SON
A BRAVE SOLDIER
AND A VERY PERFECT GENTLEMAN

202185 Lance Corporal
John Watson HOLMES
6th Battalion, Yorkshire Regiment
Died 11 October 1917, aged 20

THESE ARE THEY WHICH CAME
OUT OF GREAT TRIBULATION

(From Revelation, *Chapter 7, Verse 14.)*

2204125 Sapper
Alfred JAMES
5th Battalion, Canadian Railway Troops
Died 1 August 1918, aged 42

A HERO OF THREE WARS
GONE BUT NOT FORGOTTEN

(Sapper James's two previous campaigns were the
Greco-Turkish War of 1897 and the Boer War.)

11225 Private
William Heber LEWIS
5th Canadian Mounted Rifles (Quebec Regiment)
Died 30 January 1916, aged 21

MY COUNTRY,
'TIS FOR THEE

(Adapted from Samuel Francis Smith's poem,
America.*)*

181205 Driver
Arthur George LLOYD
187th Brigade, Royal Field Artillery
Died 14 June 1918, aged 21

ALWAYS WITH MOTHER
DARLING BOY

33418 Sergeant
Harold Andrew LODGE
2nd Battalion, Hampshire Regiment
Died 27 August 1918, aged 30

THEY NEVER FALL
WHO DIED IN A GREAT CAUSE
BYRON

10580 Private
William McCONNELL
'C' Company, 1st Battalion,
The King's (Liverpool Regiment)
Died 17 May 1915, aged 20

HE WAS MY BROTHER

128200 Lance Corporal
Lester Joseph McCOY
'L' Special Company, Royal Engineers
Died 26 June 1918, aged 38

A NOTABLE EXAMPLE
TO SUCH AS BE YOUNG
TO DIE WILLINGLY
AND COURAGEOUSLY

44154 Private
James McILWRAITH
9th Battalion, Royal Scots,
Died 17 April 1918, aged 40

O VALIANT HEART
WHO TO YOUR GLORY CAME
THROUGH BATTLE FLAME

(The words are adapted from Sir John Arkwright's
hymn O Valiant Hearts. *Private McIlwraith met*
his death very soon after being transferred to the
Royal Scots, having served in the Highland Light
Infantry since 1914.)

34714 Private
Frank Arthur MOORE
3rd Battalion, Worcestershire Regiment
Died 28 December 1916, aged 21

ENDURE HARDNESS
AS A GOOD SOLDIER OF CHRIST
2 TIM. II.3

Tombes de Guerre du Commonwealth
**Commonwealth
War Graves**

2376 Private
John Wilfred MOORE
Leicestershire Yeomanry
Died 15 January 1916, aged 18

HIS SUN WENT DOWN
WHILST IT WAS YET DAY
BRITONS NEVER DIE

930 Private
Montague John MYERS
7th Battalion, East Surrey Regiment
Died 4 April 1916, aged 23

HERE
CLOTHED IN YOUTHFUL GLORY
LIES OUR NOBLE SON
FOR SACRIFICE

66701 Private
Charles Keith NADEN
1st/6th Battalion, Northumberland Fusiliers
Died 13 April 1918, aged 18

ONLY THE ACTIONS OF THE GOOD
SMELL SWEET
AND BLOSSOM IN THEIR DUST

(A slightly amended extract from James Shirley's
poem Death the Leveller.*)*

Second Lieutenant
Frederick James PAGET
206th Squadron, Royal Air Force
Died 6 August 1918, aged 23

A GLORIOUS DEATH IS HIS
WHO FOR HIS COUNTRY DIES

266092 Private
John PEARCE
2nd/7th Battalion,
The King's (Liverpool Regiment)
Died 22 July 1917, aged 28

A LITTLE BIT OF ENGLAND
IN A FOREIGN LAND

1739 Private
Richard Douglas SALMAN
22nd Battalion, London Regiment
Died 24 May 1915, aged 21

"SALT" OF OUR ENGLISH EARTH

24499 Sergeant
Oliver Barnet WATKINSON
12th Brigade Heavy Artillery Group,
Royal Garrison Artillery
Died 21 June 1918, aged 32

DEATH IS SWALLOWED UP
IN VICTORY

(From I Corinthians, *Chapter 15, Verse 54.)*

46285 Private
Lewis WATSON
13th Battalion, York & Lancaster Regiment
Died 28 June 1918, aged 26

HE WAS WOUNDED
FOR OUR TRANSGRESSIONS
ISA. 53.5

L/1798 Driver
Wilfred Thomas WELLING
40th Divisional Ammunition Column,
Royal Field Artillery
Died 12 July 1916, aged 16

HE WOULD INSIST
ON SERVING HIS COUNTRY

10262 Private
Benjamin WEST
4th Regiment, South African Infantry
Died 7 August 1918, aged 24

AND THEY LOVED NOT
THEIR OWN LIVES
UNTO THE DEATH

(A slightly amended version of Revelation,
Chapter 12, Verse 11.)

Louez Military Cemetery

2497 Lance Corporal
Thomas James Watters BLYTH
1st/7th Battalion,
Argyll & Sutherland Highlanders
Died 28 May 1916, aged 22

GONE
IN THE UNUTTERABLE SPLENDOUR
OF YOUR IMMORTAL YOUTH

Lieutenant Colonel
Claude Henry CAMPBELL, *DSO*
1st Battalion, Cameron Highlanders,
commanding 1st/4th Battalion,
Seaforth Highlanders
Died 14 March 1916, aged 37

THE LORD IS WITH THEE
THOU MIGHTY MAN OF VALOUR
JUDGES VI. 12

1886 Private
William Samuel CARTER
1st/9th Battalion, Royal Scots
Died 12 March 1916, aged 48

HIS WISH
A SOLDIER'S DEATH
A SOLDIER'S GRAVE

(Private Carter had a military career encompassing
24 years' service in the Royal Artillery.)

4573 Private
Peter Rankine McLEOD
7th Battalion, Argyll & Sutherland Highlanders
Died 23 March 1916, aged 22

TO BE EXALTED THUS
WORTHY THE LAMB
LET US REPLY
FOR HE WAS SLAIN FOR US

Louvencourt Military Cemetery

Lieutenant
Roland Aubrey LEIGHTON
1st/7th Battalion, Worcestershire Regiment
Died 23 December 1915, aged 19

GOODNIGHT THOUGH LIFE
AND ALL TAKE FLIGHT
NEVER GOOD BYE

(Lieutenant Leighton died of wounds suffered the
previous night while commanding a party mending
barbed wire outside the trenches at Hébuterne. He
was the fiancé of Vera Brittain, in whose Letters
From a Lost Generation *the words used for the*
epitaph are quoted several times. They are adapted
from A Wink from Hesper, *a poem by*
W.E.Henley.)

Second Lieutenant
Robert Goldie MILLER
4th Battalion, Argyll & Sutherland Highlanders,
attached Royal Flying Corps
Died 17 March 1917, aged 27

WHO DARED
TO NOBLY STEM
TYRANNIC PRIDE
BURNS

Louverval Military Cemetery

Major
Rayner Harvey JOHNSON, *MC*
122nd Heavy Battery, Royal Garrison Artillery
Died 27 September 1918, aged 21

HE, BEING MADE PERFECT
IN A SHORT TIME
FULFILLED A LONG TIME

(From a book of Apocrypha: Wisdom, *Chapter*
1, Verse 13.)

Lowrie Cemetery

340096 Corporal
John William Francis HARRIOTT
1st Battalion, Northumberland Fusiliers
Died 27 September 1918, aged 23

HE TROD THE PATH
OF SUFFERING
TO THE LAND OF ETERNAL REST
R.I.P.

(Corporal Harriott was the only son of a widowed
mother from Whitley Bay.)

Mailly Wood Cemetery

3190 Lance Corporal
Archie FERGUSON
8th Battalion, Argyll & Sutherland Highlanders
Died 13 November 1916, aged 19

MY COUNTRY RIGHT OR WRONG

9448 Corporal
John MacLEAN, *MM*
1st/1st (Highland) Field Company,
Royal Engineers
Died 19 November 1916, aged 28

MACLEAN

Maple Copse Cemetery

Lieutenant
Gordon Stanley FIFE
Princess Patricia's Canadian Light Infantry
(Eastern Ontario Regiment)
Died 2 June 1916, aged 27

THEY GAVE
THEIR MERRY YOUTH AWAY
FOR COUNTRY AND FOR GOD

111398 Private
Lionel Wellington NUTTER
5th Canadian Mounted Rifles (Quebec Regiment)
Died 25 March 1916, aged 19

OUR BABY BOY

153099 Private
Peter WILSON
43rd Battalion, Canadian Infantry
(Manitoba Regiment)
Died 21 May 1916, aged 33

THIS IS THE SOLDIER'S
CAMPING GROUND
HIS WEARY DAY IS PAST

Maple Leaf Cemetery

19828 Sergeant
George Henry EVANS
10th Battalion, Canadian Infantry
(Alberta Regiment)
Died 20 November 1915, aged 25

HIS VIRTUES
ARE RECORDED ELSEWHERE

A SOLDIER
OF THE GREAT WAR

Maroc British Cemetery

29571 Private
James HANCOCK
13th Battalion, Yorkshire Regiment,
attached 173rd Tunnelling Company,
Royal Engineers
Died 22 February 1917, aged 33

HE LIES BENEATH
THE SOIL OF FRANCE
SOMEWHERE IN A GRAVE
UNKNOWN TO US. R.I.P.

(Private Hancock's widowed mother in Stoke-on-Trent was typical of the many thousands to whom a pilgrimage to northern France was beyond aspiration.)

Second Lieutenant
Edward Byron Atkins HARVEY
'B' Company, 8th Battalion,
The Queen's Own (Royal West Kent Regiment)
Died 15 April 1917, aged 21

"MY DELICATE ONES
HAVE GONE ROUGH WAYS"
BARUCH 4TH CHAPTER

(Baruch is a book of Apocrypha.)

240599 Lance Corporal
Percy Hartland POWIS
1st/6th Battalion, South Staffordshire Regiment
Died 25 May 1917, aged 33

HEEDLESS AND CARELESS
STILL THE WORLD WAGS ON
AND LEAVES ME BROKEN
OH MY SON MY SON

(The word 'broken', which is what should have been inscribed, appears on the headstone as 'BROMN'.)

14616 Private
Charles Richard WAYGOOD
1st Battalion, South Wales Borderers
Died 19 May 1916, aged 38

AND THEY SHALL WALK
WITH ME IN WHITE
FOR THEY ARE WORTHY
REV. 3. 4

Mazingarbe Communal Cemetery

S/9672 Private
John DOCHERTY
9th Battalion,
The Black Watch (Royal Highlanders)
Died 15 February 1916, aged 27

TOO DEARLY LOVED
TO BE FORGOTTEN

(Private Docherty was executed for desertion.)

Mazingarbe Communal Cemetery Extension

10414 Private
William Henry BURRELL
2nd Battalion, Royal Sussex Regiment
Died 22 May 1916, aged 21

THE WILL OF THE LORD BE DONE
ACTS 21.14
DAD, MUM

(Private Burrell was executed for desertion.)

Major
John de Luze SIMONDS, *DSO*
136th Siege Battery, Royal Garrison Artillery
Died 22 April 1917, aged 32

BE VERY PROUD TO NUMBER ME
AMONG THE DEATHLESS DEAD
J. DE L. S.

Méaulte Military Cemetery

46178 Bombardier
Edward George HADAWAY
16th Heavy Battery, 21st Brigade,
Royal Garrison Artillery
Died 1 May 1916, aged 23

OUR LITTLE LIFE
IS ROUNDED BY
A SLEEP

Second Lieutenant
Leslie ROBERTS, *MC*
East Surrey Regiment,
attached 6th Battalion,
The Queen's (Royal West Surrey Regiment)
Died 24 August 1918, aged 23

"HE SET A VERY FINE EXAMPLE
TO ALL RANKS"
GAZETTE NO. 31158

Mendinghem Military Cemetery

103351 Private
Harry CHANDLER
233rd Company, Machine Gun Corps (Infantry)
Died 26 September 1917, aged 25

SLEEP ON MY PEACEFUL COMRADE
THY DUTY IS WELL DONE

L/21778 Gunner
Leslie Amyas COOK
'B' Battery, 74th Brigade, Royal Field Artillery
Died 14 September 1917, aged 20

THAT GENTLENESS
THAT WHEN IT MATES
WITH MANHOOD
MAKES A MAN

---

29 Trooper
Alfred DUNNE
Household Battalion,
Died 11 October 1917, aged 17

O MONSTROUS WORLD
TO BE DIRECT AND HONEST
IS NOT SAFE

(From Shakespeare's Othello, *Act 3, Scene 3.)*

Second Lieutenant
Leonard Gordon HELLIER
3rd Battalion, attached 11th Battalion,
Border Regiment
Died 16 December 1917, aged 22

HIS BODY WITH FRANCE
HIS SOUL WITH GOD
HIS FRAGRANCE WITH US

(In fact with Belgium, not France.)

291021 Private
Norman Stanley HILL
1st Battalion, Gordon Highlanders
Died 30 September 1917, aged 20

JUST ONE
OF ENGLAND'S DEFENDERS
HE DIED FOR HOME AND DUTY

Sub-Lieutenant
Bertram Douglas LAUGHTON
Royal Naval Volunteer Reserve,
Hawke Battalion, Royal Naval Division,
attached Royal Flying Corps
Died 1 October 1917, aged 23

GREAT HEARTS ARE GLAD
WHEN IT IS TIME TO GIVE

Menin Road South Military Cemetery

80563 Private
Wilfrid John BROWNE
13th Field Ambulance,
Royal Army Medical Corps
Died 6 November 1917, aged 23

AFTER TOIL – REST
AFTER STRIFE – PEACE
AFTER DEATH – LIFE

Captain
Thomas Riversdale
COLYER-FERGUSSON, *VC*
2nd Battalion, Northamptonshire Regiment
Died 31 July 1917, aged 21

MY SON, MY SON
NO REWARD CAN BE TOO GREAT

(The second line of the epitaph is taken from the
citation for his VC award, which also summarizes
the officer's conduct in the action concerned as "an
amazing record of dash, gallantry and skill". He
was killed shortly afterwards by a sniper.)

1589 Regimental Sergeant Major
Stewart GODFREY
Princess Patricia's Canadian Light Infantry
(Eastern Ontario Regiment)
Died 18 April 1916, aged 47

PAST THE MILITARY AGE
HE RESPONDED
TO THE MOTHER COUNTRY'S CALL

(Not a newcomer to military life, Regimental
Sergeant Major Godfrey had served in the South
African Campaign.)

17506 Private
Henry Aldric Strickland HODGE

'A' Company, 1st Battalion, Royal Fusiliers
Died 19 January 1916, aged 19

FOR ENGLAND'S GLORY

138918 Sergeant
Brice Selwyn MARTELL
308th Siege Battery, Royal Garrison Artillery
Died 31 October 1917, aged 21

A LEWES GRAMMAR SCHOOL BOY
HE MOST NOBLY
PLAYED THE GAME

166292 Sapper
Leslie Harry MATTHEWS
152nd Field Company, Royal Engineers
Died 10 November 1917, aged 23

HAD ALL LIVED AS YOU DID
MY BOY
WE SHOULD NOT HAVE PARTED
IN THIS WAY

5374 Lance Corporal
Charles Joseph MESTREZ
1st Company, Australian Tunnelling Corps
Died 25 September 1917, aged 35

MY JOY-BRINGER GONE
OVER THE SUN
A BLACK CLOUD CAME
I AM LEFT ALONE

2409 Sapper
Harold MILNE
14th Field Company, Australian Engineers
Died 25 October 1917, aged 34

SONG SINKS INTO SILENCE
THE STORY IS TOLD

Lieutenant
Francis Sidney MITCHELL
Royal Army Medical Corps,
attached 9th Battalion, Royal Sussex Regiment
Died 15 February 1916, aged 26

KILLED WHEN ATTENDING
THE WOUNDED ON THE FIELD

152197 Sapper
Reginald Guy TURNER
2nd Army Wireless Company, Royal Engineers
Died 22 July 1917, aged 21

A YOUTHFUL BUT NOBLE DEATH

7357 Private
Tom Orlando March VINCENT
21st Battalion, Australian Infantry
Died 19 September 1917, aged 23

THE SUPREME DISTINCTION

Méricourt-l'Abbé Communal Cemetery Extension

3044 Private
George Alexander CONNER
39th Battalion, Australian Infantry
Died 26 April 1918, aged 29

IN THE SOLDIER'S HOME
IN GLORY
THERE REMAINS A LAND OF REST

Lieutenant
Thomas Whiteway EALES, *DCM*
21st Battalion, Australian Infantry
Died 19 May 1918, aged 22

... NOTHING BUT WELL AND FAIR
AND WHAT MAY QUIET US
IN A DEATH SO NOBLE

(From Milton's Samson Agonistes.*)*

2631 Private
John FAGAN
29th Battalion, Australian Infantry
Died 29 July 1918, aged 25

DARLING JACK
HOW I MISS YOU
NOBODY KNOWS BUT ME
MOTHER

13589 Corporal
Elijah GENT
12th Battalion, Northumberland Fusiliers
Died 3 July 1916, aged 25

DON'T WORRY
I'M BUT SLEEPING HERE
I'LL SEE YOU TO-MORROW
MOTHER DEAR

2915 Private
Arthur John HEALEY
59th Battalion, Australian Infantry
Died 4 July 1918, aged 25

"LOST"!
HOW CAN SUCH LIVES BE LOST?
JUST GATHERED UP:
JEWELS, RARE OF COST!

(The profusion of punctuation marks in this resounding epitaph is very unusual. Often, on the contrary, they are conspicuous by their absence.)

Messines Ridge British Cemetery

Second Lieutenant
James John CADUSCH
38th Battalion, Australian Infantry
Died between 7 and 9 June 1917, aged 29

HE HELPED TO MAKE
AUSTRALIA'S NAME
THE WONDER & PRIDE
OF THE WORLD

(Australia's nationhood dated only from 1901, and the deeds and sacrifices of its armed forces in the First World War contributed enormously to the forging of the young country's national identity.)

35 Private
Bernie CLAPHAM
34th Battalion, Australian Infantry
Died 21 July 1917, aged 22

HE SHOULDERED HIS GUN
IN HONOR'S CAUSE
AND IN THE BATTLE DIED
THY WILL BE DONE

4274 Private
Ernest William COLLINS
32nd Battalion, Australian Infantry
Died 20 November 1917, aged 24

ASLEEP
AWAITING THE GREAT REVEILLE

Second Lieutenant
John Philip DE BURIATTE
2nd Battalion, East Surrey Regiment
Died 12 March 1915, aged 27

UNDER THE WIDE
AND STARRY SKY
DIG THE GRAVE AND LET ME LIE

(Before being commissioned, Second Lieutenant De Buriatte had served as a sergeant in the Artists' Rifles.)

6998 Private
Alfred James HART
13th Battalion, Australian Infantry
Died 8 August 1917, aged 27

HONOUR DEFIED DEATH
LOVE DESPISED IT
MEMORY VENERATES IT

---

388 Lance Corporal
Roland Charles HIGGS
41st Battalion, Australian Infantry
Died 8 July 1917, aged 21

HIS LIFE'S WORK TRULY DONE
ERE LIFE HAD SCARCE BEGUN
MANLY, UNSELFISH

5768 Private
Oscar KEAST
14th Battalion, Australian Infantry
Died 11 August 1917, aged 20

RESPONSIVE TO HUMANITY'S CALL
A GALLANT ACTION
MARKED HIS FALL

2932 Corporal
Ralph Oswald KIRBY, *MM*
36th Battalion, Australian Infantry
Died 3 July 1917, aged 25

WE SHALL NOT ALL SLEEP
BUT WE SHALL ALL BE CHANGED

---

120 Private
Ernest Henry PETERS
11th Company, Australian Machine Gun Corps
Died 11 June 1917, aged 21

UNDER FOREIGN SKIES
HE'S LYING
HIS DUTY NOBLY DONE
R.I.P.

44164 Lance Corporal
Arthur Thomas WRIGHT
2nd Battalion, Royal Irish Rifles
Died 6 September 1918, aged 29

HE HAD HIS MARCHING ORDERS
LIKE A SOLDIER HE OBEYED
HIS LAST CALL

Millencourt Communal Cemetery Extension

2500 Private
Arthur Henry BOWEN
24th Battalion, London Regiment
Died 19 September 1916, aged 22

PASS FRIEND ALL WELL

Lieutenant
George Musgrove CARTMEL
205th Squadron, Royal Air Force
Died 6 April 1918, aged 19

ALL YE THAT PASS THIS WAY
TELL ENGLAND THAT
HE WHO LIETH HERE
RESTS CONTENT

(Lieutenant Cartmel was shot down and killed while flying a DH4. His epitaph, of which there are many slight variations in the Western Front cemeteries, is based on a Spartan tribute of ancient times.)

17027 Sergeant
Herbert George PHELPS
2nd Company, Machine Gun Corps
Died 20 August 1916, aged 22

AFTER THE CROSS, THE CROWN
MONS TO THE SOMME
THEN REST

5261 Private
Crawford Rupert WILSON
46th Battalion, Australian Infantry
Died 3 April 1918, aged 23

OUR LITTLE BROTHER

Mill Road Cemetery

Llewellyn BRICK
1st/5th Battalion,
Duke of Wellington's (West Riding Regiment)
Died 3 September 1916, aged 23

AU REVOIR LLEW

G/18075 Private
Charles COTTERELL
7th Battalion,
The Queen's Own (Royal West Kent Regiment)
Died 29 September 1916, aged 20

BRAVE VOLUNTEER

185 Rifleman
Samuel GLENN
13th Battalion, Royal Irish Rifles
Died 1 July 1916, aged 38

2 TIM. CH.2 V.3
"A GOOD SOLDIER
OF JESUS CHRIST"

17865 Rifleman
William HERON
13th Battalion, Royal Irish Rifles
Died 1 July 1916, aged 23

CALL HIM NOT DEAD
WHO FELL AT DUTY'S FEET

Lieutenant
Herbert William HITCHCOCK
Machine Gun Corps (Infantry),
attached 11th Battalion, Tank Corps
Died 13 November 1916, aged 22

I WILL GO FORTH
WHEN I FALL IT MATTERS NOT
SO AS GOD'S WORK IS DONE

Second Lieutenant
Cedric Stewart HOWARD
'F' Company, 2nd Battalion,
Bedfordshire Regiment
Died 28 September 1916, aged 22

HE HATH DELIVERED
MY SOUL IN PEACE
FROM BATTLE

15849 Lance Corporal
Donald McGOWAN
'B' Company, 10th Battalion,
Royal Inniskilling Fusiliers
Died 1 July 1916, aged 22

BY THE CROSS
O CHRIST DRAW NEAR
THOSE WHO DIE
THAT THEY MAY HEAR

240892 Private
William STOKES
1st/5th Battalion,
Duke of Wellington's (West Riding Regiment)
Died 3 September 1916, aged 21

ALSO IN MEMORY
OF HIS BROTHER JACK, AGE 23
KILLED IN ACTION SAME DAY
THY WILL BE DONE

(Brother Jack – Private John Henry Stokes of the
same battalion – is commemorated on Thiepval
Memorial to the Missing.)

Minty Farm Cemetery

S/3773 Private
Gordon Clark ALEXANDER
1st Battalion,
The Black Watch (Royal Highlanders)
Died 28 February 1918, aged 36

HE FOUGHT A GOOD FIGHT
AND WON

Second Lieutenant
Victor Eric GRANSDEN
10th Battalion, Royal Irish Rifles
Died 26 April 1918, aged 21

VICTORY

Monchy British Cemetery

S/9498 Private
Arthur DEAN
13th Battalion, Royal Fusiliers
Died 10 or 11 April 1917, aged 20

HE FOUGHT WITH THE BRAVE
AND JOYFULLY DIED
IN FAITH OF VICTORY

S/12427 Private
Alfred Thomas FILLINGHAM
6th Battalion, Cameron Highlanders
Died 11 April 1917, aged 23

REPOSE, BELOVED
THOU WAR WEARIED SOUL

G/18889 Corporal
Charles Henry PAYNE
6th Battalion,
The Queen's Own (Royal West Kent Regiment)
Died 3 August 1917, aged 22

GONE BUT NOT FORGOTTEN
ON ENGLAND'S ROLL OF HONOUR
YOU WILL FIND
OUR DEAR BOY'S NAME

Morbecque British Cemetery

134856 Gunner
Anthony BRAZOWSKI
254th Siege Battery, Royal Garrison Artillery
Died 3 June 1918, aged 20

SPOCZYWAJ W BOGU SYNU
KOCHANY - RODZICE

(Translation from the Polish: 'Rest in God my
beloved son – parents'. Gunner Brazowski was
from an immigrant family which had settled in
London's East End.)

68267 Private
Cyril Gimblett PARAMORE
1st Battalion, Devonshire Regiment
Died 15 April 1918, aged 18

LIFE WAS ALL TO-MORROW
BUT HE DIED TO-DAY

Mory Abbey Military Cemetery

Second Lieutenant
George Frederick FARMILOE
2nd Battalion, Honourable Artillery Company
Died 26 June 1917, aged 32

ENGLAND REMEMBERS
AND IS GRATEFUL

32041 Corporal
William Wardle Colling HALL, *MM*
1st Battalion, Duke of Cornwall's Light Infantry
Died 30 August 1918, aged 29

SAD WILLOW
SPREAD YOUR GREEN LEAVES
OVER MY BELOVED ONE'S PILLOW

210848 Sergeant
David John MORGAN, *DCM*
119th Heavy Battery, Royal Garrison Artillery
Died 17 September 1918, aged 38

SO TENDER, SO GENTLE
SO KIND, SO BRAVE
SO GLAD TO GIVE
EVEN HIS LIFE

(Sergeant Morgan was a Boer War veteran.)

46347 Private
Arthur MOTTRAM
12th Battalion, Yorkshire Regiment
Died 28 January 1918, aged 26

OF MACCLESFIELD
SPLENDID YOU PASSED
THE GREAT SURRENDER MADE

(This is just one of several extracts from Sir John Arkwright's great hymn O Valiant Hearts *which adorn the headstones of British war graves.)*

Captain
Andrew Inglis WYLLIE
4th Battalion, Royal Scots Fusiliers,
attached Tank Corps
Died 2 September 1918, aged 21

HE WAS PLEASANT IN HIS LIFE
AND HE DIED IN GLORY

Mud Corner Cemetery

415 Private
Edmund GOFF
13th Company, Australian Machine Gun Corps
Died 18 July 1917, aged 27

FAME & GLORY
EASE NOT OUR ACHING HEARTS

4818 Lance Corporal
William Gordon HUNTER
51st Battalion, Australian Infantry
Died 15 July 1917, aged 24

FOR GLORIOUS LIBERTY
AND TRUTH
HE OFFERED UP
HIS STALWART YOUTH

2586 Private
Claude Goldsmith KEOGH
43rd Battalion, Australian Infantry
Died 9 June 1917, aged 22

THEY LAID HIM BY
WITH PRAYER & SIGH
THE SPOT WHERE HE WAS KILLED

Naval Trench Cemetery

TZ/235 Leading Seaman
Matthew BURDON
Royal Naval Volunteer Reserve,
Hawke Battalion, Royal Naval Division
Died 24 April 1917, aged 27

ANCHORED
ON GOD'S WIDE SHORE LINE

PO/1629(S) Private
Cyril Edgar John RUNDLE
2nd Royal Marine Battalion,
Royal Marine Light Infantry,
Royal Naval Division
Died 31 July 1917, aged 19

FOR THREE YEARS
HE WAS THE TREBLE SOLOIST
OF TRURO CATHEDRAL

Neuville-Bourjonval British Cemetery

250755 Private
Percy COURTMAN
'D' Company, 1st/6th Battalion,
Manchester Regiment
Died 2 June 1917, aged 29

INTERNATIONAL (BREAST STROKE)
RECORD CHAMPION SWIMMER

Captain
Robert William Gordon GRANT
7th Battalion, Manchester Regiment
Died 24 May 1917, aged 21

WE HAVE GAINED
A PEACE UNSHAKEN
BY PAIN FOR EVER
WAR KNOWS NO POWER

Lieutenant Colonel
George Herbert ST HILL
Royal North Devon Hussars
Died 8 July 1917, aged 52

BEND THE KNEE, BOW THE HEAD
HONOURING OUR GLORIOUS DEAD

(A career of 18 years in the Royal North Devon
Hussars included action in the Matabele, Angoni
and South African campaigns. Much later,
Lieutenant Colonel St Hill served at Gallipoli,
where he commanded the 6th Battalion of the
Lincolnshire Regiment at the evacuation of Suvla
Bay.)

New Irish Farm Cemetery

S/30442 Rifleman
Frederick HUGHES
16th Battalion, The Rifle Brigade
Died 31 July 1917, aged 19

WEEP NOT FOR ME
DEAR MUM AND DAD
FOR I WAS TO YOU
BUT LENT

260130 Private
Thomas MARSHALL
1st/5th Battalion, Seaforth Highlanders
Died 6 September 1917, aged 22

FROM SCENES LIKE THESE
OLD SCOTIA'S GRANDEUR SPRINGS
THY WILL BE DONE

Second Lieutenant
Fairlie Russell MARTIN
1st Battalion, Royal Scots Fusiliers,
attached 57th Squadron, Royal Flying Corps
Died 29 June 1917, aged 19

A BOY
HE SPENT HIS BOY'S DEAR LIFE
FOR ENGLAND
BE CONTENT

L/14154 Gunner
William Darley SMYTH
'D' Battery, 58th Brigade, Royal Field Artillery
Died 4 October 1917, aged 22

MORE SACRED THAN IN LIFE
AND LOVELIER FAR
FOR HAVING PERISHED
IN THE FRONT OF WAR

Second Lieutenant
Keith Penecuik EWART
27th Squadron, Royal Flying Corps
Died 4 January 1918, aged 24

I HOPE TO SEE MY PILOT
FACE TO FACE
WHEN I HAVE CROSSED THE BAR

(After a DH4 piloted by Second Lieutenant Ewart failed to return from a bombing mission, he was posted 'Missing'. Enquiries through intermediaries eventually drew notification from the German authorities that two burnt bodies had been found at the crash site and buried in a small village cemetery alongside a German airfield. One body had been identified as Second Lieutenant Ewart's observer, leading to the obvious conclusion that the other could only be that of Ewart himself. These two young RFC airmen lie side by side among the graves of French villagers in a sublime location beneath wide, open skies – and beside an airfield which is still in use. [See also Captain D.M.Ewart, under Faubourg-d'Amiens Cemetery.])

Nine Elms British Cemetery

24240 Corporal
Edward Ronald ASLIN
10th Battalion, Royal Fusiliers
Died 21 March 1918, aged 21

THAT HE MAY PLEASE HIM
WHO HATH CHOSEN HIM
TO BE A SOLDIER

(From II Timothy, Chapter 2, Verse 4.)

Captain
Harold HANSON
1st/4th Battalion,
Duke of Wellington's (West Riding Regiment)
Died 1 December 1917, aged 36

I KNEW MY DUTY
REALISED THE PRICE
AND PAID IT WILLINGLY

Major
Sidney John Boileau LACON
Royal Warwickshire Regiment,
attached VIII Corps Mechanical Transport,
Royal Army Service Corps
Died 12 April 1918, aged 28

BUSTER
EVER BELOVED BY
HIS WIFE AND MOTHER
FLOREAT ETONA

(The Latin tag is a school motto – 'Long live Eton' – and marks out Major Lacon as an Old Etonian.)

39420 Private
William Alexander LOGAN, *MM*
1st Battalion,
The Queen's (Royal West Surrey Regiment)
Died 10 August 1918, aged 20

WILL YE NO COME BACK AGAIN

(From Bonnie Charlie's Now Awa', by
Carolina, Lady Nairne.)

102182 Private
Henry VAN
2nd Battalion, Sherwood Foresters
(Nottinghamshire & Derbyshire Regiment)
Died 3 June 1918, aged 26

SO SAD BUT SO TRUE
WE CANNOT TELL WHY
THE BEST ARE THE FIRST
THAT ARE CALLED TO DIE

Nine Elms Military Cemetery

132792 Sergeant
Major CAHILL
166th Siege Battery, Royal Garrison Artillery
Died 13 May 1917, aged 23

I FEAR NO FOE
WITH THEE AT HAND TO BLESS

(As in the case of Lieutenant M.W.Booth [see
under Serre Road Cemetery No 1], this soldier's
Christian name would doubtless have been the cause
of some confusion and joshing among the ranks. The
epitaph is from the Henry Francis Lyte hymn
Abide With Me.*)*

440015 Private
John James GUSTHART
28th Battalion, Canadian Infantry
(Saskatchewan Regiment)
Died 20 May 1917, aged 33

HE MARCHED
IN A DEATHLESS ARMY

Noeux-les-Mines Communal Cemetery

Major
Okill Massey LEARMONTH, *VC, MC*
2nd Battalion, Canadian Infantry
(Eastern Ontario Regiment)
Died 19 August 1917, aged 23

HE COUNTED NOT
HIS LIFE DEAR UNTO HIMSELF

(Major Learmonth was the only son of parents in
Quebec. They adapted Verse 24 of Acts, *Chapter*
20, for the epitaph. While lying mortally wounded
on the battlefield, he refused to be evacuated and
continued to give instructions and advice before being
moved to a hospital, where he died. A posthumous
VC was awarded.)

31406 Private
Gwyn WILLIAMS
16th Battalion, Royal Welsh Fusiliers
Died 23 May 1916, aged 23

WITHOUT THE SHEDDING OF BLOOD
THERE IS NO REMISSION

Noreuil Australian Cemetery

Lieutenant
Wilfred Vivian Hubert Luther BIDSTRUP
50th Battalion, Australian Infantry
Died 3 April 1917, aged 27

NO LIFE IS LOST
THAT'S NOBLY SPENT
NO HERO'S DEATH IS PREMATURE
MOTHER

2618 Lance Corporal
Arthur BURCH
55th Battalion, Australian Infantry
Died 14 May 1917, aged 37

NOBLE & GRAND HE FELL
FOR BRITAIN AND HER ALLIES
GOD REST HIS SOUL

Known to be buried in this cemetery
2634/A Private
Leslie EDGAR
50th Battalion, Australian Infantry
Died 2 April 1917, aged 24

TIRED OF WAR AND FELL ASLEEP

*(The words above Private Edgar's name signify that
the exact location of the burial was lost.)*

Known to be buried in this cemetery
2683 Private
Frank Kirby KINGSLEY
50th Battalion, Australian Infantry
Died 2 April 1917, aged 23

QUARTERED BY DEATH I REMAIN
WHEN THE BUGLE CALLS
I WILL MARCH AGAIN

2046 Private
Frederick William THOMPSON
50th Battalion, Australian Infantry
Died 2 April 1917, aged 26

THE MEMORY
OF HIS LIFE AND DEEDS
IS A PERPETUAL FEAST

Norfolk Cemetery

Lieutenant
Wolfred Reeve CLOUTMAN
178th Company, Royal Engineers
Died 21 August 1915, aged 25

HE LIVES. HE WAKES
'TIS DEATH IS DEAD
NOT HE!

*(This officer rescued a sergeant by carrying him on
his shoulder 45 feet up a ladder from the bottom of
a mine, whereupon Lieutenant Cloutman, overcome
by gas, fell to the bottom and was killed.)*

Ors British Cemetery

51873 Corporal
Herbert Stanley WADE
16th Battalion, Lancashire Fusiliers
Died 2 November 1918, aged 19

DEATH CANNOT COME
TO HIM UNTIMELY
WHO IS FIT TO DIE

(A quote by H.H.Milman.)

Ors Communal Cemetery

Second Lieutenant
James KIRK, *VC*
*10th Battalion, attached 2nd Battalion,
Manchester Regiment*
Died 4 November 1918, aged 21

BORN JANUARY 27TH 1897
FATHER FORGIVE THEM
FOR THEY KNOW NOT
WHAT THEY DO

(From Luke, *Chapter 23, Verse 34. The small
British section of this French village cemetery also
contains the grave of a second VC as well as a*

celebrated poet [see the two entries which follow].
All three were killed on the same day – one week
before the Armistice. The action in which Second
Lieutenant Kirk was killed, and for which he won
his posthumous VC, was while leading his
battalion across the Oise Canal.)

Lieutenant Colonel
James Neville MARSHALL, *VC, MC & Bar*
Irish Guards,
attached 16th Battalion, Lancashire Fusiliers
Died 4 November 1918, aged 31

SPLENDID IS DEATH
WHEN THOU FALLEST
COURAGEOUS
LEADING THE ONSLAUGHT

(See Second Lieutenant J.Kirk, above. The much-
decorated Lieutenant Colonel Marshall had also
been awarded the Officier Order of Leopold,
Chevalier Order of Leopold, and the Croix de
Guerre [Belgium]. His epitaph is taken from a
translation of Viktor Rydberg's Athenian Song,
originally in Swedish. The VC was awarded
posthumously for the action in which he was killed
while supervising repairs to a bridge, to enable his
battalion to cross the Sambre-Oise Canal.)

Lieutenant
Wilfred Edward Salter OWEN, *MC*
5th Battalion, Manchester Regiment
Died 4 November 1918, aged 25

"SHALL LIFE RENEW
THESE BODIES?
OF A TRUTH
ALL DEATH WILL HE ANNUL" W.O.

(See Second Lieutenant J.Kirk, above. This extract
from Wilfred Owen's own poem The End *is cut*
short and omits the question mark, which
completely changes the meaning of the last line.
Owen was not affirming his faith, as here he
appears to do, but was questioning it. His deeply
religious mother submitted the passage as his
epitaph without the question mark. Having enlisted
in the Artists' Rifles in October 1915, Wilfred
Owen was commissioned into the Manchester
Regiment eight months later.)

Outtersteene Communal Cemetery Extension

320976 Private
Leonard Charles BUTTIFANT
12th (Norfolk Yeomanry) Battalion,
Norfolk Regiment
Died 19 August 1918, aged 22

LIKE THE FRAGRANCE OF ROSES
IS THE MEMORY
OF OUR LOVED ONE

Second Lieutenant
Robert Cooper CLEMENTS
4th Battalion, Northumberland Fusiliers
Died 7 August 1918, aged 35

I GO ON A GREAT
AND GLORIOUS MISSION

1126 Lance Corporal
Vincent Parnell CROWHURST
10th Battalion, Australian Infantry
Died 9 May 1918, aged 22

THE HERO'S NAME
SHALL NEVER DIE
BUT EVER LIVE IN GOD

31417 Private
William DEWHURST
11th Battalion, East Lancashire Regiment
Died 13 April 1918, aged 19

JUST ONE IN THOUSANDS
BUT ALL THE WORLD TO US

2266 Private
Frank STRANGER
57th Battalion, Australian Infantry
Died 22 March 1918, aged 35

GOOD OLD FRANK
AU REVOIR FROM ALL AT HOME

2831 Private
Charles Henry WOODS
3rd Battalion, Australian Infantry
Died 15 April 1918, aged 26

I AM PROUD AND ALSO SORRY
FOR MY BRAVE BABY
HIS LOVING FATHER

Ovillers Military Cemetery

Captain
John Currie LAUDER
1st/8th Battalion,
Argyll & Sutherland Highlanders
Died 28 December 1916, aged 25

EVER LOVED
NEVER FORGOTTEN
FATHER AND MOTHER

('Father' was the music-hall entertainer Sir Harry
Lauder, who, it has been said, wrote his famous
song Keep Right on to the End of the Road
after learning of his son's death in France.)

132971 Private
Norman Willard McLAREN
'C' Company, 73rd Battalion, Canadian Infantry
Died 13 November 1916, aged 20

SAFETY
WHERE NO FOE APPROACHES
PEACE
WHERE STRIFE SHALL ALL BE O'ER

494719 Sapper
William MITCHELL
3rd/1st (South Midland) Field Company,
Royal Engineers
Died 17 December 1916, aged 39

EIGHT YEARS HAVE PASSED
A MEMORY DEAR
HIS NAME WE BREATHE
AND SHED A TEAR

Captain
Gerard Prideaux SELBY
Royal Army Medical Corps,
attached 9th Battalion, Lancashire Fusiliers
Died 26 September 1916, aged 25

A GATHERED RADIANCE
A SHINING PEACE
UNDER THE NIGHT

Oxford Road Cemetery

49296 Sergeant
Colin BLYTHE
12th Battalion,
King's Own Yorkshire Light Infantry
Died 8 November 1917, aged 38

IN LOVING MEMORY OF
MY DEAR HUSBAND
THE KENT & ENGLAND CRICKETER

(The most distinguished cricketer to die in each of
the two World Wars was a slow-left-arm bowler of
conspicuously modest disposition – 'Charlie' Blythe
and Hedley Verity, respectively. Blythe, one of the
great players of cricket's Golden Age, was deeply
sensitive, musical — he played the violin – and
widely held in great affection. He was killed on a
military railway line at the end of the Battle of
Passchendaele.)

44194 Private
Harry DYE
12th Battalion,
King's Own Yorkshire Light Infantry
Died 8 November 1917, aged 27

UNITED WITH
HIS BELOVED BROTHERS
OSBORNE & FRED
WHO FELL IN 1915

(Osborne Dye fell at Gallipoli and Fred is buried
in Aubers Ridge British Cemetery in France.)

3684 Private
George EARLE
1st Battalion, Royal Newfoundland Regiment
Died 13 March 1918, aged 26

WE ARE MORE THAN CONQUERORS
THROUGH HIM THAT LOVED US
ROMANS 8.37

37874 Private
Edward LEWIS
9th Battalion, Royal Welsh Fusiliers
Died 3 October 1917, aged 25

SLEEP EDDIE, SLEEP
THY TASK IS DONE
TAKE THY REST
SO NOBLY WON

28237 Private
William John ROFFEY
1st Battalion, Border Regiment
Died 5 April 1918, aged 33

HE SHED HIS BLOOD
BUT NONE COULD SAVE HIM

Lieutenant
William WALLACE
3rd Battalion, attached 1st Battalion,
Cameron Highlanders
Died 17 November 1917, aged 20

HE WAS –
THINK OF ALL A SON SHOULD BE
AND HE WAS THAT

Passchendaele New British Cemetery

Second Lieutenant
Stanley Lorne CROWTHER
29th Squadron, Royal Flying Corps
Died 20 September 1917, aged 21

HE DIED AT HIS POST OF DUTY
A SOLDIER OF THE AIR

810581 Corporal
Oswald Harry DOBSON
'D' Battery, 232nd Brigade, Royal Field Artillery
Died 12 October 1917, aged 24

MID THE NOISE OF WAR
CAME THE VOICE OF PEACE

696341 Private
Emanuel FULTON
31st Battalion, Canadian Infantry
(Alberta Regiment)
Died 6 November 1917, aged 21

I HAVE GIVEN MY LIFE
TO PROMOTE PEACE
BETWEEN ALL NATIONS

252338 Private
George William FURNIS
42nd Battalion, Canadian Infantry
(Quebec Regiment)
Died 3 November 1917, aged 22

SON – BROTHER
MORE OF KINDNESS
WAS IN HIS TONGUE
HIS END WAS PEACE

305113 Driver
David Sinclair VANFLEET
10th Brigade, Canadian Field Artillery
Died 6 November 1917, aged 27

HERO FOR GOD
KING AND COUNTRY

Peake Wood Cemetery

Second Lieutenant
Henry Alfred Stanley CARPENTER
103rd Company, Machine Gun Corps
Died 2 September 1916, aged 22

ALL GALLANTLY HE LIVED
AND THUS HE DIED
BUT NOT IN VAIN

15617 Private
William Ewart Gladstone CROMPTON
1st Battalion, Lincolnshire Regiment
Died 3 July 1916, aged 24

NEVER GIVE UP
PEACE AFTER PAIN

(His remains having been discovered in nearby Shelter Wood in August 1999, Private Crompton, who was identified by his 'dog-tag' and regimental shoulder-title, was buried with full military honours on 20 September 2002. An unidentified soldier whose remains had been found at the same time was buried simultaneously in an adjacent plot. Private Crompton's epitaph was composed by members of his family who attended these burials, in the knowledge that his widow had not received confirmation of his presumed death until April 1917, and the fact that the burial was taking place 85 years later. The deceased's brother Bruce, of the same battalion, was killed in action on 4 March 1915 and lies in Hooge Crater Cemetery.)

Second Lieutenant
David KERR, *MC*
6th/7th Battalion, Royal Scots Fusiliers
Died 12 August 1916, aged 22

IT IS WELL WITH THE CHILD

33497 Sergeant
George PAYNE
'B' Battery, 105th Brigade, Royal Field Artillery
Died 8 October 1916, aged 30

HE SLEEPS
WITH OTHER HEROES
IN THE WATCHFUL CARE OF GOD
KIT

('Kit' was almost certainly the widowed Catherine
Payne, whose husband had been a member of
Lancashire Constabulary.)

1536 Private
William Gaulton RICHARDSON
20th Battalion, Australian Infantry
Died 5 February 1917, aged 20

"GONE WEST"
YOUR LOVED ONES
IN FAR AUSTRALIA
WILL NEVER FORGET

Lieutenant
Thomas Kerr STEVENSON
6th/7th Battalion, Royal Scots Fusiliers,
attached 45th Trench Mortar Battery
Died 28 January 1917, aged 22

HE WAS SUCH A ONE
AS EVERY FATHER
WOULD WISH HIS SON TO BE

Second Lieutenant
Robert WARNOCK, *MC*
6th/7th Battalion, Royal Scots Fusiliers
Died 12 August 1916, aged 26

HE HAS OUTSOARED
THE SHADOW OF OUR NIGHT

(The title of a work of 1st-century Latin verse by
Publius Papinium Statius.)

3766 Private
Roy BENNETT
23rd Battalion, Australian Infantry
Died 5 October 1917, aged 23

THE SWEETEST FLOWERS
ARE GATHERED FIRST
LOVING WIFE & MOTHER

26496 Private
Alfred Spencer BUTTERWORTH
1st/5th Battalion,
Duke of Wellington's (West Riding Regiment)
Died 20 November 1917, aged 19

HE GAVE ME HIS USUAL SMILE
AND A WORD OF CHEER
AS HE PASSED

3/7217 Private
Alfred CLARKE
1st Battalion, Norfolk Regiment
Died 21 April 1915, aged 20

MEMORY KEEPS HIS VISIONS
SWEET ACROSS THE SEA

28031 Rifleman
Arthur James DOUGLASS
3rd Battalion, The Rifle Brigade
Died 2 July 1917, aged 36

ARTHUR – OUR DAD
PROUDLY REVERENCED AND LOVED
THAT WE MIGHT LIVE

32398 Driver
Alfred Outtrim GARDNER
5th Brigade, Australian Field Artillery
Died 19 October 1917, aged 20

LOVE'S STRENGTH STANDETH
IN LOVE'S SACRIFICE

36393 Private
James Stewart GREIG
1st/4th Battalion,
King's Own Yorkshire Light Infantry
Died 25 April 1918, aged 19

FAR FRAE HIS NATIVE LAND
HE FELL
HAIL CALEDONIA
HE LOVED THEE WELL

2672 Private
Lewis James KNIGHT
30th Battalion, Australian Infantry
Died 4 October 1917, aged 31

BRAVE NOBLE SOLDIER HE
A BETTER HUSBAND
NEVER COULD BE

Second Lieutenant
David Logan KYLE
Royal Engineers
Died 19 May 1915, aged 23

DEAD ERE HIS PRIME?
THEY PASSED TO HIGHER LIFE

Lieutenant
Maurice LOWE
19th Squadron, Royal Flying Corps
Died 27 June 1917, aged 26

THE KING'S, "WELL DONE!"

3085 Private
Henry Franklin PATERSON
No 3 Company, 1st Battalion,
Honourable Artillery Company
Died 30 September 1915, aged 21

HE GAVE HIS LIFE
THAT ENGLAND'S SOUL
SHOULD LIVE

Second Lieutenant
John Alexander ROSS
10th Battalion, Highland Light Infantry
Died 31 August 1918, aged 24

BE IT KNOWN TO ALL
THAT I DIED HAPPY

138295 Gunner
Alan Vernon STANIFORTH
'A' Battery, 104th Brigade, Royal Field Artillery
Died 24 June 1917, aged 19

OF CARDIFF
THE PATHS OF GLORY
LEAD BUT TO THE GRAVE

Picquigny British Cemetery

29178 Private
William GASKIN
10th Battalion, Essex Regiment
Died 17 April 1918, aged 35

AGE 35
MOTHER'S LOVE & SISTER'S JOY
LIE BURIED WITH
THEIR DARLING BOY

Second Lieutenant
George Benjamin Johnstone STODDART
65th Squadron, Royal Air Force
Died 10 April 1918, aged 18

ALSO
CAVALRY MACHINE GUNNER
IN FRANCE IN 1915
AGED 15 YEARS

(This subaltern's war service began when he enlisted
in the 2nd Dragoon Guards on 1 September 1914,
aged only 15, and he served in France with that
unit as a machine-gunner until January 1916.)

Ploegsteert Wood Military Cemetery

1281 Sergeant
Frederick Parmenas BECKLEY
*'B' Company, 1st/1st Buckinghamshire Battalion,
Oxfordshire & Buckinghamshire Light Infantry
Died 24 April 1915, aged 23*

HIS LAST WORDS WERE
"I AM NOT AFRAID
I HAVE DONE MY DUTY"

Poelcapelle British Cemetery

45595 Sergeant
Lewthwaite FOSTER, *MM*
*197th Company, Machine Gun Corps (Infantry)
Died 12 October 1917, aged 38*

THE DAY THOU GAVEST LORD
IS ENDED

*(The opening line of John Ellerton's hymn of the
same name.)*

Lieutenant
James LUNAN
*4th Battalion, Gordon Highlanders
Died 20 September 1917, aged 24*

"I LEAVE MYSELF IN GOD'S HANDS"
EXTRACT FROM HIS DIARY
WRITTEN 19.9.17

41225 Corporal
John McNEILL
*11th Battalion, Royal Scots
Died 12 October 1917, aged 20*

HE OBEYED
WENT OUT NOT KNOWING
WHITHER HE WENT

(From Hebrews, *Chapter 11, Verse 8.)*

5329 Sergeant
William Gracie ROBERTSON
*48th Battalion, Australian Infantry
Died 12 October 1917, aged 32*

HE LIVES WHILE WE REMEMBER
HE DIES IF WE FORGET

Point 110 Old Military Cemetery

14650 Private
Fred THOMSON
*'C' Company, 24th Battalion,
Manchester Regiment
Died 6 February 1916, aged 19*

HERE LIES A MOTHER'S BOY
AT HEART A MAN
WHO GAVE HIS ALL
FOR US AND MOTHERLAND

Point du Jour Military Cemetery

S/6203 Private
David ARNOTT
*10th Battalion, Argyll & Sutherland Highlanders
Died 29 April 1917, aged 21*

COMRADES
LET ME SLEEP TO-NIGHT

8865 Private
Norman Frank PERKINS
*1st Regiment, South African Infantry
Died 9 April 1917, aged 19*

"GOD AND ST. GEORGE"

Pont d'Achelles Military Cemetery

208541 Gunner
Arthur Handley BENSON
'D' Battery, 311th Brigade, Royal Field Artillery
Died 30 September 1917, aged 37

HIS LIFE FOR HIS COUNTRY
HIS HEART TO HIS HOME
HIS SOUL TO GOD

12104 Private
Ralph DENVER
9th Field Ambulance,
Australian Army Medical Corps
Died 12 December 1917, aged 22

HE WAS A TRUE BORN
AUSTRAL SON
AND FOR HIS COUNTRY
NOBLY DIED

22423 Driver
William Elphick MOON
8th Brigade, Australian Field Artillery
Died 25 June 1917, aged 21

HE WAS ONE
OF A GLORIOUS COMPANY
THE FLOWER OF OUR MEN

19603 Corporal
Charles Stanley ROBINSON
8th Brigade, Australian Field Artillery
Died 15 June 1917, aged 21

A GLORIOUS LAD

---

990 Private
Henry Michael SMYTHE
38th Battalion, Australian Infantry
Died 7 June 1917, aged 23

MY DARLING BOY IN HEAVEN

Poperinghe New Military Cemetery

Lieutenant Colonel
George Harold BAKER
5th Canadian Mounted Rifles (Quebec Regiment)
Died 2 June 1916, aged 38

DEATH IS A LOW MIST
WHICH CANNOT BLOT
THE BRIGHTNESS IT MAY VEIL

(This officer was a member of the Canadian House of Commons and the son of a member of the Senate of Canada. The epitaph is from Shelley's poem, Adonais: An Elegy on the Death of John Keats.*)*

Lieutenant
Denis Oliver BARNETT
'A' Company, 2nd Battalion, Leinster Regiment
Died 16 August 1915, aged 20

CAPTAIN OF ST. PAUL'S SCHOOL
SCHOLAR-ELECT OF
BALLIOL COLLEGE, OXFORD

(Lieutenant Barnett had first gone out to the Western Front in October 1914, with the Artists' Rifles.)

14698 Private
Peter William BISSETT
1st Battalion, Canadian Machine Gun Corps
Died 14 July 1916, aged 20

AS BOYS COME TROOPING
FROM THE WAR
OUR SKY HAS MANY
A NEW GOLD STAR

Captain
James BRUCE
256th Brigade, Royal Field Artillery
Died 25 July 1917, aged 29

HE NEVER YET
NO VILEINYE NE SAYD
IN ALL HIS LYF
UNTO NO MANER WIGHT

(Taken from the Prologue *to Chaucer's* The
Canterbury Tales.*)*

7984 Sergeant
Paul Stuart DRYDEN
2nd Battalion, Scots Guards
Died 4 May 1916, aged 25

HOW CAN A MAN DIE BETTER
THAN FACING FEARFUL ODDS
FOR THE ASHES OF HIS FATHERS
AND THE TEMPLES OF HIS GOD

(An adapted extract from Macaulay's Lays of
Ancient Rome: Horatius.*)*

---

696 Sergeant
Alfred Frank EDWARDS
2nd Battalion, London Regiment (Royal Fusiliers)
Died 9 September 1915, aged 33

FREEDOM LIVES
ON EARTH TO-DAY
BECAUSE YOU DIED
REST IN PEACE

12009 Guardsman
Alexander GIBB
2nd Battalion, Scots Guards
Died 23 July 1916, aged 28

THE PAINS OF DEATH ARE PAST
HIS LIFE'S WARFARE
CLOSED AT LAST
R.I.P.

A/1387 Rifleman
Alfred Robert HALFORD
8th Battalion, King's Royal Rifle Corps
Died 5 August 1915, aged 16

HIS FATHER, MOTHER
BROTHERS, SISTERS
MOURN THEIR LOSS
THOUGH PROUD OF HIS DEED

748276 Private
Stanley Earlton Wilson HESSE
1st Battalion, Canadian Labour Corps
Died 17 August 1917, aged 19

HIS DUTY
HE HAS NOBLY DONE
THE RIGHT HE STROVE TO SAVE
BUT HONOUR CROWNS HIS GRAVE

Second Lieutenant
Charles Bateman JAGOE
16th Battalion, Royal Irish Rifles
Died 26 July 1917, aged 23

THIS DAY
THE NOISE OF BATTLE
THE NEXT
THE VICTOR'S SONG

Second Lieutenant
Philip Gustave Adolphe TAYLOR
171st Company, Royal Engineers
Died 25 July 1917, aged 30

HEREUX CEUX
QUI ONT LE COEUR PUR
CAR ILS VERRONT DIEU
ST. MATTH. V. 8.

(... 'Blessed are the pure in heart; for they shall see
God' ... This subaltern was born in Brazil and
worked as a mining engineer in Algeria, where his
parents settled.)

159

7448 Sapper
George TOLLEY
2nd Siege Company, Royal Engineers
Died 30 July 1915, aged 23

ONE NOBLE DEED
THEN THE LORD
CALLED QUICKLY

19667 Private
Philip TOOLE
13th Battalion, The King's (Liverpool Regiment)
Died 20 December 1915, aged 25

BUGLE CALLED.
I ANSWERED

Poperinghe Old Military Cemetery

7558 Private
Nicholas ALLAN
2nd Battalion, King's Own Scottish Borderers
Died 20 April 1915, aged 46

"WE WILL DRAIN
OUR DEAREST VEINS
BUT THEY SHALL BE FREE"
BURNS

Captain
Edwin Scott BAMFORD
Adjutant, 1st Battalion,
York & Lancaster Regiment
Died 23 April 1915, aged 29

HE NOW CAN NEVER MOURN
A HEART GROWN COLD
A HEAD GROWN GREY IN VAIN

10752 Guardsman
Joseph BOND
1st Battalion, Coldstream Guards
Died 21 November 1914, aged 19

WHO IN THE GLORIOUS MORNING
OF HIS DAY
FOR ENGLAND'S SAKE LOST ALL
BUT ENGLAND'S PRAISE

7717 Private
Samuel Augustus HARRIS
Royal Army Ordnance Corps
Died 23 April 1915, aged 22

I HAVE FOUGHT A GOOD FIGHT
I HAVE FINISHED MY COURSE

(From II Timothy, *Chapter 4, Verse 7.)*

Captain
Henry Neville Baskcomb
HARRISON, *MVO*
2nd Battalion, Duke of Cornwall's Light Infantry
Died 16 March 1915, aged 36

THIS IS
THE BEAUTY OF MANHOOD
TO DIE FOR A GOOD CAUSE

3740 Private
Rowland HARVEY
3rd Battalion, Royal Fusiliers
Died 15 April 1915, aged 21

HE MAKETH WARS TO CEASE
UNTO THE END OF THE EARTH

(From Psalms, *Chapter 46, Verse 9.)*

TELL ENGLAND THAT WE WHO DIED SERVING HER
REST HERE CONTENT
An epitaph with origins in Ancient Greece. The poet
Siegfried Sassoon was deeply affected by this young
officer's death.
(Capt M.H.Goodall, Puchevillers British Cemetery)

"CROWNED WITH THE SUNSHINE
OF IMMORTAL YOUTH"
The commemoration of this officer was the subject of
confusion and a remarkable coincidence.
(Capt I.P.W.Bennett, Thiepval Anglo-French Cemetery)

VOLUNTEER FROM
COLONIA COSME, PARAGUAY
Plenty of young men returned from distant parts of
the world to enlist and fight for the cause.
(Pte D.J.Macleod, Coxyde Military Cemetery)

OH! WHY ARE WE DEAD WE YOUTH?
ALL YE THAT PASS BY FORGET NOT
Epitaphs in the form of a plea to the passer-by are
sometimes as if spoken by the deceased.
(Pte F.L.Sexton, Bapaume Australian Cemetery)

ONLY ONE IN THOUSANDS
BUT ALL THE WORLD TO ME
ONE OF THE BEST
A widow's modest and simple tribute, no less moving
than anything grand and lyrical.
(Pte J.W.Kilby, Faubourg d'Amiens Cemetery)

HIS WARFARE IS ACCOMPLISHED
HIS REST SHALL BE GLORIOUS
Much use was made of biblical phrases – slightly
amended, if appropriate, to meet the circumstances.
(Lt Col H.P.Dalzell-Walton, Bronfay Farm Military
Cemetery)

RONALD BORN 5/7/92   PURE & BEAUTIFUL   GOD BE THY PORTION, BELOVED
HUGH BORN 23/4/99   NOBLE & LOVING   MAY GOD BE THY PORTION, BELOVED
Adjacent graves for two young Australian brothers whose deaths in April 1918 were
separated by only five days.
(Lt R.G.Henderson & Pte H.G.Henderson, Adelaide Cemetery)

HIS MEMORY IS AS DEAR TO-DAY
AS AT THE HOUR HE PASSED AWAY
A reminder that war-grave epitaphs were unusual in
that they were not chosen until years after the death.
(Pte D.Niddrie, Rifle House Cemetery)

ALSO TO THE MEMORY OF
HIS TWIN BROTHER RIVERSDALE
BORN 1880. SONS OF PASCOE & SOFIA GRENFELL
While in hospital following the action for which he
won the VC, Capt Grenfell learned of 'Rivy's' death.
(Capt F.O.Grenfell, Vlamertinghe Military Cemetery)

IF THIS IS VICTORY, THEN
LET GOD STOP ALL WARS   HIS LOVING MOTHER
Many's the epitaph that movingly expresses an
upbeat sentiment. Just as movingly, this one doesn't.
(Pte F.Hitchin, Grove Town Cemetery)

IT'S NOT THE LENGTH OF LIFE THAT COUNTS
BUT WHAT IS DONE IN IT
Other kinds of burial ground await the old and the
sick. War cemeteries are for the young and active.
(Pte W.Wilby, St Symphorien Military Cemetery)

STILL ON GUARD WITH JESUS MY CAPTAIN
Christianity's fondness for military metaphor is
reflected prominently throughout the war cemeteries.
(Pte F.R.Agates, Bronfay Farm Military Cemetery)

ANCHORED ON GOD'S WIDE SHORE LINE
Not only military metaphor: nautical, too - a fact not
lost on the widowed mother of this sailor who served
in the army's Royal Naval Division.
(Leading Seaman M.Burdon, Naval Trench Cemetery)

HE WAS A GENIUS BEFORE ANYTHING ELSE
AND A HERO OF THE FIRST WATER
A talented musician and composer whose work was
used in a highly appropriate way many years later.
(Sgt C.F.G.Coles, Crouy British Cemetery)

THE SEARCH HAS ENDED. I KNEW NOT WHERE
YOU LAY. REST IN PEACE DEAR FATHER
EDITH 8TH OCTOBER 1993
A daughter's satisfaction, after 76 years.
(Gnr J.W.Wolstenhulme, Hooge Crater Cemetery)

Porte de Paris Cemetery

Flight Sub-Lieutenant
William Hayhurst HOPE
No 1 Wing, Royal Naval Air Service
Died 24 November 1916, aged 23

THERE HONOUR COMES
A PILGRIM GRAY
TO BLESS THE TURF
THAT WRAPS THEIR CLAY

(From Ode Written in the Year 1746 *by*
William Collins.)

Potijze Château Grounds Cemetery

240976 Corporal
Tom Denton HEPWORTH
1st/5th Battalion,
The King's Own (Royal Lancaster Regiment)
Died 31 July 1917, aged 24

STRONGER THAN STEEL
IS THE SWORD OF THE SPIRIT

Potijze Château Lawn Cemetery

43222 Private
Christopher BRAZIL
7th Battalion, Royal Inniskilling Fusiliers
Died 16 August 1917, aged 28

PROUD OF THE FLAG
HE SWORE TO DEFEND
HE DID HIS BEST
THEN FELL

10486 Corporal
James GRAY
8th Battalion,
The King's Own (Royal Lancaster Regiment)
Died 27 September 1917, aged 26

A BETTER SON NEVER LIVED
A BRAVER SOLDIER NEVER DIED
REST IN PEACE

Potijze Château Wood Cemetery

23785 Private
Robert CRAWFORD
12th Battalion, The King's (Liverpool Regiment)
Died 17 June 1916, aged 24

A GOOD SOLDIER
OF JESUS CHRIST
2ND TIM. 2.V.3
AND OF GREAT BRITAIN

89501 Sergeant
Clarence HOGG
'C' Battery, 49th Brigade, Royal Field Artillery
Died 28 October 1915, aged 23

GOOD-BYE MOTHER
SOMEONE MUST GO AND WE WILL
ALL HAVE TO GO YET

Second Lieutenant
Leonard Cecil Tong MANLOVE
3rd Battalion, attached 2nd Battalion,
Hampshire Regiment
Died 3 August 1916, aged 28

AND THEY SHALL BRING
THE GLORY AND HONOUR
OF THE NATIONS INTO IT

(From Revelation, *Chapter 21, Verse 26.)*

13922 Private
Walter John Thomas SPERRING
2nd Battalion, Hampshire Regiment
Died 9 August 1916, aged 21

A GRIEF TOO DEEP FOR WORDS

Pozières British Cemetery

410045 Private
Allan John BURKE
38th Battalion, Canadian Infantry
Died 15 October 1916, aged 32

ALLAN MY NAME
CANADA MY NATION
OTTAWA MY BIRTHPLACE
HEAVEN MY EXPECTATION

Second Lieutenant
Harold William COTTERELL
2nd Battalion, South Lancashire Regiment
Died 30 September 1916, aged 18

AS A SACRIFICE
GLAD TO BE OFFERED
A BOY
HE DIED FOR ENGLAND

2618 Private
Archibald Henry DAVIS
7th Battalion, Australian Infantry
Died 18 August 1916, aged 23

LEAD KINDLY LIGHT
THE PRICE OF WAR

(The title of Cardinal John Henry Newman's hymn
provides the first line of the epitaph.)

304707 Rifleman
Albert Edwin DOWDESWELL
'D' Company, 5th (City of London) Battalion,
London Regiment (London Rifle Brigade)
Died 25 March 1918, aged 19

MIGHTY THY SACRIFICE

470 Corporal
George GIESLER
5th Battalion, Australian Infantry
Died 25 July 1916, aged 24

FAREWELL MY GALLANT BOY
IN HOPES OUR SOULS
WILL MEET AGAIN

240601 Corporal
Thomas Wood GOUGH
5th Battalion, Gloucestershire Regiment
Died 23 July 1916, aged 21

A FINE
AND HONOURABLE THING IT IS
TO DIE FOR HIS COUNTRY

4214 Private
Frank Rupert GRAINGER
16th Battalion, Australian Infantry
Died 30 August 1916, aged 17

ONLY A BOY, BUT A HERO

Believed to be buried in this cemetery
3747 Private
Leslie Russell HARPER
1st Battalion, Australian Infantry
Died between 22 and 25 July 1916, aged 18

NO SHOT CAN STRIKE ME
IN THE HEART
FOR THAT
I LEFT WITH YOU MOTHER

Second Lieutenant
Reginald KEMP
8th Battalion, Manchester Regiment
Died 26 August 1918, aged 23

FAR FROM THE BATTLE'S DIN
AT REST

3559 Private
Frederick Gordon KING
58th Battalion, Australian Infantry
Died 27 March 1917, aged 18

THOUGH SO YOUNG
HE DID HIS BEST

2454 Lance Corporal
Fred LAX
3rd Battalion, Australian Infantry
Died 23 July 1916, aged 25

STILL, STILL WITH THEE
SADLY MISSED
BY EDITH PETHELRIDGE

(Lance Corporal Lax's next-of-kin was his
married sister Minnie, but the name of Miss
E.Pethelridge of Sidney was given as a second
person of whom any further enquiries could be made,
and clearly she it was who provided the epitaph.)

437650 Private
Robert Ernest LEGGE
14th Battalion, Canadian Infantry
(Quebec Regiment)
Died 7 September 1916, aged 23

DEAR THE LAND
THAT GAVE HIM BIRTH
BUT DEARER STILL
BROTHERHOOD

(The land that gave him birth was Canada –
Private Legge was born in Manitoba – but his
parents subsequently returned to England and a
home in Warrington.)

3258 Private
Theodore Bertrude Squire RICHARDSON
27th Battalion, Australian Infantry
Died 5 August 1916, aged 27

HIS BATTLE'S DONE
HIS STRIFE IS ENDED
HIS SOUL IS SAFE
HIS LIFE AMENDED

STK/1116 Lance Corporal
Robert Vernon SMITH
'D' Company, 10th Battalion, Royal Fusiliers
Died 15 July 1916, aged 24

HE GAVE HIS BOY'S DEAR LIFE
FOR ENGLAND
BE CONTENT

A SOLDIER
OF THE GREAT WAR

Prowse Point Military Cemetery

98563 Corporal
Wilfred John BEER
31st Battalion, Machine Gun Corps (Infantry)
Died 28 September 1918, aged 23

OH YET WE TRUST
THAT SOMEHOW GOOD
WILL BE
THE FINAL GOAL OF ILL

11587 Private
James Joseph MOORE
2nd Battalion, Royal Dublin Fusiliers
Died 2 March 1915, aged 21

ELDEST SON OF JAMES
AND HANNAH MOORE
WHO MOANS HIS LOSS
TALBOT STREET, DUBLIN

Puchevillers British Cemetery

2158 Private
Wilfred BARNETT
22nd Battalion, Australian Infantry
Died 16 August 1916, aged 24

SLEEP LAD, SLEEP
THY WORK IS WELL DONE

Second Lieutenant
Edward Lionel Austin BUTLER
12th Battalion, Australian Infantry
Died 23 August 1916, aged 33

IT IS AS A SOLDIER
HE WILL STAND BEFORE
THE GREAT WHITE THRONE

TZ/6356 Able Seaman
Frank CAIN
Royal Naval Volunteer Reserve,
Drake Battalion, Royal Naval Division
Died 16 November 1916, aged 24

BUT IF YOU ONLY KNEW
THE WHOLE GREAT BRITISH ARMY
WAS MADE FROM STUFF LIKE YOU

55342 Private
Edward FELLOWS
14th Battalion, Royal Welsh Fusiliers
Died 27 August 1918, aged 31

WE KISSED HIS CHEEK
BUT LITTLE THOUGHT
IT WAS OUR LAST GOODBYE

Captain
Marcus Herbert GOODALL
1st/5th Battalion, York & Lancaster Regiment
Died 14 July 1916, aged 21

TELL ENGLAND
THAT WE WHO DIED
SERVING HER
REST HERE CONTENT

*(This epitaph, adapted to the circumstances of
1914-18, has its origins in Ancient Greece. [See
also Lieutenant G.M.Cartmel, Millencourt
Communal Cemetery Extension.] While leading a
patrol "to assess the strength of the Bosch line",
Captain Goodall received wounds from which he
died eleven days later. He was a friend of fellow-
Marlburian Siegfried Sassoon, and the news of his
death affected the poet deeply at a time when he was
ill in hospital. The result was an unpublished poem
– Elegy: For Marcus Goodall, who also is
thinly disguised as 'Allgood' in Sassoon's
Memoirs of An Infantry Officer.)*

420733 Private
William Douglas HEATLEY
43rd Battalion, Canadian Infantry
(Manitoba Regiment)
Died 23 September 1916, aged 23

A HERO
WRITE UPON HIS GRAVE
HE DIED THAT
BRITAIN MIGHT ENDURE

16279 Private
John Wight KING
'B' Company, 4th Battalion,
Highland Light Infantry
Died 1 July 1916, aged 25

JUNE 30TH 1916
"TO-MORROW WE GO
ON TO VICTORY"
JULY 1ST SOMME BATTLE

452476 Sergeant
William McEWAN
2nd Battalion, Canadian Infantry
(Eastern Ontario Regiment)
Died 15 September 1916, aged 27

NO LONGER DOES
THE HELMET PRESS THY BROW
OFT WEARY WITH ITS
SURGING THOUGHTS OF BATTLE.

(This is an extract from a eulogy spoken by the
Reverend A.G.Brown at the graveside of Charles
Spurgeon, a popular 19th-century Baptist preacher.)

5229 Private
Lewis Norman SHEPHERD
52nd Battalion, Australian Infantry
Died 8 August 1916, aged 23

OUR LAD
RUDDY OF HAIR
AND STRONG OF LIMB

2952 Trooper
Alfred Edward SMOUT
'C' Squadron, 2nd Life Guards
Died 12 July 1916, aged 18

PEACE WE DO ENJOY
BECAUSE THIS BOY
DID GIVE HIS LIFE
FOR YOU AND I.

CZ/4992 Able Seaman
William STEVENSON
Royal Naval Volunteer Reserve,
Howe Battalion, Royal Naval Division
Died 19 November 1916, aged 22

ONE OF GRANGEMOUTH'S
UNRETURNING BRAVE
DIED FOR SCOTLAND

2933 Lance Corporal
Lancelot Wesley WALKER
13th Battalion, Australian Infantry
Died 2 September 1916, aged 35

AND FROM THE GROUND
THERE BLOSSOMS RED
LIFE THAT SHALL ENDLESS BE

(From George Matheson's hymn O Love That
Wilt Not Let Me Go.*)*

114087 Private
William Thomas WEEKS
5th Canadian Mounted Rifles (Quebec Regiment)
Died 17 September 1916, aged 23

HIS LIFE WAS BUT A VAPOUR
SOON IT VANISHED AWAY

(Adapted from James, Chapter 4, Verse 14.*)*

2946 Private
William John WILSON
48th Battalion, Australian Infantry
Died 8 August 1916, aged 31

"SWEET IT IS TO HAVE DONE THE
THING ONE OUGHT"
TENNYSON

Quatre-Vents Military Cemetery

424500 Private
Wesley John BELL
'D' Company, 5th Battalion, Canadian Infantry
(Saskatchewan Regiment)
Died 9 April 1917, aged 23

WE WILL KEEP FAITH
WITH HIM WHO SLEEPS
IN FLANDERS' FIELDS

(For this tribute their son, Alfred and Amelia Bell
of Minnedosa, Manitoba, adapted the closing
sentiments of fellow-Canadian John McCrae's
celebrated poem In Flanders Fields.*)*

Quéant Communal Cemetery British Extension

Lieutenant
Leslie Willoughby FRANKLIN
10th Battery, 147th Brigade, Royal Field Artillery
Died 16 October 1918, aged 20

SO YOUNG, SO DEAR
HE LEFT US BUT THE FLOWERS
OF MEMORY

Lieutenant
Samuel Lewis HONEY, *VC, DCM, MM*
78th Battalion, Canadian Infantry
(Manitoba Regiment)
Died 30 September 1918, aged 24

DEAR LEW
THE THINGS
WHICH ARE NOT SEEN
ARE ETERNAL

(The action for which Lieutenant Honey won his
VC included locating and rushing an enemy
machine-gun nest, and single-handedly capturing the
guns and ten prisoners.)

1087292 Sergeant
Eric Mackay SULLIVAN, *MM*
21st Battalion, Canadian Infantry
(Eastern Ontario Regiment)
Died 12 October 1918, aged 39

O VALIANT HEART
TAKE COMFORT WHERE YOU LIE
HOW SWEET TO LIVE
MAGNIFICENT TO DIE

Quéant Road Cemetery

462 Private
Alfred Adolphus BRENNAN
22nd Company, Australian Machine Gun Corps
Died 25 April 1917, aged 36

HE BRAVELY DEFENDED
THOSE HE HELD DEAR
& PRINCIPLES
HE CONSIDERED SACRED

3776 Private
George Walter BUCKRIDGE
17th Battalion, Australian Infantry
Died 15 April 1917, aged 21

HE SERVED
THAT WE MIGHT SAFELY STAY
AND DYING WAS HIS FEE

---

402 Private
Charles Thomas GREEN
21st Company, Australian Machine Gun Corps
Died 26 April 1917, aged 22

WE LONGED
FOR HIS SAFE RETURN
SOMETIME WE'LL MEET AGAIN

Major
Benjamin Bennett LEANE
48th Battalion, Australian Infantry
Died 10 April 1917, aged 27

HE DIED
FOR THE GREATEST CAUSE
IN HISTORY
EVER REMEMBERED

(Major Bennett was a recipient of Serbia's Order of
the White Eagle.)

Lieutenant
Harry William Francis PONTER
4th Battalion,
The Queen's (Royal West Surrey Regiment)
Died 3 September 1918, aged 29

"THEY NEVER FAIL
WHO DIE IN A GREAT CAUSE"
BYRON
MY DEAR, MY BETTER HALF

Angus Oswald PATERSON,
served as
5396 Private
William Charles RICHARDS
18th Battalion, Australian Infantry
Died 20 April 1917, aged 22

THY WORK IS DONE
THOU'ST LAID
THINE ARMOUR DOWN

6306 Private
James SAVAGE
1st Battalion, Australian Infantry
Died between 5 and 8 May 1917, aged 45

FAR FROM THE LAND
OF SUN & WATTLE
HE SLEEPS IN A HERO'S GRAVE

Lieutenant
Herbert Keith SOWELL
18th Battalion, Australian Infantry
Died 3 May 1917, aged 23

HE SERVED

Queens Cemetery, Puisieux

6933 Sergeant
Arthur ABBOTT
2nd Battalion, Suffolk Regiment
Died 13 November 1916, aged 31

DEFEND THE RIGHT
PUT UP THE SWORD
AND THROUGH THE WORLD
MAKE PEACE

Querrieu British Cemetery

624 Bombardier
Eric James RICHARDSON
3rd Brigade, Australian Field Artillery
Died 19 July 1918, aged 25

THE PARENT MOURNS
THE PATRIOT IS PROUD

(In a cemetery not far away lies his elder brother,
Corporal F.W.L.Richardson, who died less than
three months earlier. They have identical epitaphs.)

Railway Château Cemetery

Second Lieutenant
George Frederick COTTRELL
108th Heavy Battery, Royal Garrison Artillery
Died 11 May 1915, aged 22

HIGHEST SACRIFICE
LABOUR WITHOUT PAUSE
EVEN TO DEATH
FOR ENGLAND

Railway Dugouts Burial Ground

Believed to be buried in this cemetery
46298 Private
Bruce Malcolm CAMERON
16th Battalion, Canadian Infantry
(Manitoba Regiment)
Died 13 June 1916, aged 20

READY! AYE READY

(Private Cameron's enlistment in August 1914 testified to his readiness. He survived being wounded in October 1915, but met his death eight months later.)

274 Private
Archibald Charles DIXON
43rd Battalion, Australian Infantry
Died 4 October 1917, aged 20

ARCHIE'S MOTTO
& FAVOURITE HYMN
"FIGHT THE GOOD FIGHT"

140059 Private
Cecil Edgar DODGSON
3rd Battalion, Canadian Infantry
(Central Ontario Regiment)
Died 9 July 1916, aged 18

FREEDOM AND HONOUR
CALLED HIM
NOBLY HE MADE REPLY
FOR RIGHT AND TRUTH
AND JUSTICE
BRAVELY HE WENT TO DIE

(The headstone bears no Christian cross, perhaps because there was insufficient room left by an epitaph which extends some way beyond the stipulated maximum length.)

Second Lieutenant
Leonard EWBANK
5th Battalion, Border Regiment
Died 23 February 1916, aged 23

AN ENGLISHMAN
BRAVE, HONEST, LOYAL

434118 Sergeant
Magnus Henry GILBERTSON
49th Battalion, Canadian Infantry
(Alberta Regiment)
Died 10 August 1916, aged 26

MAC'S TOTEM

581 Sapper
Kenneth George HAMILTON
1st Company, Australian Tunnelling Corps
Died 26 April 1917, aged 21

OUR LITTLE HERO, KEN.
DEARLY LOVED
AND SADLY MISSED

6/1893 Private
John Longrigg HORNER
6th Battalion, Northumberland Fusiliers
Died 2 March 1916, aged 19

MOTHER
COULD I DIE A NOBLER DEATH

44054 Gunner
Briggs MAYERS
130th Battery, Royal Field Artillery
Died 25 September 1915, aged 28

MAY OUR DEATH
FOR CIVILISATION
BE NOT IN VAIN

(Gunner Mayers had returned from Cuba in October 1914 to join his brigade.)

444652 Private
Vernon Keith MERCHANT
58th Battalion, Canadian Infantry
(Central Ontario Regiment)
Died 6 June 1916, aged 16

THE ONLY CHILD
OF AGED PARENTS

(A Canadian immigrant who was born in
Colchester, Essex, this young soldier falsely stated
his date of birth to have been 4 December 1897 in
order to enlist in April 1915. He was actually only
15 years old, and was dead long before his 17th
birthday. William and Annie Merchant were 64
and 50, respectively, when their son died – not
young, certainly, but hardly "aged".)

758 Private
Frederick MILLER
18th Battalion, Australian Infantry
Died 5 October 1917, aged 22

TRANSPLANTED
HUMAN WORTH WILL BLOOM
TO PROFIT OTHERWHERE

(From Tennyson's poem In Memoriam.*)*

Captain
Hugh Rivers Hamilton O'BRIEN
112th Battery, attached 19th Anti-Aircraft Battery,
Royal Field Artillery
Died 1 June 1916, aged 25

LOOKING AFTER HIS MEN.
R.I.P.

Lieutenant
John Rookhurst PLATT
3rd (Northumbrian) Brigade,
Royal Field Artillery
Died 26 March 1916, aged 25

IN THE SECURITY OF DUTY DONE

397 Sapper
James THOMPSON
1st Company, Australian Tunnelling Corps
Died 1 March 1917, aged 29

UNPAID DUTY
IS PAID BEST OF ALL

Railway Hollow Cemetery

12/929 Private
Alfred GOODLAD
12th Battalion, York & Lancaster Regiment
Died 1 July 1916, aged 23

"THE FRENCH ARE
A GRAND NATION
WORTH FIGHTING FOR"
VIDE ALF'S LETTER 22.3.16

Ration Farm Military Cemetery

1641 Rifleman
Harold Henry SAXTON
1st/16th Battalion, London Regiment
(Queen's Westminster Rifles)
Died 10 December 1914, aged 19

HE LIVED PURELY
SPOKE TRULY
AND DIED BRAVELY

523 Private
Michael Noble SMITH
53rd Battalion, Australian Infantry
Died 19 July 1916, aged 24

THESE DEEDS
WHICH SHOULD NOT PASS AWAY
NAMES THAT MUST NOT WITHER

30885 Private
Samuel TURTLE
15th Battalion, Royal Scots
Died 15 October 1916, aged 19

SO – A CROWN OF WILD OLIVES

Redan Ridge Cemetery No 2

5334 Private
Tom TAYLOR
1st Battalion, Lancashire Fusiliers
Died 1 July 1916, aged 36

MY TASK ACCOMPLISHED
THE SUNDOWN
SPLENDID AND SERENE
DEATH

Red Farm Military Cemetery

44325 Gunner
John Joseph DYAS
'V' 8th Heavy Trench Mortar Battery,
Royal Garrison Artillery
Died 27 April 1918, aged 28

FOR COUNTRY
AND HIS CHILDREN

Reninghelst New Military Cemetery

294 Driver
Walter George BIRKETT
2nd Divisional Ammunition Column,
Canadian Field Artillery
Died 25 August 1916, aged 25

YET HE IS HERE
WITH US TODAY
A THOUSAND THINGS
HIS TOUCH REVEAL

1030 Corporal
Hylton Lance CAMPBELL
5th Battery, Australian Field Artillery
Died 16 August 1917, aged 23

OUR DEAR BOY
HE DIED
WE LIVE IN FREEDOM
TO SERVE GOD

Second Lieutenant
Eckley Oxtoby ETHEREDGE
149th Brigade, Royal Field Artillery
Died 12 July 1917, aged 19

"EITHER EDGE"
OF MY SWORD
FOR ENGLAND

(An inherited fondness for exotic Christian names
and the use of a pun in the epitaph indicate a
quirky relish for language on the part of this
officer's father, Augustus Eglinton Etheredge.)

Lieutenant
Charles Richard Magrath GODWIN
1st Brigade, Canadian Field Artillery
Died 4 April 1916, aged 24

"UNTIL HIS COMING AGAIN"
HIS BROTHER JOHN
BURIED PLOT 1 – ROW E – GRAVE 14

(Only a few weeks separated their deaths, and only
a few yards separate their graves. Lieutenant
J.L.Godwin's headstone bears a corresponding
epitaph indicating his brother's grave reference.)

1943 Private
Frederick LAST
27th Battalion, Australian Infantry
Died 30 September 1917, aged 34

SLEEP ON
OH GALLANT HEART
YE BRAVELY PLAYED
YOUR LOYAL PART

Captain
William Raymond PASTEUR, *MC*
'D' Battery, 102nd Brigade, Royal Field Artillery
Died 10 July 1917, aged 21

HE LEAVES
A WHITE UNBROKEN GLORY
A SHINING PEACE
UNDER THE NIGHT

(From Rupert Brooke's poem 1914 IV: The
Dead.*)*

21609 Private
Arthur ROWE
10th Battalion, Sherwood Foresters
(Nottinghamshire & Derbyshire Regiment)
Died 24 February 1916, aged 24

LOVELY AND PLEASANT
IN THEIR LIVES
IN DEATH NOT DIVIDED

49835 Private
Charles TREWIN
20th Battalion, Durham Light Infantry
Died 20 August 1918, aged 21

PEACEFUL BE
THY REST DEAR CHARLIE
'TIS SWEET
TO BREATHE THY NAME

Ribemont Communal Cemetery Extension

4186 Private
William John DUNN
51st Battalion, Australian Infantry
Died 5 April 1918, aged 21

ON THE RED FIELD OF BATTLE
YOU ARE LAID FAR AWAY

---

63 Private
Ernest Trafalgar FARRIS
28th Battalion, Australian Infantry
Died 19 May 1918, aged 20

THE DEDICATION OF A MAN'S LIFE
AND MIND TO A CAUSE
THERE'S HEROISM

84435 Sapper
John GOODMAN
203rd Field Company, Royal Engineers
Died 26 March 1918, aged 25

UNKNOWN TO THE WORLD
HE STANDS BY OUR SIDE
AND WHISPERS, DEAR MOTHER
DEATH CANNOT DIVIDE

67440 Driver
Thomas Grant HAMILTON
72nd Battery, Royal Field Artillery
Died 3 October 1916, aged 22

YE BABBLING WINDS
THROUGH SILENCE SWEEP
DISTURB YE NOT
OUR LOVED ONE'S SLEEP

(Driver Hamilton was executed for striking a
senior officer. His epitaph is adapted from Ode for
General Washington's Birthday *by Robert*
Burns.)

2498 Private
Charles Herbert HOWELL
23rd Battalion, Australian Infantry
Died 23 April 1918, aged 23

HIS LIFE'S SHORT JOURNEY O'ER
GIVEN FOR FREEDOM AND HOME
GRAN'S BOY

Lieutenant
Reginald Valentine MANFORD
59th Battery, 18th Army Brigade,
Royal Field Artillery
Died 8 August 1918, aged 26

TILL THE BARRAGE LIFTS

KNOWN UNTO GOD

Rifle House Cemetery

40256 Sapper
Henry Clarence DEXTER
64th Field Company, Royal Engineers
Died 15 May 1916, aged 25

ASLEEP
IN THE GARDEN OF THE BRAVE

8468 Private
Duncan NIDDRIE
10th Battalion, Argyll & Sutherland Highlanders
Died 26 March 1916, aged 25

HIS MEMORY IS AS DEAR TO-DAY
AS AT THE HOUR HE PASSED
AWAY

(This epitaph serves as a reminder that the Imperial
War Graves Commission's task of erecting
headstones began only after the war, and that the
personal inscriptions were not chosen by the families
until years after the death.)

68 Rifleman
Edward John WARD
'H' Company, 5th Battalion, London Regiment
(London Rifle Brigade)
Died 8 December 1914, aged 23

PARDON & PEACE

Roclincourt Military Cemetery

Captain
Ernest Stewart HERON
1st/5th Battalion, Cheshire Regiment
Died 28 March 1918, aged 30

ENGLAND HE LOVED
AND LOVING, GAVE HIS BEST

Lieutenant
Percival George Havelock HUNT
92nd Trench Mortar Battery,
Royal Field Artillery,
attached 9th Battalion, East Yorkshire Regiment
Died 8 November 1917, aged 26

HE WHO EVER ACTS
AS CONSCIENCE CRIES
SHALL LIVE, THOUGH DEAD

(From Pupil and Tutor, *a poem by Eliakim*
Littell.)

204684 Private
William Sidney MARSHALL
2nd Battalion, London Regiment (Royal Fusiliers)
Died 22 December 1917, aged 31

BROWN EARTH ABOVE
LIE LIGHT, LIE LIGHT
SWEET SOUL, GOODNIGHT

95961 Sapper
Giraldus PRICE
184th Tunnelling Company, Royal Engineers
Died 22 June 1916, aged 26

IN LOVING MEMORY
OF MY DEAR HUSBAND
AND OUR DEAR DAD
FROM HIS TWO LITTLE SONS

Roclincourt Valley Cemetery

Major
Philip Gerald BAILEY
36th Brigade, Royal Field Artillery
Died 26 April 1917, aged 31

THESE LAID THE WORLD AWAY
POURED OUT
THE RED SWEET WINE OF YOUTH

(From Rupert Brooke's poem The Dead.*)*

4957 Private
Arthur William STEPHENS
3rd Regiment, South African Infantry
Died 9 April 1917, aged 37

I FOUGHT MY BATTLE
WIFE AND CHILD DEAR
I AM NOT DEAD
BUT SLEEPING HERE

275751 Private
Matthew STEVENSON
1st/7th Battalion,
Argyll & Sutherland Highlanders
Died 9 April 1917, aged 23

THE DEEP THINGS OF GOD

Rocquigny-Équancourt Road British Cemetery

Lieutenant
Edward William HORNER
18th (Queen Mary's Own) Hussars,
Died 21 November 1917, aged 28

SMALL TIME, BUT IN THAT
SMALL MOST GREATLY LIVED
THIS STAR OF ENGLAND

*(Lieutenant Horner, who had been severely
wounded before eventually rejoining his unit in*

*1916, was a brother-in-law of the Prime Minister's
son, Raymond Asquith, whose headstone in
Guillemont Road Cemetery bears the same epitaph.
It is taken from Shakespeare's* Henry V, *Act 5,
Scene 2.)*

Roisel Communal Cemetery Extension

Lieutenant Colonel
Bernard Hedley CHARLTON, *MC*
4th Battalion, Yorkshire Regiment
Died 22 March 1918, aged 32

IT IS NOT CHAOS AND DEATH
IT IS ETERNAL LIFE

5357 Private
William DONOHUE
55th Battalion, Australian Infantry
Died 30 September 1918, aged 30

FOR FREEDOM WE ARE TOLD
LIES HERE A WARRIOR BOLD

2376 Corporal
Percy Bertram HARRISON
1st Battalion, Australian Machine Gun Corps
Died 18 September 1918, aged 27

HE WAS A MAN
AND A MAN'S DEATH DIED HE
FOR WHOM?
FOR YOU AND ME

Lieutenant
Gilbert Gordon HOWARD
6th Battalion, Gloucestershire Regiment
Died 29 October 1918, aged 21

A GENTLEMAN – UNAFRAID

Rookery British Cemetery

Second Lieutenant
Henry James WARNER
6th Battalion, Northamptonshire Regiment
Died 3 June 1917, aged 31

TIME FLIES AND SORROW DIMS
MEMORY REMAINS

Royal Irish Rifles Graveyard

Captain
Wyndham HALSWELL
1st Battalion, Highland Light Infantry
Died 31 March 1915, aged 32

"WYNDHAM"

(Wyndham Halswell won the Olympic 400 metres
gold medal in 1908 in a controversial re-run which
was the only walkover in the history of the Games,
and was a record-holder over 220 yards, 300 yards
and the quarter-mile. He was killed by a sniper's
bullet at Neuve Chapelle.)

Lieutenant
Thomas Edward Geoffrey
LEIGH PEMBERTON
13th (Kensington) Battalion, London Regiment
Died 11 January 1915, aged 21

NONE DIE UNTIMELY
WHO FOR ENGLAND DIE

Rue-du-Bacquerot Military Cemetery No 1

12286 Private
Thomas Langford ROBERTS
'B' Company, 6th Battalion,
King's Shropshire Light Infantry
Died 9 October 1915, aged 23

THE BRAVEST
ARE THE TENDEREST
THE LOVING ARE THE DARING

Rue Pétillon Military Cemetery

631 Private
Victor Alexander CAMPS
30th Battalion, Australian Infantry
Died 20 July 1916, aged 26

HE HEARD THE CALL
HE GAVE IT HEED
AND NOW HE SLEEPS IN FLANDERS

2188 Private
Alfred Edward WILLIAMS
30th Battalion, Australian Infantry
Died 20 July 1916, aged 27

HIS NAME SHALL BE REMEMBERED
TILL THE DREAM OF EARTH
SHALL CLOSE

Sailly-Labourse Communal Cemetery

Second Lieutenant
The Honourable Yvo Alan CHARTERIS
1st Battalion (Special Reserve), Grenadier Guards
Died 17 October 1915, aged 19

THEY CARRY BACK BRIGHT
TO THE COINER
THE MINTAGE OF MAN

(From A.E.Housman's poem A Shropshire
Lad. *The verse continues: 'The lads that will die in*
their glory and never be old'. Lord Elcho, elder
brother of the above and heir to the earldom of
Wemyss, also lost his life six months later, but in a
different theatre of war. He has no known grave
and is commemorated on the Jerusalem Memorial to
the Missing, Israel.)

Sailly-sur-la-Lys Canadian Cemetery

2763 Private
Frederick William CARTMAN
1st/6th Battalion,
Duke of Wellington's (West Riding Regiment)
Died 5 June 1915, aged 26

HE HAS GONE
FROM SHADES & FENCES
TO THE TRUTH

4868 Private
Bernard TURNER
3rd Battalion, East Lancashire Regiment
Died 9 May 1915, aged 20

HE SLEEPS WITH
THE GREAT GRAND ARMY OF
ENGLAND'S GLORIOUS DEAD

Sanctuary Wood Cemetery

5894 Private
Aubrey Rupert BLOOMER
10th (Prince of Wales's Own Royal) Hussars
Died 4 June 1915, aged 20

WE SHALL NEVER FORGET
MUD, STAN AND RED

22783 Lance Corporal
William ELLIOTT
47th Company, Machine Gun Corps (Infantry)
Died 16 August 1917, aged 21

HE SLEEPS IN DEATH
FAR, FAR FROM HOME
HE OWNS A SOLDIER'S GRAVE
R.I.P.

57174 Private
Leonard HOMER
12th Battalion, North Staffordshire Regiment
Died 11 September 1918, aged 23

MOTHER I AM HAPPY
THOUGH 'TWAS HARD TO PART
STILL MY SPIRIT LINGERS
NEAR THY ACHING HEART

William CRAIGIE
served as
42764 Driver
Walter WARREN
3rd Brigade, Canadian Field Artillery
Died 30 April 1915, aged 29

HONOUR IS THEIRS
WHO FOR THEIR COUNTRY DIED
BUT FOR US
THE GLORIOUS EXAMPLE

Sandpits British Cemetery

S/18749 Private
George KILPIN
1st Battalion, Gordon Highlanders
Died 2 August 1918, aged 32

ONE OF THE FIRST 100,000
"THE CONTEMPTIBLES"
WHILE ENGLAND HAS SUCH SONS
SHE NEED FEAR NAUGHT

(As his epitaph proclaims, Private Kilpin was a regular soldier, having previously served in the 12th Lancers and the Royal Garrison Artillery, and served in the campaigns in Tibet [1903-04] and on the North-West Frontier of India.)

21156 Lance Corporal
James KINNISH
13th Battalion, The King's (Liverpool Regiment)
Died 18 June 1918, aged 33

A MANX VOLUNTEER OF 1914
WHO GAVE HIS LIFE
FOR KING AND EMPIRE

(Lance Corporal Kinnish was one of four brothers
who enlisted in 1914.)

38598 Private
Cecil MITCHELL
7th Battalion, King's Shropshire Light Infantry
Died 27 July 1918, aged 18

FORGET NOT THOSE
WHOSE HEARTS STILL STRIVE
AND ACHE
FOR HONOUR'S SAKE

Serre Road Cemetery No 1

2355 Corporal
Harry James BENWELL
8th Battalion, Royal Warwickshire Regiment
Died 1 July 1916, aged 26

HIS CHILD RISETH UP
AND CALLETH HIM
HIS WIFE ALSO PRAISETH HIM

Lieutenant
Major William BOOTH
15th Battalion,
West Yorkshire Regiment (Prince of Wales's Own)
Died 1 July 1916, aged 29

IN PROUD AND LOVING MEMORY
OF OUR DEAR BROTHER

(Major by name, lieutenant by rank, this
Yorkshire and England cricketer fell on the first
day of the Battle of the Somme. [An England

footballer serving in the same battalion, Lieutenant
E.H.Lintott, was killed the same day.] Reluctant
to accept the reality of Lieutenant Booth's death, his
sister kept a room for him in her cottage at Pudsey
for nearly 50 years.)

15145 Private
Charles DAWKINS
14th Battalion, Hampshire Regiment
Died 3 September 1916, aged 24

THE LAND OF GLORY
LIES ON HIGH
THERE ARE NO FIELDS
OF BATTLE THERE

K/24 Private
Paul Jean DESTRUBÉ
and
1236 Lance Corporal
Charles Guy DESTRUBÉ
both 22nd Battalion, Royal Fusiliers
both Died 17 February 1917,
aged 26 and 27 respectively

UNIS DANS LA MORT
COMME ILS L'ÉTAIENT
DANS LA VIE

(Brothers in a shared grave. The epitaph translates
from the French as "United in death as they were in
life", although "vie" is incorrectly inscribed as
"wie". These were two of three French-Canadian
brothers described in an officer's diary as "the most
delightfully independent mad folk you ever saw ….
always deserting when we were in England". The
third sibling was wounded earlier in the war and
returned to Canada. The others were then told that
one of them had to become a lance corporal, and the
one who lost the toss took the stripe. They were
killed near Miraumont and the bodies were found
in each other's arms.)

419 Private
Gavin Park HAMILTON
15th Battalion,
West Yorkshire Regiment (Prince of Wales's Own)
Died 1 July 1916, aged 27

BORN AT LEEDS, YORKS
SCOTCH PARENTAGE
FINE LAD BELOVED BY ALL

Serre Road Cemetery No 2

267 Private
James ARBON
51st Battalion, Australian Infantry
Died between 14 and 16 August 1916, aged 31

YOU DIED FIGHTING
FOR THE HONOUR
OF BRITAIN'S GLORIOUS NAME
MY SON

2807/B Private
Daniel Colombus THOMAS
10th Battalion, Australian Infantry
Died 20 August 1916, aged 32

HE CAREFULLY DID HIS DUTY
WHAT MORE COULD
OUR DEAR FATHER DO

Solferino Farm Cemetery

Lieutenant
Derek Edward Lewis Venn BAUMER
32nd Brigade, Royal Field Artillery
Died 21 October 1917, aged 20

DEATH OPENS UNKNOWN DOORS
IT IS MOST GRAND TO DIE

(From The Tragedy of Pompey the Great, *a*
play by John Masefield.)

682 Guardsman
Ebenezer James LEWIS
1st Battalion, Welsh Guards
Died 12 October 1917, aged 22

LOVE THAT HATH US IN THE NET
CAN HE PASS AND WE FORGET?
DEAR WIFE

200760 Private
John Edward SCHOLES
2nd/5th Battalion, Lancashire Fusiliers
Died 10 October 1917, aged 25

WORTHY THE NAME
OF AN ENGLISHMAN

Spoilbank Cemetery

5702 Private
Walter Leonard GREGORY
1st Battalion, Australian Infantry
Died 11 March 1918, aged 23

LOST IN FRANCE
OUR TREASURED LOVE
NOW HE WAITS US SAFE ABOVE
R I P

(Lost, certainly, but in Belgium, not France.)

7637 Gunner
David Bishop Mary McENIRY
61st Trench Mortar Battery,
Royal Garrison Artillery
Died 1 March 1916, aged 33

JESUS MERCY MARY HELP
PRIDE OF HIS PARENTS
PULSE OF THEIR HEARTS

St Acheul French National Cemetery

Second Lieutenant
Evelyn Walter Copland PERRY
No 3 Squadron, Royal Flying Corps
Died 16 August 1914, aged 23

FIRST ON THE ROLL OF HONOUR
ALL GLORY TO HIS NAME

(This RFC pilot was the first British officer to be
killed on active service in France in the Great War.
Airman 2nd Class H.E.Parfitt, who is buried in
the adjacent grave, perished with him when their
aircraft crashed at Amiens.)

1050 Lance Corporal
Evan RICHARDS
'A' Company, 2nd Battalion, Welsh Regiment
Died 11 December 1914, aged 23

THE GREAT WAR
FOR THE WORLD'S FREEDOM
HE GAVE HIS LIFE
FOR AN EARLY GRAVE

Ste Catherine British Cemetery

832033 Private
Earl Orington MacKINNON
10th Battalion, Canadian Infantry
(Alberta Regiment)
Died 9 April 1917, aged 19

SPIRIT IN HEAVEN
BODY IN FRANCE
MEMORY IN CANADA

S/40367 Private
Allan RINTOUL
9th Battalion,
The Black Watch (Royal Highlanders)
Died 9 April 1917, aged 20

THE GREATEST HERO IN THE STRIFE
FOR FREEDOM CAN BUT GIVE HIS LIFE

St Nicolas British Cemetery

335725 Private
Robert BINNIE
1st/8th Battalion, Royal Scots
Died 19 May 1917, aged 20

HE WAS A BOY
THINK WHAT A BOY SHOULD BE
& HE WAS THAT

St Pierre Cemetery

Major
Walter Linney HAWKSLEY
98th Field Ambulance,
Royal Army Medical Corps
Died 3 April 1916, aged 33

AND THIS MAN DIED
AS AN EXAMPLE OF COURAGE
AND A MEMORIAL OF VIRTUE
UNTO ALL HIS NATION

35433 Sergeant
Henry Evin IRONS
'A' Battery, 14th Brigade, Royal Field Artillery
Died 24 April 1918, aged 33

HEROIC UNTIL DEATH
THE PRICE OF PEACE

St-Quentin Cabaret Military Cemetery

Second Lieutenant
William James DOBBIE
2nd Battalion, Royal Irish Rifles
Died 7 June 1917, aged 34

FAREWELL MY WIFE
AND CHILDREN DEAR
I AM NOT DEAD
BUT SLEEPING HERE

St Sever Cemetery

Second Lieutenant
Jack Harry Frogley BARNES
46th Battalion, Australian Infantry
Died 8 May 1917, aged 26

HE DID HIS BEST
ALONG WITH THE REST
FOR HE WAS ONE OF THE BOYS

Colonel
William Leslie DAVIDSON, *CB*
Royal Horse Artillery
Died 3 August 1915, aged 65

R.I.P.
JUBE ME VENIRE AD TE
GOD KEEP THEE, BELOVED

(The Latin line in the epitaph is from an anonymous 14th-century prayer and translates as 'Order me to come to you'. Colonel Davidson, who was within two years of being the oldest-known Great War death on active service overseas, had lived a distinguished life, both military and civilian. His army experience dated back to the Zulu War of 1879 and he later became a Gentleman Usher to the King. His widow, Lady Theodora, was to suffer a further blow later in the war when their son was killed while serving in the Royal Flying Corps.)

Second Lieutenant
Gordon Minter FRIEAKE
1st/4th Battalion,
Oxfordshire & Buckinghamshire Light Infantry
Died 1 August 1916, aged 19

JOINED 1914
I HAVE ONLY DONE MY DUTY
HAVE NO REGRETS FOR RESULT
SICKLE TRENCH, POZIERES 1916

(It was with the London Rifle Brigade that Second Lieutenant Frieake originally enlisted at the start of the war.)

Second Lieutenant
Charles Salkeld GILHESPIE
3rd Battalion, Loyal North Lancashire Regiment,
attached 1st/5th Battalion,
South Lancashire Regiment
Died 12 December 1917, aged 19

TO US A GRAVE
TO HIM THE RAINBOW'S END

Second Lieutenant
Edmund Henry GRANT
16th Battalion, King's Royal Rifle Corps
Died 2 August 1916, aged 27

"STAND FAST"
HE SPRANG TO DUTY'S CALL
AND STOOD THE TEST
"ALL'S WELL"

Second Lieutenant
Arthur Annan JOHNSTON
'B' Battery, 291st Brigade, Royal Field Artillery
Died 16 April 1917, aged 26

HIS BODY TO THAT
PLEASANT COUNTRY'S EARTH
AND HIS PURE SOUL
UNTO HIS CAPTAIN CHRIST

Second Lieutenant
Frederick Thomas Averay JONES
3rd/1st Battalion, Herefordshire Regiment
Died 5 December 1917, aged 34

HIS LAST WRITTEN WORDS
GOOD-BYE TO ALL
WE SHALL MEET AGAIN

Lieutenant
Anthony PERCIVAL
9th Battalion, Machine Gun Corps
Died 15 October 1917, aged 25

TONY AND LEILA'S
DARLING ONLY CHILD
LOVED AND MOURNED BY MANY

Captain
Frederick Brockwall RATCLIFFE
1st (Royal) Dragoons,
attached 6th Battalion,
Machine Gun Corps (Cavalry)
Died 30 March 1918, aged 36

ON THIS
YOUR WIFE'S BIRTHDAY
YOU GAVE YOUR LIFE FOR ME

(Captain Ratliffe had served for over 18 years.)

Lieutenant Colonel
Skinner Raymond SEBASTIAN, *MC*
3rd Battalion, Hampshire Regiment,
commanding 5th Battalion,
Oxfordshire & Buckinghamshire Light Infantry
Died 27 March 1918, aged 31

ROTTINGDEAN, WINCHESTER
OXFORD, LINCOLN'S INN
SHANGHAI, FRANCE

Captain
Edward Wingfield SHAW, *DSO*
1st Battalion, Middlesex Regiment
Died 7 December 1916, aged 21

THANKS BE TO GOD
THAT SUCH HAVE BEEN
THOUGH THEY ARE HERE NO
MORE

8554 Sergeant
Harold Edgar TOMS
2nd Battalion, Border Regiment
Died 23 December 1915, aged 26

MAY THE LAD HE SAVED
SO WORTHY BE
OUR LOSS – HIS GAIN
FOR ALL ETERNITY

Lieutenant
Edwin Roy WILMSHURST
'A' Company, 20th Battalion, Royal Fusiliers
Died 1 December 1916, aged 21

THE GOAL HE SOUGHT
WAS FOUND IN YOUTH
AND IN A NOBLE FIGHT

St Souplet British Cemetery

6426 Lance Corporal
James DOHERTY
1st Battalion, Royal Irish Fusiliers
Died 24 March 1918, aged 19

'TIS EVER SO
THE GOOD, THE BEAUTIFUL
THE BRAVE ARE FIRST TO GO

St Symphorien Military Cemetery

25886 Private
William WILBY
7th (South Irish Horse) Battalion,
Royal Irish Regiment
Died 23 October 1918, aged 25

IT'S NOT THE LENGTH OF LIFE
THAT COUNTS
BUT WHAT IS DONE IN IT

Lieutenant
John Rothes Marlow WILKINSON
4th Battalion, Middlesex Regiment
Died 23 August 1914, aged 26

THESE WHO DESIRED TO LIVE
WENT OUT TO DEATH

St Vaast Post Military Cemetery

12593 Private
Henry William Robert CHALMERS
14th Battalion, Hampshire Regiment
Died 30 June 1916, aged 19

WILL GLORY O' ENGLAND
EVER DIE
SO LONG AS WE'VE LADS
LIKE THESE?

Second Lieutenant
Frederick Niven GERDS
176th Tunnelling Company, Royal Engineers
Died 1 June 1915, aged 26

COME FROM THE FOUR WINDS
O BREATH
AND BREATHE UPON THESE SLAIN
THAT THEY MAY LIVE

(From Ezekiel, *Chapter 37, Verse 9.)*

Second Lieutenant
Bernard Richard PENDEREL-BRODHURST
82nd Field Company, Royal Engineers
Died 1 October 1918, aged 27

HIS BODY TO FAIR FRANCE
HIS PURE SOUL
UNTO HIS CAPTAIN CHRIST

(This officer had previously served in the London
Regiment with both the 13th (Kensington)
Battalion and the Artists' Rifles.)

Strand Military Cemetery

853 Private
Eric Stanley HINGSTON
40th Battalion, Australian Infantry
Died 14 May 1917, aged 21

GOOD, STAN

Believed to be buried in this cemetery
1208 Lance Corporal
Herbert Leslie PRIOR
34th Battalion, Australian Infantry
Died 10 June 1917, aged 26

AN ANZAC HERO
LIES NEAR HERE
TREAD SOFTLY

Sucrerie Military Cemetery

10/25 Private
Herbert GALE
10th Battalion, East Yorkshire Regiment
Died 30 May 1916, aged 21

HOW SLEEP THE BRAVE
WHO SINK TO REST
BY ALL THEIR COUNTRY'S
WISHES BLEST – WM. COLLINS

(From Collins's Ode Written in the Year
1746. *Although they named their son Herbert,*
Private Gale's parents also had it recorded on his
headstone that he was known as 'Bob'.)

12/388 Private
Harry HANDBURY
'B' Company, 12th Battalion,
York & Lancaster Regiment
Died 8 April 1916, aged 21

IS IT WELL WITH THE LAD?
YEA IT IS WELL

(An adaptation of words in II Kings, *Chapter 4,*
Verse 26.)

Second Lieutenant
John Walter Rees MORGAN
4th Battalion, attached 2nd Battalion,
Royal Dublin Fusiliers
Died 1 July 1916, aged 23

"WHO HAD IT NOT IN HIM
TO FEAR"
R.I.P.

Sunken Road Cemetery, Contalmaison

455068 Private
William Edward DAILEY
4th Battalion, Canadian Infantry
(Central Ontario Regiment)
Died 7 September 1916, aged 16

MOTHER'S DARLING

(Sixteen is the age inscribed on his headstone, but
Private Dailey was, if the date of birth he gave on
enlistment is to be believed, actually a year older –
not that any of this would have made a jot of
difference to the maternal anguish of Florence
Dailey, three-and-a-half thousand miles away in
Gananoque, Ontario.)

3037 Lance Corporal
John DEEVY
48th Battalion, Australian Infantry
Died 6 August 1916, aged 50

IN MEMORY OF DAD
FROM HIS LOVING DAUGHTERS
MAY & FRANCES

(This is a very unusual instance of an epitaph from
grown-up children of the deceased.)

3925 Private
Joseph RAMSHAW
48th Battalion, Australian Infantry
Died 6 August 1916, aged 25

PAUSE OH YOU WINDS OF FRANCE
AS AROUND HIS GRAVE
YOU MOAN & WHISPER

497 Corporal
Christian SORENSEN
46th Battalion, Australian Infantry
Died 12 August 1916, aged 24

IN ANSWER
TO HIS COUNTRY'S CALL
HE GAVE HIS BEST
HIS LIFE, HIS ALL

1994 Private
George Patrick Power TOLHURST
27th Battalion, Australian Infantry
Died 31 August 1916, aged 19

HIS SUN HAS GONE DOWN
WHILE IT IS YET DAY

Sun Quarry Cemetery

427211 Private
Reginald ADDIS
29th Battalion, Canadian Infantry
(British Columbia Regiment)
Died 9 September 1918, aged 20

HE DID HIS BEST
WITHOUT A MURMUR
AND DIED THAT WE MIGHT LIVE

Captain
James Lloyd EVANS
5th Battalion, Canadian Infantry
(Saskatchewan Regiment)
Died 1 September 1918, aged 39

WITH LOFTIEST COURAGE
IN GLORIOUS DEATH
ENTERED LIFE EVERLASTING

(Captain Evans was a Boer War veteran.)

171250 Private
John McDOWELL
24th Battalion, Canadian Infantry
(Quebec Regiment)
Died 28 August 1918, aged 27

HE GAVE HIS LIFE FREELY
AND WE ARE PROUD OF OUR BOY

436853 Private
Fred TOWNS
15th Battalion, Canadian Infantry
(Central Ontario Regiment)
Died 30 August 1918, aged 27

SOLDIER REST
THY WARFARE O'ER
DREAM OF FIGHTING FIELDS
NO MORE

3230199 Private
Arthur Hirsch WOODROW
4th Battalion, Canadian Infantry
(Central Ontario Regiment)
Died 31 August 1918, aged 20

OH, OUR SON
A BLOOMING FLOWER THOU WERT
PLUCKED UP BEFORE ITS TIME

Suzanne Communal Cemetery Extension

17/8432 Private
George Herbert BAGSHAWE
17th Battalion, Manchester Regiment
Died 28 January 1916, aged 25

MANY WATERS
CANNOT QUENCH LOVE
NEITHER CAN THE FLOODS
DROWN IT

(From The Song of Solomon, *Chapter 8, Verse 7.*

Suzanne Military Cemetery No 3

G/63097 Private
George Harry LARNER
7th Battalion, Middlesex Regiment
Died 7 August 1918, aged 19

HE LEAPT TO ARMS UNBIDDEN

G/92923 Private
Walter Frederick PITFIELD
4th Battalion, London Regiment (Royal Fusiliers)
Died 25 August 1918, aged 18

ACROSS THE RIVER OF DEATH
LOVE LIVES TODAY
YESTERDAY AND FOREVER

Talana Farm Cemetery

Z/1828 Rifleman
Percy Walter BUSS
1st Battalion, The Rifle Brigade
Died 6 July 1915, aged 26

TAKEN FROM WARFARE
INTO THE PEACE OF GOD

Second Lieutenant
Bernard GIBBS, *MC*
6th Battalion, attached 1st Battalion,
The Rifle Brigade
Died 6 July 1915, aged 22

I WILL GO DOWN
INTO THE GRAVE
UNTO MY SON MOURNING

17989 Lance Corporal
Edward John MACE
5th Battalion,
Oxfordshire & Buckinghamshire Light Infantry
Died 24 January 1916, aged 20

I SPRANG TO THE CALL
HAVE NO REGRETS
PRIZE IS MORE THAN SACRIFICE

---

475 Rifleman
Frank Francis MAY
1st Battalion, The Rifle Brigade
Died 6 July 1915, aged 27

WELL DONE FRANK
LOTTIE

('Lottie' was Rifleman May's sister
Charlotte, of Peckham, south-east London.)

A SOLDIER
OF THE GREAT WAR

Tank Cemetery

Second Lieutenant
Alfred NOEL
2nd Battalion, London Regiment (Royal Fusiliers)
Died 3 May 1917, aged 25

IS IT NOTHING TO YOU
ALL YE THAT PASS BY?

(From Lamentations, *Chapter 1, Verse 12.)*

Terlincthun British Cemetery

877148 Private
Reginald BAGNELL
5th Battalion, Canadian Machine Gun Corps
Died 17 September 1918, aged 21

DARLING YOUR RACE IS RUN
AND VICTORY WON, AND NOW
YOUR RECORD'S IN THE SKY
FATHER & MOTHER

Lieutenant
John Dobree BELL
19th Headquarter Company,
Royal Field Artillery,
attached Intelligence Corps
Died 30 October 1918, aged 31

WHATEVER IS, IS BEST

3372 Squadron Corporal Major
William Westrop BROWN
1st/1st Life Guards Battalion,
Guards Machine Gun Corps
Died 10 September 1918, aged 40

THANK GOD FOR ONE
WHO COUNTING NOT THE COST
FACED DEATH
AND WOULD NOT YIELD

(Squadron Corporal Major Brown, a Boer War
veteran, held Long Service and Good Conduct
medals and the Belgian Croix de Guerre.)

1030934 Lance Corporal
Albert James CLINGAN
72nd Battalion, Canadian Infantry
(British Columbia Regiment)
Died 11 September 1918, aged 26

ENGLISH BY BIRTH
AMERICAN BY ADOPTION
DIED FOR BOTH.
WIFE, DAUGHTER

(The deceased's father was an inspector in the
Liverpool Police Force and his widow and daughter
lived in Massachusetts.)

49415 Rifleman
George Cyril DENNIS
1st Battalion, The Rifle Brigade
Died 11 November 1918, aged 18

AGE 18 YRS. 9 MONTHS
IN UNDYING MEMORY
NEVER SHALL WE FORGET
FROM HOME

(If there was any rejoicing at 148 Clarendon Road,
Dover, the home of Mr & Mrs G.Dennis, when
the hostilities ceased, it would soon have been cut
short. Their young son died of wounds in hospital
on the day the Armistice was signed.)

195189 Private
Maxwell PATERSON
20th Battalion, Canadian Infantry
(Central Ontario Regiment)
Died 21 September 1918, aged 21

HUSHED THE SONG
HE SCARCE BEGAN
THERE SOME TIME
WE'LL UNDERSTAND

(Private Paterson had enlisted in October 1915 as
a bugler in the 93rd Battalion.)

133176 Private
Hugh Gordon ROSS
Survey Section, Canadian Engineers
Died 5 February 1919, aged 22

LOST LIFE
NOT HONOUR
AND DIED
IN THE BRITISH WAY

157057 Private
John Edward STEELE
'H' Company, 51st Battalion,
Machine Gun Corps
Died 4 September 1918, aged 22

THEY ARE NOT DEAD
WHO'VE FOUGHT
OLD ENGLAND'S BATTLES
FROM MOTHER

40433 Private
Henry WADD
1st/4th Battalion,
Loyal North Lancashire Regiment
Died 12 September 1918, aged 20

NEVER FROM MY MIND
DEAR HARRY BOY
MUM

The Huts Cemetery

16401 Private
George ANSTEE
1st Battalion, Royal Fusiliers
Died 1 August 1917, aged 24

BUT YE SHALL DIE LIKE MEN
AND FALL
LIKE ONE OF THE PRINCES
PSALM 82

672 Bombardier
Jack Thwaites BARRY
74th Siege Battery, South African Heavy Artillery
Died 10 August 1917, aged 26

COME WEARY SOUL
FROM WAR AND VIGIL CEASE
LORD HAVE MERCY

(The first two lines are from a hymn entitled
There's Peace and Rest in Paradise.*)*

752 Private
George Edward BEAVIS
28th Battalion, Australian Infantry
Died 21 September 1917, aged 21

WHEN THE FIELDS
ARE WHITE WITH DAISIES
I'LL RETURN
IN LOVING MEMORY

Major
Clarence Evelyn BEERBOHM
'D' Battery, 167th Brigade, Royal Field Artillery
Died 26 September 1917, aged 32

IN LOVING RADIANT MEMORY
WITH UNDAUNTED HEART
HE BREASTED LIFE'S LAST HILL

116106 Gunner
Harry Wallace DANIEL
'C' Battery, 95th Brigade, Royal Field Artillery
Died 15 October 1917, aged 22

OVER THERE
OUR SON SLEEPETH
HIS MEMORY CLINGS
AS YEARS PASS AWAY

Second Lieutenant
Wellesley Venables DEANE
'D' Battery, 95th Brigade, Royal Field Artillery
Died 24 September 1917, aged 21

DIDSBURY – WATERLOO

(This strange inscription might be a cryptic reference
to some family connection with the Duke of
Wellington: Didsbury was Second Lieutenant
Deane's birthplace, and his first name was the Iron
Duke's family name.)

22301 Gunner
James Walter Dundas GALE
7th Brigade, Australian Field Artillery
Died 28 September 1917, aged 22

HEAVENLY FATHER IN THY KEEPING
I LEAVE MY DARLING WALLIE SLEEPING

3638 Gunner
Francis Joseph HALL
2nd Brigade, Australian Field Artillery
Died 29 October 1917, aged 23

NEVERMORE
WILL HIS MOTHER GREET HIM
UNDER THE SOUTHERN CROSS
R.I.P.

L/42626 Gunner
Francis HAZZLEDINE
'C' Battery, 102nd Brigade, Royal Field Artillery
Died 15 October 1917, aged 19

AN ONLY BOY
HIS PARENTS' PRIDE & JOY

Lieutenant
William HILL
'C' Battery, 86th Army Brigade,
Royal Field Artillery
Died 30 October 1917, aged 33

NOT ALL IN VAIN
HAS YOUTH GONE FORTH
WITH CHRIST TO CALVARY

Captain
John Lindsay KELSALL
'B' Battery, 86th Brigade, Royal Field Artillery
Died 28 August 1917, aged 26

HE DIED AT THE GUNS
HEARTENING HIS MEN
AT ZILLEBEKE LAKE

(Commissioned as a Royal Army Service Corps
officer in the first month of the war, Captain Kelsall
was Mentioned in Despatches between his transfer
to the RFA and being killed in action six months
later.)

Lieutenant Colonel
Courtenay Talbot Saint PAUL, *DSO*
36th Battery, 45th Brigade, Royal Field Artillery
Died 31 July 1917, aged 35

AN OLD CLIFTONIAN
PRAISE GOD FOR THESE
AND PRAY THEIR LIKE TO BE

21041 Corporal
Alfred Haroldston PERROTT
6th Brigade, Australian Field Artillery
Died 28 October 1917, aged 28

HOW CAN MAN DIE BETTER?
THE UNIVERSE ITSELF SHALL BE
HIS IMMORTALITY

(The first line is from Macaulay's Lays of
Ancient Rome: Horatius.*)*

7076 Private
Louis Henry SALAMITO
6th Battalion, Australian Infantry
Died 20 September 1917, aged 22

A LIFE GIVEN
IN ITS MORNING
PART PURCHASE OF OUR FREEDOM

Thiepval Anglo-French Cemetery

Captain
Ivan Provis Wentworth BENNETT
7th Battalion,
The Queen's (Royal West Surrey Regiment)
Died 14 July 1916, aged 25

"CROWNED WITH THE SUNSHINE
OF IMMORTAL YOUTH"

(In the course of research for this book it was
discovered that, despite being commemorated on the
Thiepval Memorial to the Missing, Captain
Bennett actually rests in a named grave which, by
an extraordinary coincidence, is in the front row of
the cemetery which faces the Memorial. Different
versions of his name and date of death lay at the
heart of the confusion, which was drawn to the War
Graves Commission's attention, as a result of which
steps were taken towards correcting the details on
the headstone and removing tthe name from the
Memorial.)

Tigris Lane Cemetery

311796 Gunner (Signaller)
Thomas KELLY
59th Siege Battery, Royal Garrison Artillery
Died 1 September 1918, aged 21

THE BLOOD OF HEROES
IS THE SEED OF FREEDOM

Tilloy British Cemetery

Second Lieutenant
Randolph COOK
7th Battalion, The Cameronians (Scottish Rifles),
attached 9th Battalion, King's Royal Rifle Corps
Died 9 April 1917, aged 33

LOVE WHO SENT FORGOT TO SAVE
THE YOUNG, THE BEAUTIFUL
THE BRAVE

X/99 Corporal
Cecil King EDWARDS
125th Siege Battery,
South African Heavy Artillery
Died 23 April 1917, aged 22

HE DIED
IF IT IS DEATH TO DIE
THAT WE MIGHT LIVE

Captain
Douglas Stanley HIGGINS
9th Battalion, attached 5th Battalion,
Oxfordshire & Buckinghamshire Light Infantry
Died 9 April 1917, aged 37

THESE WERE HONOURED
IN THEIR GENERATIONS
THE GLORY OF THE TIMES

(Taken from Apocrypha – Ecclesiasticus,
Chapter 44, Verse 7.)

C/9341 Rifleman
Augustus Bertie HORSEY
9th Battalion, King's Royal Rifle Corps
Died 9 April 1917, aged 22

'TIS AS A SOLDIER
HE WILL STAND BEFORE
THE GREAT WHITE THRONE

Second Lieutenant
William Tordiff JOHNSTON
12th Battalion, Manchester Regiment
Died 13 April 1917, aged 20

A FINE BOY
SO FRANK AND FRIENDLY
SO FULL OF ENERGY
AND KEENNESS

24060 Private
Charles Frank Stephen LUSTY
7th Battalion, King's Shropshire Light Infantry
Died 9 April 1917, aged 20

HE WAS OUR ONLY CHILD

476041 Sergeant
Charlie RODGERS
455th Field Company, Royal Engineers
Died 11 May 1917, aged 21

GOD ONE DAY
WAS GATHERING FLOWERS
ON HIS WAY HE GATHERED OURS

57668 Saddler
John William SEAVERS
'B' Battery, 77th Brigade, Royal Field Artillery
Died 31 August 1918, aged 31

PEACE WHERE THE TEMPEST
WHERE THE SIGHING IS
YES PEACE WHERE HE IS

S/17388 Private
Donald John STEWART
9th Battalion, Gordon Highlanders
Died 4 April 1918, aged 20

THE WAR AND CHASE
GIVE LITTLE CHOICE
OF RESTING PLACE

Second Lieutenant
James Parker SUTHERLAND
2nd Battalion, Royal Scots
Died 9 April 1917, aged 20

ALL THAT THEY HAD
THEY GAVE – THEY GAVE

Second Lieutenant
Horace George WALNE
2nd Battalion, Suffolk Regiment
Died 11 April 1917, aged 27

HE WAS LOVED
BY HIS MEN IN ACTION
AND IS FONDLY REMEMBERED
AT HOME

Second Lieutenant
Arthur Pelham WEBB
'D' Company, 5th Battalion,
King's Shropshire Light Infantry
Died 9 April 1917, aged 32

HE DIED FOR AN IDEAL

Tincourt New British Cemetery

270227 Private
Ernest Rannie FOORD
16th Battalion, Royal Scots
Died 27 August 1917, aged 20

HE WANTED TO DO HIS BIT

14318 Private
A.D. HANSEN
2nd Regiment, South African Infantry
Died 25 January 1918, aged 15

A LITTLE THING
FOR BRITAIN DONE
BUT OH HOW FINE

Captain
Godfrey Beaumont LOYD, *MC*
'D' Company, 12th Battalion,
King's Royal Rifle Corps
Died 1 December 1917, aged 24

OH! TRUE BRAVE HEART
GOD BLESS THEE WHERESOE'ER
IN HIS WIDE UNIVERSE
THOU ART TODAY

1635 Private
John Thomas NIXON
22nd (Tyneside Scottish) Battalion,
Northumberland Fusiliers
Died 27 August 1917, aged 24

THE WORD OF FREEDOM IS WRITTEN
IN THE BLOOD OF HEROES

Toutencourt Communal Cemetery

Second Lieutenant
Thomas Alington ROYDS
59th Squadron, Royal Air Force
Died 20 April 1918, aged 33

WITH GOOD WILL
DOING SERVICE

(The Royal Air Force, formed when the Royal
Flying Corps and Royal Naval Air Service were
amalgamated, was less than three weeks old when
this officer died.)

Track X Cemetery

Captain
Ian Grant FLEMING, *MC*
6th Battalion, Gordon Highlanders
Died 31 July 1917, aged 25

LIFE IS NOT LOST
FOR WHICH IS BOUGHT
ENDLESS RENOWN
SPENSER

Tranchée de Mecknes Cemetery

1203 Private
Stanley William AFFLECK
17th Battalion, Royal Fusiliers
Died 25 April 1916, aged 19

HE PLAYED THE GAME
AND THE SUN SHINES
ON HIS MEMORY

---

559 Private
Reginald Howard BENNETT
17th Battalion, Royal Fusiliers
Died 27 April 1916, aged 20

IF ONE HAS SERVED THEE
TELL THE DEED TO MANY
HAST THOU SERVED MANY?
TELL IT NOT TO ANY

8532 Sergeant
James Joseph BUTLER
8th Battalion, Yorkshire Regiment
Died 28 May 1916, aged 33

A CALM AND UNDISTURBED REPOSE
A SAFE RETREAT FROM ALL OUR FOES

Trois Arbres Cemetery

45750 Lance Corporal
Herbert Willie CASTLING
23rd (Tyneside Scottish) Battalion,
Northumberland Fusiliers
Died 8 April 1918, aged 32

SLUMBER SUCH
AS NEEDS MUST BE
AFTER HARD WON VICTORY

2845 Private
Richard FORREST
12th Battalion, Australian Infantry
Died 3 January 1918, aged 33

HAD WE A DEAREST WISH
FULFILLED
DEAREST DADDY
WE WOULD ASK FOR YOU

26965 Gunner
William GRANT
5th Siege Battery, Royal Garrison Artillery
Died 2 November 1914, aged 39

FIGHTING TO SAVE
A WORLD'S MORALITY
HE DIED THE NOBLEST DEATH
A MAN MAY DIE

---

512 Private
Charles Harold McCARTHY
36th Battalion, Australian Infantry
Died 12 June 1917, aged 23

THE FITTEST PLACE
WHERE MAN CAN DIE
IS WHERE HE DIES FOR MAN

(From a verse by Michael J.Barry)

3207 Lance Corporal
Malcolm McCASKILL
28th Battalion, Australian Infantry
Died 2 January 1918, aged 34

NEHEMIAH XI CHAP. 2 VERSE

('And the people blessed all the men ... ')

Second Lieutenant
Thomas Waldegrave NOPS
9th Kite Balloon Section, Royal Flying Corps
Died 21 October 1916, aged 23

"HE DIED AS GAMELY
AS ANY MAN THAT FELL
IN THIS WAR"
HIS SENIOR OFFICER

1691 Lance Corporal
Norman Gordon PIPER
43rd Battalion, Australian Infantry
Died 22 April 1917, aged 25

BEHOLD FRANCE
THOU HOLDEST ONE OF
AUSTRALIA'S
BRAVEST & BEST

1904/A Private
Selwyn Kemp SKIPWORTH
34th Battalion, Australian Infantry
Died 24 July 1917, aged 26

FOR MOTHER'S HONOUR
HOME'S SECURITY
AND COUNTRY'S FREEDOM

18390 Private
Arthur SMITH
'B' Company, 11th Battalion, Suffolk Regiment
Died 6 September 1916, aged 27

HE LEFT HIS HOME
& DID HIS DUTY FOR US ALL
FROM LOVING WIFE
SON & DAUGHTER

260802 Pioneer
Robert VINES
339th Railway Construction Company,
Royal Engineers
Died 8 May 1917, aged 36

IN LIFE AS IN DEATH
"OTHERS"

---

982 Corporal
Clifford Limen WALLIS
33rd Battalion, Australian Infantry
Died 23 July 1917, aged 22

HE DIED AN AUSTRALIAN HERO
THE GREATEST DEATH OF ALL

Tyne Cot Cemetery

266376 Private
Herbert BARKER
8th Battalion, Seaforth Highlanders
Died 22 August 1917, aged 20

THROUGH GOD
WE SHALL DO VALIANTLY

(From Psalms, Chapter 108, Verse 13.)

1306 Private
Fred BEER
14th Battalion, Royal Warwickshire Regiment
Died 4 October 1917, aged 21

THOUGH SEAS
MAY ROLL BETWEEN US
ALWAYS IN MEMORY
OF FLO & JOE. R.I.P.

Captain
Thomas Henry BONE
44th Battalion, Australian Infantry
Died 5 October 1917, aged 26

DEARLY LOVED HUSBAND
OF EFFIE
& LOVED DADDY
OF LITTLE MARJORIE

43338 Private
Albert Henry CLARK
9th Battalion, Royal Irish Fusiliers
Died 16 August 1917, aged 20

WHAT NOBLER OFFERING
COULD HE GIVE
THAN YIELD HIS LIFE
FOR YOURS AND MINE

Second Lieutenant
George COWIE
54th Squadron, Royal Flying Corps
Died 22 October 1917, aged 18

ONLY SON OF
ALEXANDER & SYLVIA COWIE
DUFFTOWN, SCOTLAND
IN THE DAYS OF THY YOUTH

(The concluding phrase is taken from
Ecclesiastes, *Chapter 12, Verse 1.)*

6983 Private
Justus Frederick DARR
3rd Battalion, Australian Infantry
Died 4 October 1917, aged 27

IN FOND RESPECT
AND LOVING MEMORY
OF OUR DEAR SOLDIER BOY

56677 Private
John Samuel EDMUNDS
2nd Battalion, Royal Welsh Fusiliers
Died 25 November 1917, aged 20

"AND HIS SUN WAS SET
WHILE IT WAS YET DAY"
JERM. XV.9

Second Lieutenant
Wilfred Charles GOULDEN
2nd Battalion, Middlesex Regiment
Died 12 February 1918, aged 20

DEAR LADDIE
ALWAYS CHEERY & WILLING
ALWAYS HAPPY & BUSY

5172 Private
Henry GRAHAM
1st Battalion, Cameron Highlanders
Died 11 November 1914, aged 33

ALSO IN MEMORY
OF WILLIE & BOB
BROTHERS
KILLED IN ACTION

3055 Lance Corporal
Joseph Marcus HARWOOD
45th Battalion, Australian Infantry
Died 13 October 1917, aged 20

AUSTRALIA
WILL HAVE OTHER SONS
BUT NONE MORE HONOURED
THAN THESE

S/7089 Private
John Telfer HIDDLESTON
8th Battalion, Seaforth Highlanders
Died 22 August 1917, aged 22

I LAY IN DUST
LIFE'S GLORY DEAD

3249 Private
William Keith HOOPER
48th Battalion, Australian Infantry
Died 12 October 1917, aged 21

GRANDSON
OF VIRGINIE COURTOIS
LATE OF TOURS, FRANCE

202768 Rifleman
Harry HULM
1st/5th Battalion,
The King's (Liverpool Regiment)
Died 20 September 1917, aged 30

THEY WIN OR DIE WHO WEAR
THE ROSE OF LANCASHIRE
IN GOD IS MY TRUST

235185 Corporal
James INCE
13th Battalion, The King's (Liverpool Regiment)
Died 23 September 1917, aged 21

O ENGLAND
KEEP THY BRIGHT BANNERS
WITHOUT BLOT OR STAIN

Second Lieutenant
Joseph IRVINE
4th Battalion, Australian Infantry
Died 4 October 1917, aged 30

BREAK BREAK BREAK
ON THY COLD GREY STONES
O SEA

(From Tennyson's poem Break, Break, Break.
This is an unusually subtle epitaph: the significance
is not in the words themselves, but in those which
follow: '.... And I would that my tongue could utter
– The thoughts that arise in me.')

Captain
Clarence Smith JEFFRIES, *VC*
34th Battalion, Australian Infantry
Died 12 October 1917, aged 22

ON FAME'S ETERNAL CAMPING
GROUND
THEIR SILENT TENTS ARE SPREAD

(The VC was awarded posthumously, for the action
in which Captain Jeffries was killed at the Battle of
Passchendaele. His age at death was notified
correctly by his next-of-kin but wrongly recorded as
23 by the Australian military authorities, and is
inscribed thus on the headstone.)

---

957 Corporal
Reginald KILLICK
1st Battalion, Australian Infantry
Died 21 September 1917, aged 25

SLEEP ON BRAVE HEART
OUR LOSS IS SOFTENED
BY OUR PRIDE

26035 Corporal
Thomas LIVERMORE
10th Battalion, Durham Light Infantry
Died 23 August 1917, aged 25

HE LOVED ME
AND GAVE HIMSELF FOR ME

212 Private
William McKERROW
2nd Battalion, Gordon Highlanders
Died 29 October 1914, aged 26

SOLDIER REST
THY WARFARE'S O'ER
DREAM OF BATTLE-FIELDS
NO MORE

Brigadier General
James Foster RIDDELL
2nd/5th Battalion, Northumberland Fusiliers,
commanding
149th (1st/1st Northumberland) Brigade
Died 26 April 1915, aged 52

KILLED LEADING HIS BRIGADE
BUT 5 DAYS LANDED

SOLDIER AND GREAT GENTLEMAN

3286 Private
William Arthur ROWE
58th Battalion, Australian Infantry
Died 25 September 1917, aged 24

IN LOVING MEMORY
OF MY DEAR SON
FOR EMPIRE AND HONOUR

Second Lieutenant
John Henry Raymond SALTER
Royal Flying Corps
Died 13 October 1917, aged 18

"AND SO HE PASSED OVER
AND THE TRUMPETS
SOUNDED FOR HIM"
BUNYAN

170 Private
Bert Arthur SIMPSON
36th Battalion, Australian Infantry
Died 12 October 1917, aged 26

IN THE GARDEN OF SLEEP
WHERE THE POPPIES BLOOM

2977 Private
Harley Randolph SLOGGETT
54th Battalion, Australian Infantry
Died 21 October 1917, aged 20

HERE LIES
THE NOBLEST WORK OF GOD

52360 Rifleman
Gerald Oscar SMITH
15th Battalion, Royal Irish Rifles
Died 14 October 1918, aged 25

LIFE IS VERY SWEET BROTHER
WHO WOULD WISH TO DIE

S/22809 Private
John Walker STEWART
7th Battalion, Seaforth Highlanders
Died 12 October 1917, aged 24

HE CAME AND BOUGHT A GRAVE
AMONG THE ETERNAL

488181 Private
Christopher ST JOHN
24th Battalion, Canadian Infantry
(Quebec Regiment)
Died 6 November 1917, aged 32

DEAR SON OF MY HEART
BENEATH A FOREIGN CLAY
GOD REST YOUR SOUL
IT IS A MOTHER'S PRAYER

6346 Private
Ernest Roy STONE, *MM*
8th Battalion, Australian Infantry
Died 20 September 1917, aged 21

OUR HERO AT REST
A BONZER BOY

9584 Lance Corporal
Alexander Gibbon STRACHAN
1st/8th Battalion,
West Yorkshire Regiment (Prince of Wales's Own)
Died 9 October 1917, aged 20

NEITHER SHALL
THEY LEARN WAR ANY MORE
ISA. 11.4.

3210 Private
Archie Stuart THOM
47th Battalion, Australian Infantry
Died 12 October 1917, aged 33

THE PIPERS PLAYED
THE GATHERING OF THE CLANS

(Private Thom was a son of Crieff, Perthshire.)

201458 Lance Corporal
Benjamin Arthur TYLER
2nd/4th Battalion,
Oxfordshire & Buckinghamshire Light Infantry
Died 22 August 1917, aged 20

WAR HATH DESTROYED
BUT LOVING MEMORY LIVES

3892 Private
Robert Alfred WALLACE
47th Battalion, Australian Infantry
Died 12 October 1917, aged 24

THEY SHALL RETURN
TO THEIR OWN BORDER

(Adapted from Jeremiah, *Chapter 31, Verse 17.)*

Upton Wood Cemetery

2355888 Private
Robert Scott CHALMERS
5th Battalion, Canadian Infantry
(Saskatchewan Regiment)
Died 1 September 1918, aged 37

SIX BROTHERS IN ALL
ANSWERED THE CALL
ONE CRIPPLED, THREE KILLED

888110 Private
Victor GRANT
5th Battalion, Canadian Infantry
(Saskatchewan Regiment)
Died 1 September 1918, aged 28

THE ONLY SON
OF A SORROWFUL MOTHER

552963 Lance Corporal
Sophus Rasmus LARSON
8th Battalion, Canadian Infantry
(Manitoba Regiment)
Died 31 August 1918, aged 26

THE PATHS OF GLORY
LEAD BUT TO THE GRAVE

(From Thomas Gray's Elegy Written in a
Country Churchyard.*)*

737123 Private
Owen Berkley PESTELL
10th Battalion, Canadian Infantry
(Alberta Regiment)
Died 2 September 1918, aged 26

A GENEROUS BOY
GOD BLESS HIM

183253 Private
Earl Elijah SMITH
10th Battalion, Canadian Infantry
(Alberta Regiment)
Died 3 September 1918, aged 36

THEY HAVE REACHED A LAND
BEYOND THE VALE OF TEARS
THOSE WHO DIED FOR OTHERS

Vailly British Cemetery

6918 Private
Edward ROBINSON
1st Battalion,
The Queen's (Royal West Surrey Regiment)
Died 9 October 1914, aged 35

THROUGH STRAIGHTNESS
TO GREATNESS

D/3177 Sergeant
Bertram STAIRMAND
2nd Dragoon Guards (The Queen's Bays)
Died 12 September 1914, aged 28

THE LOVE THAT PAID UNDAUNTED
THE FINAL SACRIFICE

Second Lieutenant
Eric Vickers TINDALL
4th Battalion, attached 2nd Battalion,
King's Royal Rifle Corps
Died 12 September 1914, aged 21

ONE GLORIOUS HOUR
OF GLORIOUS LIFE
IS WORTH AN AGE
WITHOUT A NAME

**Vaulx Australian Field Ambulance
Cemetery**

4328 Private
William Albert HAMMOND
12th Battalion, Australian Infantry
Died 6 May 1917, aged 19

COULD THIS MOTHER
HAVE CLASPED HIS HAND
MY BOY SO BRAVE AND TRUE

Vaulx Hill Cemetery

Second Lieutenant
John BILLING
East Yorkshire Regiment,
attached 5th Battalion,
King's Own Yorkshire Light Infantry
Died 2 September 1918, aged 20

I PRAYED FOR COURAGE
AND GOT IT

Second Lieutenant
Reginald William COOK, *MC*
3rd Battalion, attached 1st Battalion,
Devonshire Regiment
Died 1 September 1918, aged 26

FOR THE GLORY OF ENGLAND AND
THE HONOUR OF BRISTOL

Lieutenant
Guy Kennedy DAVENPORT, *MC*
4th Brigade, Australian Field Artillery
Died 10 April 1917, aged 26

SAME MESSAGE

(This is an example of a very 'Personal Inscription'
– 'epitaph' was not a word ever used by the War
Graves Commission – which would have been
understood by the deceased but which defies
interpretation by anyone else. The first reaction to it

of this book's author was that the next-of-kin had probably submitted a second form in respect of another member of the family who had died in the war, and that the two forms had got separated. Subsequent research revealed that the Australian Army authorities of the time had made exactly the same assumption and replied to the widowed Mrs Mabel Davenport accordingly. Her response was to confirm that there was no second form and to emphasize that the two words she had written were indeed what she wanted inscribed on her husband's headstone. Lieutenant Davenport, a Sydney solicitor in the family firm, was killed only four days after rejoining his unit, having recovered from bronchitis and laryngitis in a London hospital. His Military Cross had earlier been awarded for "consistent gallantry and devotion to duty" in operations around Pozières during the Battle of the Somme.)

49805 Private
John HUNT
'C' Company, 2nd/4th Battalion,
Duke of Wellington's (West Riding Regiment)
Died 31 August 1918, aged 36

A NOBLE LIFE
A NOBLE DEATH

Second Lieutenant
Lionel Bruce MABY
2nd Battalion, Scots Guards
Died 12 September 1918, aged 20

HE WON FOR HIMSELF GLORY
WHICH IS EVER YOUNG

---

723 Bombadier
Frank McDONNELL
5th Brigade, Australian Field Artillery
Died 19 April 1917, aged 34

HONOUR THE FALLEN BRAVE
FLAG, FLOWER AND TREE

23069 Gunner
Horace Russell MAYERS
12th Brigade, Australian Field Artillery
Died 23 April 1917, aged 21

ONE OF MANY WHO PERISHED
NOT IN VAIN
AS A TYPE OF OUR CHIVALRY

3679 Gunner
George Stephen SMITH
4th Brigade, Australian Field Artillery
Died 31 March 1917, aged 20

ONLY A YOUTH
WITH A LOYAL HEART

Vermelles British Cemetery

33221 Private
George Marlin BLUNT
6th Battalion, Leicestershire Regiment
Died 25 February 1917, aged 21

HE WAS THE ONLY SON
OF HIS MOTHER
AND SHE WAS A WIDOW

(From Luke, *Chapter 7, Verse 12.)*

Y/1804 Rifleman
Harry Reyland CABLE
2nd Battalion, King's Royal Rifle Corps
Died 28 August 1915, aged 31

HIS WATCHWORD WAS
GOD SAVE ENGLAND
R.I.P.

276793 Private
George CANE
2nd/7th Battalion, Manchester Regiment
Died 16 April 1917, aged 20

AGE 20.
HE SHALL GROW UP BEFORE HIM
AS A TENDER PLANT.
MOTHER.

(From Isaiah, *Chapter 53, Verse 2.)*

40090 Private
Henry James COOMBS
7th Battalion, Leicestershire Regiment
Died 14 October 1916, aged 27

THE PARENT MOURNS
THE PATRIOT IS PROUD

4946 Trooper
Thomas William COOPER
19th (Queen's Alexandra's Own) Royal Hussars
Died 10 February 1916, aged 21

IF THE TRUMPET GIVE
AN UNCERTAIN SOUND
WHO SHALL PREPARE HIMSELF
TO THE BATTLE. I COR. XIV. 8

S/1992 Private
James DOCHERTY
10th Battalion, Argyll & Sutherland Highlanders
Died 30 August 1915, aged 19

HE FOUGHT NOT TO DESTROY
BUT TO DEFEND
A NOBLE BRITISH SOLDIER
TO THE END

19647 Private
Henry Frederic Noel FALKNER
2nd Battalion, Northamptonshire Regiment
Died 11 October 1916, aged 33

RELINQUISHED HIS CAPTAINCY
LINCS. REGT.
TO QUICKER FIGHT THE FOE

(Private Falkner was a solicitor who relinquished
his army commission in order to enlist as a private
in the Northamptonshire Regiment after
ascertaining that by doing so he would straightaway
go out to the Front.)

28866 Private
Benjamin FERGUSON
14th Battalion, Highland Light Infantry
Died 21 June 1916, aged 18

HERE'S WHERE
MY HERO'S ASLEEP
LET STARS BE MY EYES
DEW, TEARS THAT I WEEP

S/16169 Private
Alexander GEEKIE
'B' Company, 6th Battalion,
Cameron Highlanders
Died 6 July 1916, aged 27

A TRUE SCOT
HE RETURNED FROM CANADA
TO FIGHT IN SCOTTISH RANKS

Second Lieutenant
Mark HOVELL
1st Battalion, Sherwood Foresters
(Nottinghamshire & Derbyshire Regiment)
Died 12 August 1916, aged 28

ON EARTH
THE BROKEN ARCS
IN THE HEAVEN
A PERFECT ROUND

(From Abt Vogler, *by Robert Browning.)*

16947 Lance Corporal
Lawrence HUTCHINSON
7th Battalion, Cameron Highlanders
Died 18 July 1916, aged 20

DIED FIGHTING
SLEEP ON BRAVE CAMERON
SLEEP ON

6820 Private
William Joseph MACE
6th Battalion,
The Queen's (Royal West Surrey Regiment)
Died 24 February 1916, aged 19

THIS ENGLAND ASKED OF HIM
THIS UNGRUDGINGLY HE GAVE
HIS LIFE

Major
George Frederick
MOLYNEUX-MONTGOMERIE
3rd Battalion, Grenadier Guards
Died 22 October 1915, aged 46

SO HE PASSED OVER
AND ALL THE TRUMPETS
SOUNDED FOR HIM
ON THE OTHER SIDE

(From John Bunyan's Pilgrim's Progress.
Another Grenadier officer who died four days
earlier and is buried in this cemetery has the same
epitaph – see Captain E.F.Penn.)

22/447 Private
John Edward PAYNE
22nd (Pioneer) Battalion, Durham Light Infantry
Died 13 August 1916, aged 20

NO MOTHER NEAR
TO CLOSE HIS EYES

Captain
Eric Frank PENN
4th Battalion, Grenadier Guards
Died 18 October 1915, aged 37

SO HE PASSED OVER
AND ALL THE TRUMPETS
SOUNDED FOR HIM
ON THE OTHER SIDE

(Captain Penn played first-class cricket, as did
many of his relations, and won Cambridge blues in
1899 and 1902, either side of military service in
the Boer War. His age is incorrectly inscribed on
the headstone as 33. The epitaph is an extract from
John Bunyan's Pilgrim's Progress.*)*

38252 Private
George Frederick REED
9th Battalion,
King's Own Yorkshire Light Infantry
Died 27 December 1916, aged 24

FOR THEE
O DEAR COUNTRY
TO THAT DEAR LAND OF REST

20279 Lance Corporal
John RETSON
7th Battalion, Cameron Highlanders
Died 4 June 1916, aged 18

PEACE
THY OLIVE WAND EXTEND
AND BID WILD WAR
ITS RAVAGE END

S/13163 Private
John TINTO
8th/10th Battalion, Gordon Highlanders
Died 13 July 1916, aged 18

COULD NOT RESIST THE CALL
I WANT YOU
A BRAVE HIGHLANDER

Captain
Philip Stafford Gordon WAINMAN
6th Battalion, attached 2nd Battalion,
Worcestershire Regiment
Died 26 September 1915, aged 35

KILLED
WHILE LEADING HIS MEN
ON THE EVE
OF HIS 36TH BIRTHDAY

(Captain Wainman had also served in the Boer
War.)

Vertain Communal Cemetery Extension

Captain
Richard d'Arcy MAXWELL
2nd Battalion, Royal Scots
Died 23 October 1918, aged 32

CLASPED BY THE LAND
YOU BRAVELY STROVE TO FREE

Vichte Military Cemetery

140423 Bombardier
Frank Allan BARTLETT
268th Siege Battery, Royal Garrison Artillery
Died 31 October 1918, aged 23

HE DIED THAT WE MIGHT LIVE

(With the Armistice only eleven days away,
Bombardier Bartlett was killed in the final advance,
east of the village of Vichte. His elder brother,

Sapper E.J.Bartlett, died in 1916 at the same age,
and his headstone in Bailleul Communal Cemetery
Extension bears the same epitaph.)

Vieille Chapelle New Military Cemetery

Second Lieutenant
Clive Marston BEAUFOY
10th Battalion, Royal Warwickshire Regiment
Died 25 September 1918, aged 21

SACRIFICED

99368 Private
Charles ENGLAND
2nd/6th Battalion, Durham Light Infantry
Died 25 September 1918, aged 20

THEY WERE A WALL UNTO US
BOTH BY DAY AND NIGHT
AND WE WERE NOT HURT

(Based on I Samuel, *Chapter 25, Verse 16.)*

21203 Private
Samuel Norman ROBINSON
1st Battalion, Loyal North Lancashire Regiment
Died 18 April 1918, aged 36

SAM'S ALWAYS NEAR AND DEAR

Vignacourt British Cemetery

1878 Private
Matthew Richard BLACK
57th Battalion, Australian Infantry
Died 8 August 1918, aged 21

YOUNG HE DIED
BUT DEEDS OF MERCY
BEAUTIFIED
HIS LIFE'S SHORT SPAN

6509 Private
Arthur Percival FERGUSON
32nd Battalion, Australian Infantry
Died 28 June 1918, aged 27

IN A DREAM
HE STANDS BY MY SIDE
WHISPERS MOTHER
DEATH CANNOT DIVIDE

294259 Gunner
Fergus INNS
144th Heavy Battery, Royal Garrison Artillery
Died 19 June 1918, aged 19

THIS BOY WAS BRAVE
FOR THOSE AT HOME
HIS LIFE HE GAVE
AGE 19 YEARS

6068 Lance Corporal
Maurice MOLLOY, *MM*
21st Battalion, Australian Infantry
Died 22 May 1918, aged 21

PETIT FILS DE ALBERT KELLE
QUI NAQUIT A NANCY
ET QUITTA LA FRANCE
POUR L'AUSTRALIE EN 1863

(The epitaph highlights the poignancy of Lance Corporal Molloy's death in France, his French grandfather having emigrated to Australia 55 years earlier.)

Lieutenant
Lancelot Joseph Wollard PAYNE, *MC*
25th Battalion, Australian Infantry
Died 30 May 1918, aged 21

IN THE LAND OF
ETERNAL SUNSHINE
WE SHALL HEAR
THAT SONG AGAIN

Second Lieutenant
Sydney Arnold SMITH
65th Squadron, Royal Air Force
Died 6 August 1918, aged 23

HE GAVE HIMSELF
WITH A GALLANT PRIDE

Villers-Bocage Communal Cemetery Extension

23787 Sergeant
Cecil Claud SAUNDERS, *MM*
222nd Field Company, Royal Engineers
Died 25 July 1917, aged 23

O FAREWELL HONEST SOLDIER

Villers-Bretonneux Military Cemetery

28053 Gunner
Henry James BEZER
7th Brigade, Australian Field Artillery
Died 22 August 1918, aged 21

SHOULD I FALL, GRIEVE NOT,
I SHALL BE ONE WITH THE SUN,
WIND AND FLOWERS

Second Lieutenant
Victor George BRINDLEY
80th Squadron, Royal Air Force
Died 30 August 1918, aged 27

HELD WE FALL TO RISE,
ARE BAFFLED TO FIGHT BETTER,
SLEEP TO WAKE

(From the epilogue to Robert Browning's poem Summum Bonum (Asolando). *Second Lieutenant Brindley, whose home was in Orange Free State, had joined the 3rd Regiment, South African Infantry, right at the start of the war, in August 1914.)*

5473 Sapper
Frederick William JEEVES
6th Field Company, Australian Engineers
Died 1 August 1918, aged 30

BETTER A WOODEN CROSS
THAN BE ONE
WHO COULD HAVE GONE
AND DID NOT

5448 Corporal
Guthrie Wilberforce REILLY
26th Battalion, Australian Infantry
Died 8 August 1918, aged 33

SLEEP SON BENEATH
THE SOLDIER'S RUGGED CROSS
YOUR DUTY NOBLY DONE

3204 Private
John Henry VENN
2nd Battalion, Australian Pioneers
Died 13 June 1918, aged 25

GATHERED TO THE QUIET WEST
HIS SUNDOWN SPLENDID
AND SERENE TO REST

820831 Private
Stanley WALKER
44th Battalion, Canadian Infantry
(New Brunswick Regiment)
Died 11 August 1918, aged 21

TREAD SOFTLY,
OUR DEAR HERO BOY
SLEEPS HERE.
FATHER, MOTHER AND BROTHERS

Villers Station Cemetery

429512 Private
Harrison Raymond ALLEN
16th Battalion, Canadian Infantry
(Manitoba Regiment)
Died 2 December 1916, aged 25

FOR KING AND COUNTRY
THUS HE FELL
A TYRANT'S ARROGANCE TO QUELL

703917 Private
Francis Reuben BROWN
102nd Battalion, Canadian Infantry
(Central Ontario Regiment)
Died 23 March 1917, aged 18

SCARCE BOY
YET MAN WITH TORCH HELD HIGH
HIS SCROLL FOR US TO DIE

454482 Private
Harold George CARTER
73rd Battalion, Canadian Infantry
(Quebec Regiment)
Died 20 April 1917, aged 21

SO SOON PASSETH IT AWAY
AND WE ARE GONE
PS. 90.10

(Having been captured five days after deserting,
Private Carter was convicted by court martial, and
executed.)

911995 Private
William DONNAN
46th Battalion, Canadian Infantry
(Saskatchewan Regiment)
Died 3 May 1917, aged 45

ONLY SON OF ROBERT DONNAN
BALLYCRAN, CO. DOWN, IRELAND
KILLED NEAR LENS
IN HIS FIRST ENGAGEMENT

Lieutenant
John Llewellyn EVANS
'D' Company, 54th Battalion, Canadian Infantry
(Central Ontario Regiment)
Died 1 March 1917, aged 23

"HE RUSHED INTO THE FIELD
AND FOREMOST FIGHTING FELL"
BYRON

(From Childe Harolde.)

164410 Corporal
William MacKendrick HENRY
75th Battalion, Canadian Infantry
(Central Ontario Regiment)
Died 28 June 1917, aged 20

HIS LIFE WAS A SONG
HIS SACRIFICE A JOY
HE IS WITH THE HEROES

Lieutenant
Donald MACLEAN
Princess Patricia's Canadian Light Infantry
(Eastern Ontario Regiment)
Died 5 July 1917, aged 26

COMRADE'S TRIBUTE
"THE ATMOSPHERE OF HIS LIFE
DREW US HEAVEN-WARD"

790564 Private
Alastair FRASER
47th Battalion, Canadian Infantry
(Western Ontario Regiment)
Died 31 March 1917, aged 32

CLOSE UPON
THE FIELD OF STRIFE
OPEN STANDS
THE GATE OF LIFE

1015102 Private
Christopher MARSDEN
72nd Battalion, Canadian Infantry
(British Columbia Regiment)
Died 28 June 1917, aged 19

REMEMBER ME
O MIGHTY ONE
OUR ONLY CHILD

754318 Private
Clarence GIBSON
73rd Battalion, Canadian Infantry
Died 4 April 1917, aged 21

HIS AMBITION WAS
NO HONOURS
ONLY A CLEAN SHEET

28107 Private
Thomas John HENRY
9th Battalion, East Surrey Regiment
Died 12 October 1916, aged 22

MILES AWAY
BUT ALWAYS NEAR US

Major
Edward Cecil Horatio MOORE
38th Battalion, Canadian Infantry
(Eastern Ontario Regiment)
Died 9 April 1917, aged 40

OBJECTIVE GAINED

192573 Private
Harry NUTTALL
15th Battalion, Canadian Infantry
(Central Ontario Regiment)
Died 2 June 1917, aged 42

TIME
LIKE AN EVER ROLLING STREAM
BEARS ALL ITS SONS AWAY

(From the hymn O God Our Help in Ages
Past, *by Isaac Watts.)*

234852 Private
Charles Albert ROLLINGS
52nd Battalion, Canadian Infantry
(Manitoba Regiment)
Died 18 July 1917, aged 26

"THE UNDONE YEARS
THE CRUELTY OF WAR"
SADLY MISSED BY
MOTHER, FATHER, SISTERS, BROS.

Lieutenant
Thomas Alexander ROWAT
38th Battalion, Canadian Infantry
(Eastern Ontario Regiment)
Died 28 June 1917, aged 38

IT IS WELL
2ND KINGS 4TH CHAP.
26TH VERSE

629567 Lance Corporal
Ernest Muncaster TURNER
47th Battalion, Canadian Infantry
(Western Ontario Regiment)
Died 16 March 1917, aged 36

MARCH
IN HEAVENLY ARMOUR CLAD

(From the hymn Oft in Danger *by Henry Kirke*
White.)

Vis en Artois British Cemetery

Second Lieutenant
Alfred CHAVENTRE
2 'A' Battery, 126th Brigade,
Royal Field Artillery
Died 1 September 1918, aged 20

I GAVE MY ALL, MY LIFE
AT CALL OF ENGLAND'S NEED

Major
John Kenrick Lloyd FITZWILLIAMS, *MC*
25th Army Brigade, Royal Field Artillery
Died 30 August 1918, aged 33

THE PEOPLE
THAT DO KNOW THEIR GOD
SHALL BE STRONG
AND DO EXPLOITS

(From Daniel, *Chapter 11, Verse 32. Major*
Fitzwilliams held the Order of St Stanislaus, 2nd
Class [Russia].)

Lieutenant
Gilbert Dennis James GRUNE
8th Squadron, Royal Flying Corps,
and Royal Field Artillery
Died 13 March 1916, aged 22

KILLED IN AIR FIGHT
HE BORE HIM BRAVELY
TILL LIFE'S SPLENDID CLOSE

2383605 Private
John Albert NADON
52nd Battalion, Canadian Infantry
(Manitoba Regiment)
Died 28 August 1918, aged 26

GOD, MOTHER, ENGLAND

26633 Private
William James RIPPIN
7th Battalion, King's Shropshire Light Infantry
Died 19 June 1917, aged 21

ALSO IN MEMORY OF CHARLIE
SOMEWHERE IN FRANCE
KILLED 29 JUNE 1917

('Charlie' – Private Charles Henry Rippin – is
commemorated on the Arras Memorial to the
Missing. Only ten days separated their deaths.)

Vlamertinghe Military Cemetery

Lieutenant
Alfred Ray Lancaster BELL
2nd Battalion, Royal Dublin Fusiliers
Died 17 May 1915, aged 19

HE HATH DELIVERED MY SOUL
IN PEACE
FROM THE BATTLE
THAT WAS AGAINST ME

(From Psalms, *Chapter 55, Verse 18.)*

Second Lieutenant
Thomas Lloyd BLACK
171st Field Company, Royal Engineers
Died 2 June 1915, aged 22

HE WAS EARLY IN THE FIELD
& GAVE HIS ALL FOR OTHERS

6421 Private
Geoffrey William CAMPBELL
4th/5th Battalion,
The Black Watch (Royal Highlanders)
Died 12 January 1917, aged 18

ALL OUR FREEDOM, HOPE AND JOY
WE OWE TO THE LADS LIKE YOU

97297 Gunner
George DRAPER
197th Battery, Royal Garrison Artillery
Died 29 April 1917, aged 34

IN LOVING MEMORY OF
MY DEAR HUSBAND
AND FATHER OF
HIS SIX CHILDREN

204467 Rifleman
William GOOCH
5th Battalion, The King's (Liverpool Regiment)
Died 18 March 1917, aged 25

LIKE A HERO HE FELL
IN THE RUSH OF BATTLE
THAT WE MIGHT LIVE
IN PEACE

267017 Private
Francis GOOLEY
1st/7th Battalion,
The King's (Liverpool Regiment)
Died 23 March 1917, aged 20

OF YOUR CHARITY
PRAY FOR THE SOUL OF
FRANCIS GOOLEY ALSO JOHN
R.I.P.

(Brother John has no known grave and is
commemorated on the Loos Memorial to the
Missing.)

Captain
Francis Octavius GRENFELL, *VC*
9th (Queen's Royal) Lancers
Died 24 May 1915, aged 35

ALSO TO THE MEMORY OF
HIS TWIN BROTHER
RIVERSDALE
BORN 1880. SONS OF
PASCOE & SOFIA GRENFELL

*(Captain Grenfell had been Master of the Beagles
and a member of the cricket XI at Eton, following
which he served in Egypt with the Seaforth
Highlanders, in the Boer War with the King's
Royal Rifle Corps and in India with the 9th
Lancers. He won the VC for gallantry in action on
24 August 1914. Whilst in hospital recovering
from wounds sustained in that action, he learned
that his twin brother Rivy had been killed in
France. The photograph shows the twins with the
beagles at Eton; Francis is on the right.)*

2014 Corporal
Herbert Victor Wilson HASLEGRAVE
16th Battalion, Middlesex Regiment
Died 15 September 1916, aged 25

JUST A VOLUNTEER

Lieutenant
John Christopher HEBBLETHWAITE
43rd Battery, Royal Field Artillery
Died 22 June 1916, aged 20

A BOY
HE SPENT HIS BOY'S DEAR LIFE
FOR ENGLAND

710960 Gunner
Edward Henry Harold HUSBAND
'C' Battery, 298th Brigade, Royal Field Artillery
Died 9 May 1917, aged 22

PROMOTED TO GLORY
AN EARNEST SOUL WINNER
OF THE SALVATION ARMY

Second Lieutenant
Alan Williamson KENT
7th Battalion, Northumberland Fusiliers
Died 27 April 1915, aged 21

HIS LAST WORDS
ON LEAVING HOME
FAREWELL
I WILL DO MY BEST

---

483 Acting Bombardier
Brian Innis McCARTHY
71st Siege Battery, South African Heavy Artillery
Died 4 June 1916, aged 22

FACING DANGER HE PASSED
FROM THE SIGHT OF MEN
BY THE PATH OF DUTY

R/2013 Lance Corporal
Percy Charles ROBINSON
10th Battalion, King's Royal Rifle Corps
Died 25 June 1916, aged 17

CALLED HOME
TO HIGHER SERVICE
AGE 17 YEARS

2460 Private
Hugh Gordon STEPHENS
16th Battalion, Middlesex Regiment
Died 12 September 1916, aged 22

LATE OF BANGALORE, S. INDIA
NOW WITH CHRIST
WHICH IS FAR BETTER

(The bleak humour which arises from this epitaph
through the juxtaposition of two separate statements
– one a simple fact, the other a biblical quote
[Philippians, Chapter 1, Verse 23] – was
presumably unintended.)

5980 Company Sergeant Major
George WELLS
14th Battalion, Hampshire Regiment
Died 9 June 1917, aged 35

HE DIED
IN THAT FULL SPLENDOUR
OF HEROIC PRIDE
THAT WE MIGHT LIVE

Vlamertinghe New Military Cemetery

622053 Corporal
Arthur Samuel BENNELL
298th Brigade, Royal Horse Artillery
Died 17 September 1917, aged 21

THE LAST ENEMY
TO BE DESTROYED
IS DEATH

159585 Gunner
Richard BROOKS
V/5th Trench Mortar Battery,
Royal Field Artillery
Died 31 July 1917, aged 32

HIS LAST WRITTEN WORD
"RESTING"
REST ON BELOVED

Major
Frank FISHER
470th (North Midland) Field Company,
Royal Engineers
Died 26 September 1917, aged 42

"FOR HIS HIGH COURAGE
AND SELF-SACRIFICE
WE THANK THEE LORD!"

Captain
Frank Edward GATLIFF
14th Brigade, Australian Field Artillery
Died 6 August 1917, aged 22

BRAVE AND NOBLE ACTIONS
COUNT FOR MORE
THAN LENGTH OF YEARS

161909 Gunner
Emanuel HOY
'B' Battery, 307th Brigade, Royal Field Artillery
Died 15 August 1917, aged 27

FOR THIS MAN IS WORTHY OF
MORE HONOUR AND GLORY

285030 Private
Robert HUGHES
1st/6th Battalion,
The Black Watch (Royal Highlanders)
Died 2 July 1917, aged 19

FRIENDS MAY FORGET HIM
HIS MOTHER WILL NEVER

Captain
William Johnstone KNOX, *MC*
13th Brigade, Australian Field Artillery
Died 20 August 1917, aged 30

THE LUCK OF THE GAME

Lieutenant
Walter John McMULLIN, *MC*
1st Brigade, Australian Field Artillery
Died 4 October 1917, aged 27

'TIS THE LUCK OF THE GAME

Lieutenant
Illaesus Faustus PASCOE-WEBBE
13th Brigade, Australian Field Artillery
Died 19 August 1917, aged 30

O GOD WHY THIS SACRIFICE

Lieutenant
Patrick Randal PLAYFORD
'A' Battery, 1st (West Lancashire) Brigade,
Royal Field Artillery
Died 1 July 1917, aged 25

THE GOLD OF HIS YOUTH
HE SO GLADLY GAVE
YET TO US
HE'LL NEVER BE DEAD

43350 Private
Trefor Stanley ROBERTS
11th Battalion, Leicestershire Regiment
Died 8 May 1918, aged 20

MY REAL SON CAN NEVER DIE

675188 Gunner
Ralph Osborne ROTHWELL
'C' Battery, 275th Brigade, Royal Field Artillery
Died 2 August 1917, aged 22

GOOD OLD RALPH

Voormezeele Enclosure No 3

65559 Private
John Donald Mackintosh CAMPBELL
26th Battalion, Royal Fusiliers
Died 7 June 1917, aged 18

THE HORN OF DERMID
HAS SOUNDED

(Dermid is a hero of Celtic legend.)

S/2664 Private
George DAVIE
'D' Company, 1st Battalion, Gordon Highlanders
Died 15 March 1915, aged 27

RED, RED IS THE PATH TO GLORY

---

595 Private
Francis Guy DWYER
Princess Patricia's Canadian Light Infantry
(Eastern Ontario Regiment)
Died 4 February 1915, aged 20

"GOD REST MY SOUL"
THE LAST WORDS HE SAID

1862 Private
Francis Henry Buckley FAWLEY
Honourable Artillery Company
Died 15 May 1915, aged 19

SO YOUNG, SO BRAVE, SO TRUE

2168 Private
Maxwell GREEN
No 1 Company, Honourable Artillery Company
Died 22 April 1915, aged 19

O SOLDIER SAINT
WHO PUT HIS BREAST
BETWEEN THE SPEARS AND ME

1113 Private
Ronald Young HEDDERWICK
Honourable Artillery Company
Died 16 May 1915, aged 27

HE FOUGHT HIS WAY
TO EVERLASTING LIFE
MET BY HIS GOD'S "WELL DONE"

Second Lieutenant
Victor ROBERTS
9th Battalion, Welsh Regiment
Died 19 July 1917, aged 20

MY PURPOSES ARE BROKEN OFF

Second Lieutenant
William Albert SEEDS
10th Battalion,
The Queen's (Royal West Surrey Regiment)
Died 6 or 7 June 1917, aged 33

FOR HIM THE FIGHT
THE VICTORY
FOR US BUT LOVING MEMORY

A SOLDIER
OF THE GREAT WAR

Vraucourt Copse Cemetery

13331 Private
Albert Edward PARKINSON
12th Field Ambulance,
Australian Army Medical Corps
Died 11 April 1917, aged 26

THE NIGHT IS DARK
AND I AM FAR FROM HOME

(From Cardinal Newman's poem The Pillar of
Cloud: Lead Kindly Light.*)*

Wancourt British Cemetery

513324 Private
William Gilbert BROWN
1st/14th Battalion, London Regiment
(London Scottish)
Died 16 April 1917, aged 26

FAR FROM HOME HIS MANLY FORM
IN MEMORY EVER LIVES

PS/8274 Lance Corporal
Geoffrey Thurnam FAIRBANK
20th Battalion, Royal Fusiliers
Died 16 April 1917, aged 19

DUTY FIRST – LIFE LAST

875201 Private
George Gibson FRENCH, *DCM*
27th Battalion, Canadian Infantry
(Manitoba Regiment)
Died 27 August 1918, aged 23

WE WERE PROUD OF HIS LIFE
WE MUST BE PROUD
OF HIS DEATH

392448 Rifleman
Henry Walter MUMFORD
1st/9th Battalion, London Regiment
(Queen Victoria's Rifles)
Died 29 April 1917, aged 20

NOW HEAVEN IS
BY THE YOUNG INVADED

Believed to be buried in this cemetery
492922 Private
Stanley WAIN
13th (Kensington) Battalion, London Regiment
Died 6 May 1917, aged 20

DEAR OLD STAN
JUST WE FOUR
MOTHER, FATHER & RALPH

Warlencourt British Cemetery

5191 Private
Thomas CAFE
22nd Battalion, London Regiment
Died 8 October 1916, aged 22

WEEP NOT FOR ME
BUT PITY TAKE
AND LOVE MY MOTHER
FOR MY SAKE

8718 Private
Abraham Bernard GREEN
'B' Company, 3rd Regiment,
South African Infantry
Died 18 October 1916, aged 26

YEA, THOUGH I WALK

('...... through the valley of the shadow of death, I
will fear no evil ......' – Psalms, Chapter 23,
Verse 4.)

Warlincourt Halte British Cemetery

105662 Private
Wilfred Louis BRADSHAW
177th Company, Labour Corps
Died 17 May 1917, aged 24

MY ALL – MY ONLY CHILD
NOT DEAD – FOR LIFE ETERNAL
CROWNS THY FAIR YOUNG HEAD

472773 Rifleman
Alfred CHAPNESS
12th Battalion, London Regiment (The Rangers)
Died 12 April 1917, aged 22

GOD SENT FROM ABOVE
AND DREW HIM
FROM THE ENEMY
TO HIS BOSOM

Lieutenant
Harold George COLLINS
48th Squadron, Royal Flying Corps
Died 9 April 1917, aged 22

NO WORDS EXPRESS
THE MEASURE OF
OUR THANKFULNESS
TO YOU – OUR DEAD

(At the time of Lieutenant Collins's death, the life
expectancy of a Royal Flying Corps subaltern was
less than three weeks.)

Captain
Eric William COULSON-MAYNE
'D' Company, 5th Battalion,
Durham Light Infantry
Died 25 April 1917, aged 20

BELOVED YOU LIVE
FOR EVER IN OUR HEARTS
BRAVE, SWEET, DARLING SON

(The only son of Eric and Nellie Coulson-Mayne of
Richmond Green, Surrey, this young officer had
passed his entrance-exam for Sandhurst in 1914
but preferred to accept an immediate commission
into the Bedfordshire Regiment [Special Reserve].
He was wounded in 1915 and recovered to serve as
a recruiting officer during convalescence, and then as
an intelligence officer at Albert in 1916.)

Lieutenant
David Grant DAVIDSON
23rd Battalion, Canadian Infantry,
attached 11th Squadron, Royal Flying Corps
Died 23 August 1917, aged 21

OUR WORK MUST BE BROUGHT
TO A SATISFACTORY CONCLUSION
OR WE DIE IN THE ATTEMPT

102034 Gunner
Frederick GILBERT
196th Siege Battery, Royal Garrison Artillery
Died 20 May 1917, aged 36

DEAREST LOVE
FROM YOUR TWO LITTLE GIRLS
SLEEP ON DEAR ONE AND REST

Second Lieutenant
George Archibald Edward Fitzgeorge
HAMILTON
1st Battalion, Grenadier Guards
Died 18 May 1918, aged 19

TRULY YE ARE OF THE BLOOD

266233 Private
William Ernest HORNER
1st/7th Battalion, Sherwood Foresters
(Nottinghamshire & Derbyshire Regiment)
Died 14 March 1917, aged 20

HE HATED WAR
BUT VOLUNTARILY GAVE
HIS LIFE FOR FREEDOM

15722 Sergeant
Hubert Francis SMITH
17th Battalion, Manchester Regiment
Died 29 April 1917, aged 24

ONE DIETH
IN HIS FULL STRENGTH
NOW BEING
WHOLLY AT EASE AND QUIET

(From Job, *Chapter 21, Verse 23.)*

Warloy-Baillon Communal Cemetery Extension

22780 Private
Sidney BRADLEY
1st Battalion,
West Yorkshire Regiment (Prince of Wales's Own)
Died 5 July 1916, aged 38

WE WONDER WHY?
HIS WIFE AND 3 CHILDREN

THEIR NAME LIVETH
FOR EVERMORE

341083 Gunner
Frederick Thomas GORDON
267th Siege Battery, Royal Garrison Artillery
Died 24 July 1918, aged 33

THE BATTLE DRUMS
NO LONGER BEAT
HIS SOUL FINDS REST
AT JESU'S FEET

39644 Lance Corporal
Arthur Leonard HALLIWELL
24th Battalion, Manchester Regiment
Died 28 November 1916, aged 20

LET THOSE WHO COME AFTER
SEE THAT THEIR SACRIFICE
BE NOT IN VAIN

1745 Private
Frank Noel HINDE
45th Battalion, Australian Infantry
Died 5 April 1918, aged 24

THOU OH FRANCE
HOLDEST ONE OF GOD'S NOBLEST

16240 Private
Robert James HOLMES
6th/7th Battalion, Royal Scots Fusiliers
Died 12 August 1916, aged 21

HE DIED YOUNG, CLEAN, ARDENT
TO SAVE OTHERS
FROM DEATH OR WORSE

---

723 Private
Lawrence HUFFAM
48th Battalion, Australian Infantry
Died 15 August 1916, aged 24

ONE OF SIX BROTHERS
ALL OF WHOM
ANSWERED AT ONCE

G/90028 Private
Charles Edwin MORRIS
'C' Company, 2nd/4th Battalion,
London Regiment (Royal Fusiliers)
Died 30 May 1918, aged 18

THEY CROWDED ALL THEIR YOUTH
INTO AN HOUR
& FOR ONE FLEETING DREAM
OF RIGHT THEY DIED

3899 Private
Alfred ROBINSON
4th Battalion, Australian Infantry
Died 17 August 1916, aged 20

IN DARK
AND BITTER HOURS APART
WE BROOD ABOVE
THE ASH OF SACRIFICE

13297 Sergeant
George STANGOE
8th Battalion, Gloucestershire Regiment
Died 18 November 1916, aged 27

HIS LIFE
A RANSOM FOR MANY

131581 Sapper
Joseph VICKERS
236th Army Troop Company, Royal Engineers
Died 7 September 1916, aged 20

ALL THAT FOR WHICH HE FOUGHT
LIVES ON

White City Cemetery

Lieutenant
Leslie Benito FISHER
12th Battalion, King's Royal Rifle Corps
Died 14 August 1915, aged 30

TRIUMPHANT BE THEIR DIRGE
WHO WERE THE FLOWER
OF MOURNING ENGLAND

White House Cemetery

28881 Sergeant
William BARRY
66th Siege Battery, Royal Garrison Artillery
Died 4 October 1917, aged 28

LOVE TO MY BOY IN ST. JEAN
MAY HIS SOUL HEAVEN OBTAIN
IRISH MOTHER

(St Jean, now known by the Flemish version of its
name, Sint-Jan, is the location of White House
Cemetery.)

Captain
George Townshend BROOKE
1st (North Midland) Field Company,
Royal Engineers
Died 5 May 1915, aged 36

ALLELULIA! ALLELULIA! ALLELULIA!

Lieutenant Colonel
Henry William Ernest HITCHINS
1st Battalion, Manchester Regiment
Died 26 April 1915, aged 49

NOBLE-HEARTED GALLANT SOLDIER
HONOURABLE, TRUE, BRAVE
LOVING AND BELOVED
GOD BLESS YOU

(Lieutenant Colonel Hitchins had been Mentioned
in Despatches for gallant and distinguished service
at the capture of Givenchy on 20 December 1914,
and again at Ypres in April 1915. His late father
was a major general.)

13254 Lance Corporal
Ernest HORROD
2nd Battalion, Coldstream Guards
Died 26 March 1916, aged 27

HE RAN THE RACE
THAT WAS SET BEFORE HIM

266929 Private
George MITCHELL
2nd/7th Battalion, Sherwood Foresters
(Nottinghamshire & Derbyshire Regiment)
Died 29 September 1917, aged 24

FAR FROM MOTHER
BUT NEARER TO GOD

306754 Private
Frank Joseph SELBY
2nd/8th Battalion, Sherwood Foresters
(Nottinghamshire & Derbyshire Regiment),
attached 178th Light Trench Mortar Battery
Died 29 September 1917, aged 21

DARLING FRANK
LOVED, REMEMBERED
LONGED FOR ALWAYS
MOTHER

M/225505 Private
John William TAYLOR
884th Mechanical Transport Company,
Royal Army Service Corps
Died 19 August 1917, aged 20

NOW HE SERVES IN PARADISE
UNDER THE PRINCE OF PEACE

---

513 Sergeant
Kenneth William VEAR
37th Battalion, Australian Infantry
Died 3 October 1917, aged 25

GOOD OLD KEN
A MAN'S MAN

Wimereux Communal Cemetery

The Reverend
Armar Edward ACTON
Chaplain to the Forces 4th Class,
attached 2nd Battalion, Border Regiment
Died 4 November 1917, aged 28

FATALLY WOUNDED
WHEN VISITING HIS MEN
MENIN ROAD
FAITHFUL UNTO DEATH

9559 Private
George Harold ALDRIDGE
2nd Battalion,
The Queen's (Royal West Surrey Regiment)
Died 5 November 1914, aged 25

MAY PEACE HER SWAY EXTEND
AND BRITAIN'S POWER DEPEND
ON WAR NO MORE

6351 Private
John William BRYANT
17th Lancers (Duke of Cambridge's Own),
attached 2nd Life Guards
Died 22 November 1914, aged 26

THE DEVOTED SON OF
AN INVALID MOTHER

365037 Gunner
Oliver Nelson CARMICHAEL
151st Siege Battery, Royal Garrison Artillery
Died 17 June 1917, aged 20

BORN 21.1.1897
A SOLDIER
IN THE GREAT WAR

93926 Gunner
Frederick George CLARKE
114th Battery, Royal Field Artillery
Died 30 July 1916, aged 37

A MORTAL ARROW
PIERCED HIS FRAME
HE FELL
BUT FELT NO FEAR

(Lines from The Christian Soldier *by James*
Montgomery.)

Lieutenant
Edward CRAWFORD
3rd Battalion, Royal Inniskilling Fusiliers
Died 27 May 1915, aged 35

HIS LIFE FOR THE LIFE
FRANCE GAVE US
OFF USHANT, 6TH OCT. 1779

(This is a reference to a sea-battle between the
frigates Quebec *(British) and* Surveillante
(French). The surgeon's-mate of the former, an
ancestor of Lieutenant Crawford, was among 36 of
the British officers and crew who, having been cast
into the Atlantic waters, were saved by being taken
aboard the enemy ship.)

18424 Private
Charles DONKIN
8th Battalion, North Staffordshire Regiment
Died 7 October 1917, aged 29

MAY HIS VICTORY RIBBON
BE PURE WHITE
BORN FEB. 28TH. 1888
AGE 30

(A miscalculation here by the soldier's widow – the
date of birth is correct; the age at death is not.)

41484 Private
David DUNN
18th Battalion, Highland Light Infantry
Died 29 October 1917, aged 21

MY SON
WE MISS YOU
NIGHT AND DAY
WE MISS YOU EVERYWHERE

402502 Private
William John ELLINS
3rd Battalion, Canadian Infantry
(Central Ontario Regiment)
Died 24 June 1916, aged 40

WE ARE BROTHERS & COMRADES
WE LIE SIDE BY SIDE
AND OUR FAITH & OUR HOPES
ARE THE SAME

Captain & Quarter Master
Frank Stephen FORD
1st Battalion, Essex Regiment
Died 24 March 1918, aged 47

HE WAS A MAN
TAKE HIM FOR ALL IN ALL
WE SHALL NOT LOOK UPON
HIS LIKE AGAIN

(Adapted from Shakespeare's Hamlet, *Act 1,*
Scene 2.)

15607 Private
Horace GAMBIE
11th Battalion, Suffolk Regiment
Died 7 February 1917, aged 23

WE PICTURED HIM
SAFELY RETURNING
WE LONGED
TO CLASP HIS HAND

301088 Private
John Catto HAY
1st/2nd Highland Field Ambulance,
Royal Army Medical Corps
Died 21 October 1917, aged 21

FOR BRITAIN'S GLORY

54 Private
Magdal HERMANSON
8th Battalion, Canadian Infantry
(Manitoba Regiment)
Died 3 May 1915, aged 19

HE WAS THE FIRST ICELANDER
TO GIVE HIS LIFE
FOR CANADA
I THANK YOU MY SON

17931 Rifleman
William James IRWIN
14th Battalion, Royal Irish Rifles
Died 23 June 1917, aged 21

FAREWELL
SUNSHINE OF OUR HOME
YOUR DUTY NOBLY DONE
MY FAIR YOUNG SON

436 Private
James Aloysius KINLAY
4th Regiment, South African Infantry
Died 21 July 1916, aged 38

CI GIT UN SOLDAT IRLANDAIS
DE SUD AFRIQUE
FILS DE J. KINLAY
DUBLIN

(Translation from the French: 'Here lies an Irish
soldier from South Africa, son of J.Kinlay,
Dublin'.)

629123 Private
George Lyall McLAUCHLAN, *MM*
47th Battalion, Canadian Infantry
(Western Ontario Regiment)
Died 16 April 1917, aged 40

A SON OF
THE PERTHSHIRE MOUNTAINS
LIES HERE

Major
Hugh McMASTER, *DSO, MC*
'A' Battery, 46th Brigade, Royal Field Artillery
Died 2 December 1917, aged 30

AGED 30
10 YEARS SERVICE
WITH THE BRITISH ARMY

(The only son of a widow, Major McMaster first
joined the 48th Brigade in 1907, at Dundalk. He
had been seriously wounded in 1914 and 1916.)

266828 Private
Harry MARSDEN
2nd/7th Battalion, Sherwood Foresters
(Nottinghamshire & Derbyshire Regiment)
Died 6 October 1917, aged 21

NO CONSCRIPT
A VOLUNTEER FOR THE RIGHT
FOR CHRIST'S SAKE

439522 Private
Lawrence MARTIN
52nd Battalion, Canadian Infantry
(Manitoba Regiment)
Died 5 October 1916, aged 33

ONE OF THE MANY
CANADIAN INDIANS
WHO DIED
FOR THE EMPIRE

2111 Lance Corporal
Peter PENNINGTON
'C' Company, 4th Battalion,
South Lancashire Regiment
Died 29 April 1915, aged 22

HE DIED
AS FIRM AS SPARTA'S KING
BECAUSE HIS SOUL
WAS GREAT

(Adapted from Sir Francis Doyle's poem The
Private of the Buffs.*)*

285121 Private
James Henderson RANKIN
1st/6th Battalion, Seaforth Highlanders
Died 8 August 1917, aged 20

ALSO HIS BROTHER "BILLY"
FELL AT ROEUX, 16TH MAY 1917
OUR HOPES, OUR LIFE

(Brother Billy – Private W.H. Rankin of the
Argyll & Sutherland Highlanders – has no
known grave and is commemorated on the Arras
Memorial to the Missing.)

202261 Private
Albert ROEBUCK
1st/4th Battalion, York & Lancaster Regiment
Died 13 October 1917, aged 23

DAYS OF SADNESS
OFT COME O'ER US
GOD'S WILL BE DONE

303701 Private
Reginald Whitworth SABINE
2nd/5th Battalion, Manchester Regiment
Died 11 October 1917, aged 19

HOPE IS GRIEF'S BEST MUSIC

L/1922 Shoeing Smith
John SCOTT
'A' Battery, 4th Brigade, Royal Field Artillery
Died 17 July 1916, aged 29

WE MAY BE HERE,
OUR HEARTS
ARE WHERE A GALLANT
BRITISH SOLDIER LIES

Lieutenant
Cecil Frederick TAYLOR
(Queen's Own Royal) Glasgow Yeomanry
Died 20 January 1918, aged 21

IN EVER SORROWING AND
GLORIOUS MEMORY OF
OUR DARLING & GALLANT BOY

73564 Gunner
Herbert TEAGLE
'C' Battery, 107th Brigade, Royal Field Artillery
Died 5 June 1917, aged 33

ONE LESS AT HOME
ONE FAREWELL WORD UNSPOKEN
ONE MORE IN HEAVEN

687 Private
William Edward **TRIBE**
19th Battalion, Australian Infantry
Died 6 August 1916, aged 23

FAR FROM THE LAND
WHERE HIS FOREFATHERS SLEEP

1468 Sergeant
Walter James **WEEDON**
83rd (2nd/3rd Home Counties) Field Ambulance,
Royal Army Medical Corps
Died 24 March 1915, aged 22

WHEN THE EAST
WAS BATHED IN SPLENDOUR
AND THE DAY
HAD BUT BEGUN

Ypres Reservoir Cemetery

9/11835 Private
James Willie **BATES**
9th Battalion,
Duke of Wellington's (West Riding Regiment)
Died 19 December 1915, aged 19

ONE OF THE FIRST
TO ANSWER THE CALL
MEMORY CLINGS
TO BYGONE HAPPY DAYS

KNOWN UNTO GOD

42764 Gunner
Charles Caton **BATTERSBY**
301st Siege Battery, Royal Garrison Artillery
Died 7 August 1917, aged 22

MAY THIS SACRIFICE
BE A MEANS OF PROMOTING
PEACE THROUGHOUT THE LAND

Major
The Honourable
William George Sidney **CADOGAN**, *MVO*
10th (Prince of Wales's Own) Hussars,
and General Staff
Died 12 November 1914, aged 35

TELL ENGLAND
YE THAT PASS THIS WAY
THAT HE WHO RESTS HERE
DIED CONTENT

(This son of the 5th Earl Cadogan served in the
Boer War and was equerry of the Prince of Wales
from 1912 to 1914. The epitaph is an adaptation
of words which originated in Ancient Greece.)

Major
Colin Archibald Henson **CAMPBELL**
'C' Battery, 296th Brigade, Royal Field Artillery
Died 29 September 1917, aged 37

IN LABOURS BY KINDNESS,
HONOUR, GOOD REPORT:
AS DYING AND BEHOLD WE LIVE

(Major Campbell, whose military career had
encompassed the Boer War, was the sixth successive
generation of his family to have served in the Royal
Navy or army. His epitaph is a very condensed
version of a sequence of verses in II Corinthians,
Chapter 6.)

130804 Gunner
Cyril Ernest CLINCH
146th Heavy Battery, Royal Garrison Artillery
Died 25 September 1917, aged 30

TU NE VIENDRAS PU A MOI
UN JOUR J'IRAI A TOI
M C

(French was the native tongue of 'MC' – the
widowed Marguerite Clinch of Neuilly-sur-Seine.
Her words translate as: 'You will not be able to
come to me; one day I will go to you'.)

Major
Hugh ELLIOT
11th Battalion, The King's (Liverpool Regiment)
Died 26 July 1915, aged 51

NEC ASPERA TERRENT
PEACE SHALL FOLLOW BATTLE
NIGHT SHALL END IN DAY

(Born in India and a regular soldier for more than
three decades, Major Elliot had served in the
Burma Campaign of 1885-86. The Latin tag
means: 'Nor do difficulties deter'.)

92566 Flight Sergeant
Edward Thomas FOWLER
18th Balloon Section, Royal Flying Corps
Died 1 October 1917, aged 32

THE PATH OF DUTY
WAS THE WAY TO GLORY

(From Tennyson's Œnone.)

Second Lieutenant
Archibald Forster GRAHAM
Royal Garrison Artillery
Died 11 November 1915, aged 22

SURELY FOR HIM
HIGH SERVICE WAITS
THOUGH EARTH'S LAST FIGHT
IS FOUGHT

Major
James Leadbitter KNOTT, *DSO*
10th Battalion,
West Yorkshire Regiment (Prince of Wales's Own)
Died 1 July 1916, aged 33

DEVOTED IN LIFE
IN DEATH NOT DIVIDED

(Major Knott's was one of over nineteen thousand
British deaths on the first day of the Battle of the
Somme. After the war his body was taken to Ypres
for burial next to his brother, a Northumberland
Fusiliers officer who died in 1915. The brothers'
epitaphs are identical.)

3419 Private
Harry Noel LEA
17th Battalion, Australian Infantry
Died 14 October 1917, aged 21

HAPPY WARRIOR

361452 Sapper
Frederick Wesley LEWIS
4th Field Survey Company, Royal Engineers
Died 11 October 1918, aged 20

AND THEN
O HOW PLEASANT
THE CONQUEROR'S SONG

(A line from John Newton's hymn Be Gone,
Unbelief; My Saviour is Near.)

Second Lieutenant
Clarence John LOVELL
274th Siege Battery, Royal Garrison Artillery
Died 19 October 1917, aged 19

WHERE THE LINES
SWEPT ON IN TRIUMPH
AND HEROES STAYED BEHIND

868 Gunner
John McCARTHY
36th Group, Australian Heavy Artillery
Died 4 October 1917, aged 24

BELOVED SON
OF D. & M. MCCARTHY
GRANDSON OF CORPORAL D. MCCARTHY
(CRIMEA)

Brigadier General
Francis Aylmer MAXWELL,
VC, CSI, DSO & Bar
18th (King George's Own) Lancers, Indian Army,
commanding 27th Infantry Brigade,
9th (Scottish) Division
Died 21 September 1917, aged 46

AN IDEAL SOLDIER AND
A VERY PERFECT GENTLEMAN
BELOVED BY ALL HIS MEN

(This senior officer's VC was won in the Boer
War.)

Lieutenant Colonel
Athelstan MOORE, *DSO*
1st Battalion, Royal Dublin Fusiliers
Died 14 October 1918, aged 38

"SAIL FORTH!
STEER FOR
THE DEEP WATERS ONLY!
RECKLESS O SOUL, EXPLORING"

(These lines are by the American poet Walt
Whitman.)

28118 Gunner
John Philip MORGAN
36th Group, Australian Heavy Artillery
Died 4 October 1917, aged 30

LEAVING A SORROWING WIFE
MOTHER, SISTER
AND 3 YOUNG CHILDREN

13010 Private
Percy George ROWLEY
6th Battalion, Duke of Cornwall's Light Infantry
Died 1 August 1915, aged 38

BUT NONE OF THE RANSOMED
WILL EVER KNOW
HOW DEEP
WERE THE WATERS CROSSED

(Adapted from The Joy of the Lord, *a poem by*
Elizabeth C.Clephane.)

Second Lieutenant
Cecil Owen SMITH
36th Battery, 33rd Brigade, Royal Field Artillery
Died 20 August 1917, aged 19

A DAILY THOUGHT
AN EVERLASTING SORROW

19599 Private
William John SOLOMON
6th Battalion, Duke of Cornwall's Light Infantry
Died 17 September 1915, aged 18

DUTY CALLED HIM
HE DID HIS BEST
NOW HE'S A SOLDIER
IN HEAVEN AT REST

Second Lieutenant
Osmer Noel STEWART, *MC*
'B' Battery, 71st Brigade, Royal Field Artillery
Died 31 July 1917, aged 19

OUR ONLY SON
GOD KEEP HIM

L/6356 Bombardier
Alfred George TAYLOR
192nd Brigade, Royal Field Artillery
Died 13 December 1917, aged 19

LOVE HE FOUND AND PEACE
WHERE FIRE AND WAR HAD BEEN

966 Private
Ronald George TULLOCH
Motor Transport,
2nd Divisional Supply Column,
Australian Army Service Corps
Died 21 October 1917, aged 27

SIMPLE DUTY
HAD NO PLACE FOR FEAR
MOTHER

Ypres Town Cemetery

Captain
Percy Stuart BANNING
2nd Battalion, Royal Munster Fusiliers
Died 4 November 1914, aged 27

WHO STANDS IF FREEDOM FALL?
WHO DIES IF ENGLAND LIVE?

(Captain Banning's father had served in the same
regiment as a Lieutenant Colonel. The epitaph is
from Rudyard Kipling's poem For All We Have
and Are.*)*

Lieutenant
Edward Wynne CHAPMAN
3rd Dragoon Guards (Prince of Wales's Own)
Died 17 November 1914, aged 27

HE LEAVES A WHITE
UNBROKEN GLORY
A GATHERED RADIANCE
A SHINING PEACE

(From Rupert Brooke's poem 1914. IV: The
Dead.*)*

Major
John Gwynne GRIFFITH
32nd Lancers and
Brigade Major, 9th Cavalry Brigade, Indian Army
Died 24 May 1915, aged 40

THERE WAS A MAN
SENT FROM GOD
WHOSE NAME WAS JOHN

(St John the Divine's words in reference to St John
the Baptist are in John, *Chapter 1, Verse 6.)*

Lieutenant
His Highness Prince
MAURICE Victor Donald
of BATTENBERG, *KCVO*
1st Battalion, King's Royal Rifle Corps
Died 27 October 1914, aged 23

GRANT HIM WITH ALL
THY FAITHFUL SERVANTS
A PLACE
OF REFRESHMENT AND PEACE

(Prince Maurice, a grandson of Queen Victoria,
had been Mentioned in Despatches.)

Major
Lord Charles George Francis Mercer
NAIRNE, *MVO*
1st (Royal) Dragoons,
attached 6th Cavalry Brigade
Died 30 October 1914, aged 40

"NOT IN VAIN
NOT UNHONOURED
NOT FORGOTTEN
THEY GAVE UP THEIR LIVES"

(This much-decorated son of the 5th Marquess of
Lansdowne was Equerry-in-Ordinary to the King
and a former ADC to Field Marshal Lord
Roberts. His awards included the MVO, the South
African Medal [5 clasps], the Legion of Honour
[France], the Order of Military Merit [Spain], the

Order of the Crown *[Russia]* and the Order of the *Iron Crown, Class II [Austria].)*

Lieutenant
Humfrey Richard TALBOT
3rd (Prince of Wales's) Dragoon Guards
Died 13 November 1914, aged 25

PEACE SHALL FOLLOW BATTLE
NIGHT SHALL END IN MORN

(Lines from Christian, Dost Thou See Them, *a hymn translated by John M.Neale from the 7th-century Greek of Andrew of Crete.)*

Ypres Town Cemetery Extension

41103 Sergeant
Hugh McLENNAN
2nd Brigade, Canadian Field Artillery
Died 26 April 1915, aged 27

ALL'S WELL
FOR OVER THERE
AMONG HIS PEERS
A HAPPY WARRIOR SLEEPS

7718 Private
Johnstone MACPHERSON
1st Battalion,
The Black Watch (Royal Highlanders)
Died 1 November 1914, aged 34

MY SON DIED BY
THE HAND OF FOES
A STRANGER'S HAND
HIS LIMBS REPOSED

(Private Macpherson was a Boer War veteran.)

Y Ravine Cemetery

1634 Private
Michael John HOLLAND
1st Battalion, Royal Newfoundland Regiment
Died 1 July 1916, aged 19

MY SON, MY SON
A CROWN THOU HAST WON
OF EVERLASTING GLORY

541 Private
Francis Thomas LIND
1st Battalion, Royal Newfoundland Regiment
Died 1 July 1916, aged 37

HOW CLOSELY BRAVERY
AND MODESTY ARE ENTWINED

(After volunteering at the start of the war, 'Mayo' Lind, who perished on the first day of the Battle of the Somme, became Newfoundland's unofficial war correspondent through his letters to The Daily News. *The nickname derived from a letter in which he drew attention to the shortage of Mayo, a popular brand of tobacco, as the result of which an abundance of the stuff was sent out as gifts to the men of the Newfoundland Regiment.)*

898 Lance Corporal
George Edward PIKE
1st Battalion, Royal Newfoundland Regiment
Died 1 July 1916, aged 33

BE ASHAMED TO DIE
UNTIL YOU HAVE GAINED
SOME VICTORY FOR HUMANITY

Captain
William STEPHEN
5th Battalion, Gordon Highlanders
Died 13 November 1916, aged 35

M.A. GRADUATE
OF ABERDEEN UNIVERSITY

Second Lieutenant
James Martyn Strickland SYKES
5th Battalion, Gordon Highlanders
Died 13 November 1916, aged 19

BEATI MUNDO CORDE

(Translation from the Latin: 'Blessed are the pure
in heart' – Matthew, Chapter 5, Verse 8.)

Zantwoorde British Cemetery

Captain
Robert Sefton ADAMS
12th Battery, 35th Brigade, Royal Field Artillery
Died 5 October 1917, aged 29

TO THEM THAT SAVED
OUR HERITAGE
AND CAST THEIR OWN AWAY

240693 Sergeant
Louis McGUFFIE, *VC*
1st/5th Battalion, King's Own Scottish Borderers
Died 4 October 1918, aged 25

OH FOR THE TOUCH
OF THE VANISHED HAND
AND THE SOUND OF THE VOICE
THAT IS STILL

(The epitaph is an adapted extract from the poem
Break, Break, Break, *by Alfred, Lord Tennyson.*
Sergeant McGuffie's VC was awarded
posthumously, he having been killed by a shell six
days after the action for which he won it. His age is
engraved incorrectly on the headstone as 24.)

TAILPIECE

Poelcapelle British Cemetery

Believed to be buried in this cemetery
Second Lieutenant
Hugh Gordon LANGTON
4th Battalion, London Regiment (Royal Fusiliers)
Died 26 October 1917, aged 32

"Inscriptions requiring the use of special alphabets such as Greek, etc, cannot be accepted." Despite this unequivocal condition, there are unexplained instances of epitaphs in, for instance, Hebrew. (There are also inscriptions which exceed the stipulated maximum of 66 characters and spaces – including one which runs to no fewer than exactly 400.)

The epitaph in this case is another which was clearly in breach of what was officially permitted, and it is unique. It consists of a piece of music. The officer to whom it is dedicated was a gifted violinist who had studied with some of the best teachers in Europe.

Efforts to identify the piece of music having failed, it was assumed that the notes are purely figurative. And yet ..... they closely resemble a line from the old sentimental song After the Ball, *albeit with the final note missing. The line in question is: "Many a heart is aching". The temptation to believe that this was the family's intended tribute is difficult to resist.*

The deceased's father, devastated by the loss of his son, fell ill and died exactly a week after the war ended.

Bartletts Battlefield Journeys Ltd
Broomhill, Edlington, Horncastle, Lincolnshire, LN9 5RJ
Tel: +44 (0) 1507 523128
Email: Info@battlefields.co.uk
www.battlefields.co.uk

BARTLETTS BATTLEFIELD JOURNEYS provide the ultimate battlefield experience for the discerning traveller and have an established reputation for their unique and very personal service. After escorting pilgrims to the Western Front and Normandy for many years, our team of four dedicated guides have widened their interests to offer a study of conflict over the ages, thereby extending our service to encompass all theatres of war and battle sites throughout mainland Europe.

Bartletts' speciality in leading small groups of between five and seven is particularly attractive to clients who seek an informal, unhurried and friendly experience. Each tour is meticulously researched and it is the composition and wishes of the group members which determine the programme.

Our renowned battlefield tours are <u>all-inclusive</u>, with all the following features covered by the tour price –

- Travel in a comfortable air-conditioned vehicle
- Accommodation at 3- and 4-star hotels, including breakfast and evening meals with wine
- Ferry crossings and meals
- Lunch each day, plus morning and afternoon coffee/tea
- Museum entrance-fees
- The services of a dedicated tour-guide who dines with the group each evening
- Detailed research into a soldier or army unit of specific interest to the guest
- Individual packs of handouts, maps and other documents
- Unparalleled quality of personal service and care

Bespoke tours can be arranged for guests wishing for a more exclusive experience who may be unable to fit in with our scheduled programme or who seek broader battlefield explorations. Bespoke tours are especially recommended for a combination of theatres of war, such as Waterloo and Arnhem, or Normandy and the Somme. Advantages include the opportunity to travel at your own speed and direction, personal arrival and departure times, and an individually-tailored itinerary. Just tell us where to go and your wishes will be accommodated.

For details and prices of our journeys and facilities, please visit our web-site or e-mail us (see above for addresses). Bespoke quotations are available on request.